New Generations of Catholic Sisters

NEW GENERATIONS OF CATHOLIC SISTERS

The Challenge of Diversity

—◄◆►—

MARY JOHNSON, S.N.D. de N.
PATRICIA WITTBERG, S.C.
MARY L. GAUTIER

OXFORD
UNIVERSITY PRESS

OXFORD
UNIVERSITY PRESS

Oxford University Press is a department of the University of
Oxford. It furthers the University's objective of excellence in research,
scholarship, and education by publishing worldwide.

Oxford   New York
Auckland   Cape Town   Dar es Salaam   Hong Kong   Karachi
Kuala Lumpur   Madrid   Melbourne   Mexico City   Nairobi
New Delhi   Shanghai   Taipei   Toronto

With offices in
Argentina   Austria   Brazil   Chile   Czech Republic   France   Greece
Guatemala   Hungary   Italy   Japan   Poland   Portugal   Singapore
South Korea   Switzerland   Thailand   Turkey   Ukraine   Vietnam

Oxford is a registered trademark of Oxford University Press
in the UK and certain other countries.

Published in the United States of America by
Oxford University Press
198 Madison Avenue, New York, NY 10016

Library of Congress Cataloging-in-Publication Data
Johnson, Mary, 1957-
New generations of Catholic sisters : the challenge of diversity / Mary Johnson, SNDdeN,
Patricia Wittberg, SC, and Mary L. Gautier.
pages cm
Includes bibliographical references.
ISBN 978–0–19–931684–7 (cloth : alk. paper)   1. Nuns—United States—History—20th
century.   2. Monasticism and religious orders for women—United States—History—20th
century.   3. Monastic and religious life of women—United States—History—20th
century   4. Vatican Council (2nd : 1962–1965 : Basilica di San Pietro in Vaticano)   I. Title.
BX4220.U6J64 2014
271'.9007309045—dc23
2013035723

1 3 5 7 9 8 6 4 2
Printed in the United States of America
on acid-free paper

To the next generations of Catholic Sisters in the United States

Contents

Acknowledgments

WE WISH TO thank the many people who have supported this project. The Lilly Endowment provided financial assistance for the 1999 national study; we are grateful to Sister Jeanne Knoerle, SP, then-program director for religion at Lilly, for her assistance. The National Religious Vocation Conference, with the support of executive director Brother Paul Bednarczyk, CSC, and the NRVC board, permitted us to use data from the 2009 NRVC/CARA study. The Center for Applied Research in the Apostolate (CARA) provided data and analyses from several additional national studies.

Wade Clark Roof, Helen Rose Ebaugh, Sister Esther Heffernan, OP, Jay Demerath, and Michele Dillon provided key advice for the research design of the 1999 study. We are grateful to Sister Rose McDermott, SSJ, and Sister Sharon Euart, RSM, for sharing their canonical expertise in reviewing chapter 2. Sister Anne O'Donnell, SNDdeN, Mary Esslinger, Jerry Filteau, and Peter McDonough also shared important insights.

The CARA staff, Father Tom Gaunt, SJ, Melissa Cidade, Mark Gray, and M. Connie Neuman, provided much support. Faculty, administrators, and students at Emmanuel College, Trinity Washington University, and Indiana University-Purdue University in Indianapolis shared their interest in the project with us.

Four anonymous reviewers gave helpful feedback on an early draft of the manuscript. We especially thank Cynthia Read, executive editor at Oxford University Press, for her encouragement and Marcela Maxfield, editorial assistant, for her careful attention to detail in the copy edits.

Finally, we wish to thank our religious congregations, the Sisters of Notre Dame de Namur and the Sisters of Charity of Cincinnati, and our communities, families, friends, and colleagues who sustained us in our work.

New Generations of Catholic Sisters

Introduction

IN THE EARLY 1960s, the Second Vatican Council urged the Church to use the social sciences in shedding light on both its internal self-understanding and its external mission. Since the Council, the Church has often done the latter, using social science to examine and focus its mission in the world. There has been resistance, however, to doing the former: using the same sociological tools to look at the Church itself. It can be threatening to do this, because sociological analysis requires us to examine and admit what is working and what is not. No human organization is perfect, and all organizations must do a realistic examination of themselves from time to time. The Church must do it since it is a human organization with a divine mission that is essential to the life of the world. Religious life must also do this self-examination because its mission is essential to the life of the Church.

There are hundreds of charisms contained in women's religious institutes in the United States—all of which are distinct and beautiful, and all of which are needed for the complex mission of the Church today. Each institute is marked by its own rich history, structure, and culture, and each needs to conduct periodic self-examinations as internal and external pressures cause it to change. We focus on one of these changes, a generational analysis of the vocation to the vowed religious life in institutes of women religious.

Generational analysis is not a familiar lens for some, and it may challenge the conventional wisdom about the future of religious life in the United States. Indeed, depending on the social location, one hears speculation about multiple futures, some hopeful and open to new initiatives, and some pierced with fatalism. Nineteenth-century sociologist Georg Simmel's story of the "Society of the Broken Dish" is helpful here.

Simmel recounted the story of a group of French businessmen who went to dinner. During the meal, a dish fell on the floor and broke into a number of pieces. One of the businessmen noted that the number of pieces equaled the number of diners at their table. Considering it an omen, one of the men suggested that they constitute a society in which they owed one another support and aid. Each took a piece of the dish home and agreed that upon death, the piece would be sent to the president of the society who would glue the pieces together again. The last survivor was to glue the last piece of the reconstituted dish and inter it. Simmel continued: "The 'Society of the Broken Dish' will thus dissolve and disappear. The feeling within that society, as well as in regard to it, would no doubt be different if new members were admitted and the life of the group thereby perpetuated indefinitely" (1950, 124–125).

The group, not the individual, is the unit of analysis for sociologists, so Simmel knew how important new members are to the life of a group. He also knew that new members are important to how a group feels and acts, and to how it is perceived by outsiders. We know that the life of a group cannot be taken for granted, especially if it has been entrusted with a sacred mission. Theologians also remind us of how important the charism is to the life of a group and to the world outside it.

We present data on religious life from several studies conducted over the past fifteen years, and we encourage institutes to interpret the data in the light of their own charisms. We are very aware that the backdrop for this conversation, at the present time, includes multiple conversations among the laity, the clergy, and the hierarchy, as well as multiple tensions in religious life. But we believe that all of those conversations should not produce a "swamping" effect, whereby the conversation about vocations to the vowed religious life is paralyzed and fails to move forward.

It has been a privilege for us to collaborate in providing sociological analysis in this particular book. We hope that it complements the existing body of theological, psychological, and spiritual writings on religious life, and that it casts light on new voices and visions in the new generations of religious life in the United States today.

Ultimately, the decision of each institute to move into the future regarding vocations to the vowed religious life belongs to the members of that institute in their deliberative bodies of assemblies and chapters. We hope and pray that, given the great needs of the Church and the world, the Holy Spirit will inspire institutes to welcome, like the elder Elizabeth's welcome of the young Mary, new generations of talented and committed Catholic women, who bring a rich diversity of generation, age, race, ethnicity, and ecclesiology. These institutes, and the whole Church, are challenged to provide the spiritual sustenance and emotional and structural support to those who are called by God to be sisters.

Mary Johnson, S.N.D. de N.
Patricia Wittberg, S.C.
Mary L. Gautier
April 29, 2013
Feast of St. Catherine of Siena

Chapter 1

Religious Life in the United States

TOWARD A NEW DEMOGRAPHIC DEFINITION

*Maria was sitting in the lounge area of the campus min-
istry office at the Catholic university where she was in her
second year of law school. Although she had often walked
by this office, this was the first time she had actually
dropped in. As she waited to see one of the campus ministers, she reflected on what had brought her here.*

*As much as Maria was enjoying law school and preparing
to practice immigration law back in the large West Coast
city to which her parents had immigrated thirty years earlier, she felt a stirring of something deeper that she knew
she had to explore, if only for the sake of her peace of mind.
Sitting in the campus ministry office confirmed the interior
confusion she had been feeling over the last several months.
Her eyes passed over a bulletin board that included "Come
and See" invitations from several religious institutes of
women, some in various kinds of habits and some with
only a small symbol affixed to secular clothing. All of the
sisters in the pictures looked happy and were pictured in
the context of their daily lives: in one case a monastery, in
another a school, and in a third case a health clinic in a
developing nation. One poster showed a group of women
at home having a meal together. "How did all of these different women get to where they ultimately wound up?"
she mused.*

*Maria had called for an appointment to meet with one of
the four lay campus ministers who, with a priest, staffed
the office. She had not known whom to ask for, so she said*

she would meet with whomever was free that day. She was there at the urging of a law professor, a member of the Focolare movement, whom Maria had met while spending an undergraduate semester in Italy. Maria had also been inspired by the Italian lay movement Sant'Egidio and their work for peace. She had gravitated toward both, but her law professor friend had encouraged her to explore other forms of consecrated life as well. "Consecrated life," Maria had said to her friend, "What's that?"

While undergrads congregated in one corner of the office to plan their spring break trip to Honduras, Maria chuckled to herself. She was glad her mother and grandmother could not see her now, for two very different reasons. To put it mildly, her mother would not appreciate her exploring the possibility of becoming a Catholic sister. Her parents had worked hard to put her and her siblings through Catholic schools. The tuition money had not come easily, and her mother had complained that during all those years, her children had never had a sister for a teacher. Several of the other mothers in the parish had agreed that it was a shame the sisters were "dying out." Maria's mother was proud of her lawyer-to-be daughter and would not be happy to hear that she was exploring the possibility of becoming part of what many called a "dying breed."

Maria's grandmother would also react negatively to Maria's interest, but for an entirely different reason. A devout Catholic, she had been born in Mexico and had come to the United States only a few years earlier to join her daughter's family. She would be thrilled that Maria was interested in religious life, because she had had two beloved aunts who were nuns. They had lived in a monastery not too far from her home village. While Maria's great-grand aunts had died long before she was born, she had often heard her grandmother speak lovingly of them and express the hope that someone in the family would enter that monastery. Her grandmother's daughters had pursued other ways of life, so now she turned to the next generation for the fulfillment of her hope. Maria knew that *her grandmother would not look kindly on her appointment that day. Was not her inquiry at the campus ministry office like the American "shopping around for Masses and parishes" phenomenon that her grandmother could neither understand nor accept? The Mexican monastery had been good enough for other family members, so why wasn't it good enough for Maria?*

Maria's mind continued to spin. She started to think of the sisters whom she had met in recent years. Although she had never had a sister as a teacher in school, she did get to know the one who had served as a pastoral minister in her parish. Later, during her post-college year of service in an inner-city adult education center, she had met the two sisters who ran that facility. While the three sisters she had encountered were different in personality and background, they all seemed very committed to the people they served. That had impressed Maria. She had lost touch with all three over the years, so she could not contact them now. In fact, she could not remember the names of their religious institutes, if indeed she had ever known them. And so today was the day to find out more information. She had huge questions for the campus minister: How would she know if God was calling her to the religious life? If her call was real, was religious life really "dying out" in this country?

At that moment, the door opened, and a female lay campus minister younger than Maria invited her to come in. How would the campus minister respond to Maria's inquiries about the calling she felt stirring within her, and about religious life for women in general in the United States today?

MARIA'S STORY POINTS to two of the levels on which young adult Catholics live as they try to find their future paths: the personal relationships they have with God and the social contexts in which they discern and live out those relationships. The story also points to the intersection of spirituality and sociology that describes these two levels. Spirituality concerns itself with the call of God and the discernment of God's desire for the individual and the group; sociology concerns itself with the networks and institutions within which that call and discernment take place. Sociology therefore examines the issues of religious form and function, personal and institutional identity, organization, culture, gender, ethnicity, age, and generation that are manifested in this story.

Maria's first question for the campus minister, "How would I know if God is calling me to become a sister?" is a question that women ask spiritual directors, wisdom figures, vowed religious, family, and friends who know them well. The answer to the second question, "Are sisters dying out in the United States?" is one about which people have a variety of opinions. Some respond based on their own experience; others repeat what they have read or heard from Catholic commentators. In this chapter, we put forth some answers to Maria's second question. As we shall see, there are many opinions about the identity and future of Catholic sisters in the United States.

Every organization must concern itself, to some degree, with how it is seen by others—especially those organizations that, by necessity, must attract new generations of members. Since an identity can attract, repel, or do neither, it is incumbent upon the organization to determine how its identity is being defined, who is doing the defining, and with what consequences.

We shall analyze several definitions of vowed religious life that are suggested by Maria's story, including definitions found in the media, as well as those used by scholars who study institutes[1] of sisters today. We begin with the famous admonition of W. I. Thomas, an influential social scientist of the early 1920s, about the power held by those who define a situation: "If men [sic] define situations as real, they are real in their consequences" (Thomas and Thomas 1928, 571–572). Others refer to this as the notion of the self-fulfilling prophecy. References made by commentators about the decline or impending death of an organization are not to be taken lightly because of the power these definitions have on constructions of reality.

Definitions in the Media

Several prominent and influential writers have recently used the rhetoric of decline, diminishment, division, and death when speaking of institutes of Catholic sisters and have advanced widely varying reasons for this decline. In his *American Catholic: The Saints and Sinners Who Built America's Most*

Powerful Church, Charles Morris offers a typically pessimistic vision of the future of religious sisterhoods in the United States: "If the demographics of the priesthood are daunting, the future of the female religious orders is probably hopeless.... Since nuns are 'lay,' or non-ordained, religious, exit from the religious life was always much easier than for priests... by the 1990's, about half of all nuns had left" (Morris 1997, 318). Secular factors, he believed, were also involved: "The mass resignations may have related less to Vatican II reforms than to the feminist movement. Nuns filled executive positions in Catholic service institutions long before similar jobs were opened to women in secular organizations. As lay women's professional horizons broadened, the convent lost much of its comparative recruitment advantage." He concludes, "The brute fact is that in about ten or fifteen years, for all practical purposes, there will be no working nuns in America" (Morris 1997, 319).

In *A People Adrift: The Crisis of the Roman Catholic Church in America*, Peter Steinfels advanced a similar argument: "Today the number of sisters has declined dramatically, and with almost no new recruits to the convent, many of these religious orders are destined to disappear" (Steinfels 2003, 113). Later in the same book, he opines that "[a]fter the Council, women's orders were reassessing their missions and rules of life at the same times as the women's movement was transforming social attitudes and practices. Existing disciplines and loyalties could not easily survive two such simultaneous and interacting upheavals. More significant than the religious orders' loss of members has been their inability to attract new ones. Many orders of sisters are primarily devoted to caring for their own elderly, and smaller orders will soon go out of existence" (Steinfels 2003, 327).

Other journalists echo Steinfels and Morris. According to Kenneth Briggs, "Mass-going American Catholics wonder what happened to that huge cohort of remarkable, black-swathed women who appeared then disappeared from their vulnerable lives" (Briggs 2006, 230). Briggs asserts that it is the hierarchy of the Catholic Church itself that has caused the decline, by imposing rigid and unreasonable restrictions on women's institutes. In contrast, George Weigel asserted that there was a neat split in types of women's religious institutes, roughly corresponding to those that continue to wear habits and follow a traditional way of life, as compared to those that have discarded these practices. The former largely belong to the Council of Major Superiors of Women Religious (CMSWR); the latter are members of the Leadership Conference of Women Religious (LCWR). According to Weigel, "there can be no denying that the 'renewal' of women's religious life led by the LCWR and its affiliated orders has utterly failed to attract new vocations. The LCWR orders are dying, while several religious orders that disaffiliated from the LCWR are growing" (Weigel 2012, 2).

Sometimes the sisters themselves have added to this journalistic perspective. An article in *The New York Times* quoted a seventy-three-year-old sister who had recently retired as the chief executive officer of one of the largest networks of Catholic hospitals in the country: "We can't be maudlin about this. I mean, yes, we are a dying breed. We are disappearing from the face of the earth and all of that. That being said, perhaps this is a moment for people to acknowledge the contribution that has been made by women religious throughout our history in the United States." Her own order, she said, had stopped recruiting several years ago: "It was painful, but I think it was also courageous to say we're just not going to recruit anymore. Let's just live out the rest of our lives to the fullest that we possibly can and thank God for what we have been able to do. And when the time comes, as they say, the last person turn the lights out" (Sack 2011).

Social Science Research

Vocations to the religious life have also been a focus of social scientific research over the last three decades. In a 1982 national study of Catholic sisters in the United States, sociologist Sister Marie Augusta Neal, SNDdeN, listed changes in society and the Church as reasons why fewer people were entering religious orders. Neal also pointed to several of the internal policies the sisters had adopted: requiring candidates to have some college and/or work experience prior to entrance; failing to invite vocations from new immigrants; and the reduced probability of young women coming in direct contact with sisters in ministry (Neal 1984, 70–74).

Other sociologists attributed the decline in vocations to the declining power of traditional Catholic beliefs. Roger Finke and Rodney Stark argued that "[i]t is not at all clear that one can accept vows of celibacy and poverty on behalf of abstract ideas about virtue and goodness. We conclude that the crisis of vocations thus reflects a crisis of faith and the deep erosion of the power of traditional Catholic symbols and sacraments" (Finke and Stark 1992, 268). Therefore, "…unless the church is able to re-establish greater tension with its environment it will not be able to restore the rewards needed to maintain high levels of sacrifice by the religious. It takes a vivid conception of active and potent supernatural forces to motivate people to make major sacrifices on behalf of faith, because only such active forces can plausibly deliver the great rewards on which a favorable exchange ratio rests" (Finke and Stark 1992, 271). According to Finke and Stark, therefore, religious institutes of women are declining because they and the Church are no longer sufficiently challenging to appeal to the idealism and enthusiasm of youth.

Helen Rose Fuchs Ebaugh, another sociologist, examined one institute of women religious in the United States and concluded that "[d]uring the past thirty years a number of factors, external to the orders themselves, came together in time and space and led to specific structural changes within religious orders of women in the United States. These structural changes, in turn, interacted in such a way as to make the demise of the institution virtually inevitable" (Ebaugh 1993, 162). She went on to list such factors as the new collegial approach to authority articulated by Vatican II, expanding secular opportunities for women, declining birth rates, credentialism in professional associations, and the rise of feminist ideologies in the society.

In addition to sociologists, researchers from other disciplines have also studied religious life. In the early 1990s, psychologists David Nygren and Sister Miriam Ukeritis, CSJ, conducted a study of 9,999 religious sisters, brothers, and priests. These researchers were concerned with the organizational structure and strategic effectiveness of religious institutes in their mission to alleviate "absolute human need." They argued that religious sisters, brothers, and priests needed to address issues of individualism, leadership, authority, corporate identity, and role clarity if they were to take advantage of a closing window of opportunity to revitalize their institutes (Nygren and Ukeritis 1993, 245). However, Nygren and Ukeritis also believed that this would be very difficult to do: "Most religious would see some return to normative behavior as necessary, but they are reluctant to do so if that means returning to the sect-like distinction of religious life of the past" (Nygren and Ukeritis 1993, 185).

Economist Sister Mary J. Oates, CSJ, also argued that the strict lifestyle of sisters, the influence of the civil rights and feminist movements, and women's widening professional opportunities have played a role in the decline of religious life. In addition, however, she cited a "critical agent" that she felt had been overlooked by previous scholars: "It is the effect on sisters, most of whom were parochial school teachers, of the rapid progress of American Catholics to middle-class status since the 1940s." But meeting the needs of the middle class in the suburbs did not call forth the same commitment from idealistic young people as addressing the many needs of earlier immigrant generations had. Oates felt that the remedy was for the institutes to concentrate on helping the poor: "If the progressive spirit that spurred nineteenth and early-twentieth century parishioners to fund free schools for poor and working-class children again flourishes, idealistic and generous young men and women, religious and lay, will again emerge to conduct and support them" (Oates 1995, 163).

Whatever its cause, the predicted demise of all or most of the religious institutes of women in the United States has ominous implications for American Catholicism, should it come to pass. Religious life in the United States is both an organization and part of a global social movement within the universal Church. Several scholars have remarked on the great potential of international networks of religious sisters to create new solidarities and bring about social change. According to Finke and Wittberg, newly formed religious orders were a source of spiritual renewal and adaptation to changed social conditions in previous centuries, keeping the Catholic Church comparatively free of the schismatic and sectarian fission that bedeviled Protestantism (Finke and Wittberg 2000, 156; see Masini 1998 for the social change role of sisters in recent times). Some observers see this creative and adaptive role as missing in religious orders today. Father Thomas Reese, SJ, asserted: "The Franciscans, Dominicans, and Jesuits were the engine of reform in centuries when the papacy and the hierarchy were corrupt. But no major religious communities arose during the twentieth century except Opus Dei and the Legionaries of Christ. The sisters' communities, which built the American church during the late nineteenth and early twentieth centuries, were decimated after Vatican II. Today it is the conservative groups that have vocations" (Reese 2004, 150). This, he felt, will rob the future American Church of its most creative and philanthropic element. As Frank Butler, former president of Foundations and Donors Interested in Catholic Activities, Inc. (FADICA), stated, "In many ways, the charity of religious women has been the most formidable influence in the tradition of Catholic philanthropy in our day" (FADICA 2010a,b). Without women's religious institutes, or with only a limited number of traditionalist ones, these authors conclude, the Church will be less able to engage with a rapidly changing world.

Comments such as these, both the popular and the scholarly, reflect a specific "ideological frame" (Mannheim 1955). According to Mannheim, human beings must make sense of the events of their lives, and so they construct a framework to explain them. The constellation of negative beliefs about the future of religious institutes has coalesced into just such an ideological frame, leading many critics, both within and outside of institutes, to question whether young people should be encouraged to pursue a religious vocation. Two of the most prevalent ideologies focus on the young people themselves, and neither corresponds to existing data.

First, some people argue that the age gap between the members of many institutes and interested women in the new generations is too large, or that the difficulties they would face as a generational minority are too great. But that position is disputed by evidence from an organization of younger women religious whose members have made their own choices about their pursuit of a religious vocation at this time in history. According to its website, Giving Voice is a "peer-led organization that creates spaces for younger women religious to give voice to their hopes, dreams and challenges in religious life" (www.giving-voice.org). The organization coordinates communication among younger women religious in the United States who meet regularly in person and virtually across institute lines.[2] They plan to expand their membership to younger women religious internationally.[3]

Members of the Giving Voice generation, sisters under the age of fifty, are realistic about the challenges they face and hopeful about the future. One newer member, speaking on behalf of the Giving Voice core team, wrote:

> ...As I reflect on the particular mission of younger women religious I can't help but think one of the most important things we're doing now is building a network of relationships, which will somehow be the "seedbed" of the Spirit's leading us into the future. I've been in a number of conversations recently about what a smaller religious life will look like. Right now that's harder to imagine with the amount of loss on the horizon in the next 10-15 years. However, through our relationships we are planting the seeds for whatever will come (Kohles 2013).

A second ideology argues that young people are not interested in religious life. However, a 2012 study found that 8 percent of millennial Catholic women (born after 1981) considered a religious vocation at least "a little seriously." Figure 1.1 shows that even among the Post-Vatican II women born between 1961 and 1981, who are the least likely to have considered a religious vocation, 7 percent of them have also considered a religious

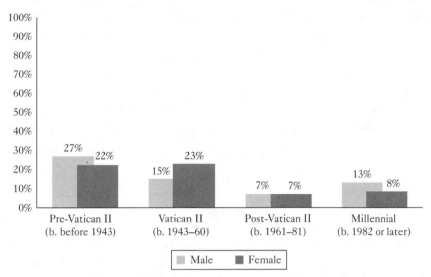

FIGURE 1.1 Never-married Catholics age fourteen and older who have considered a religious vocation at least "a little seriously" (females as a religious sister and males as clergy or a religious brother)

Source: CARA Vocations Poll, 2012

vocation at least "a little seriously." The study found that as many as 250,000 never-married Catholic women have "very seriously" considered becoming a sister at one time or other in their lives.[4]

Those who have seriously considered a religious vocation are more likely to have attended a Catholic school; those who attended a Catholic elementary school are three times more likely to consider becoming a sister than those who did not. Similarly, those who have known a sister, brother, or priest, or who have been invited by a sister, brother, or priest to consider religious life are more likely to do so. Many women still tend to first think of being a sister when they are in their teens (Gray and Gautier 2012). Women entering religious life today are a little younger than those who entered ten years ago; their average age of entrance is thirty-two. They are well-educated: About 70 percent have a bachelor's degree upon entrance (Bendyna and Gautier 2009). But they also carry educational debt: About one-third of them have at least $20,000 of such debt (Gautier and Cidade 2012).

These data raise questions about what kinds of new structures are needed to help women discern a religious vocation at various points along the life course. This is an urgent need because, in spite of pessimistic pronouncements, there are women who are interested in religious life. At least 110 women in the United States in 2012 professed perpetual vows as either sisters, who are engaged in ministries such as education, health care and social service, or nuns, who reside in monasteries and engage in several periods of prayer each day (Gautier and Saunders 2013). There are approximately 1,200 women in formation[5] at the present time, about 150 of whom are nuns in monasteries. The remaining 1,050 sisters are evenly divided between LCWR and CMSWR institutes. The retention rate across all religious institutes is 50 percent (Bendyna and Gautier 2009).

Views of Religious Leaders

The views of the sisters' leaders have also been strikingly optimistic. One of the studies in this book (see appendix I) asked the leaders of institutes of women religious about their visions for the future of religious life in this country. Contrary to the speculation put forth by both journalistic and academic commentators, the institute leaders repudiated the notion that sisters were no longer needed in the United States, that supporting religious institutes meant devaluing the role of the laity in the Church, or that religious life no longer had anything to offer young people. They also did not believe that future religious institutes would include ecumenical and interfaith members, or Catholic married and single non-vowed members. Finally, the leaders did not believe that all new members would necessarily come only from outside the United States. Instead, they envisioned their future vowed membership as multiethnic and multiracial, and felt that the poor and marginalized must be invited to become sisters in their institutes. They saw the recruitment of this new generation of sisters as an essential aspect of their institute's mission, the responsibility of each sister.

Another hopeful view of religious life is displayed in the acclaimed "Women and Spirit: Catholic Sisters in America" exhibit, sponsored and produced by the aforementioned LCWR. The exhibit, which chronicles the collective story of women religious in the United States from 1727 to the present, was displayed in several cities across the country from May 2009 to June 2012. Over a million people visited the exhibit, viewing artifacts documenting almost 300 years of the sisters' works: nursing Civil War soldiers; constructing and staffing hundreds of schools, hospitals, and settlement houses; and influencing the development of the Church and nation in a myriad of other ways. A documentary DVD of the exhibit is available through the LCWR website (www.womenandspirit.org).

If the sisters and their leaders are relatively optimistic about their past and future, why have scholars and commentators in the media advanced such a different view? The ministry of many religious today is less institutional and less parish-centered than it was immediately prior to the Second Vatican Council. Responding to the needs of those in poverty situates religious on the margins of the society, where scholars and commentators are often not found. The prevailing media and academic definitions of the situation do not always speak to these new realities in which religious find themselves. Because their work can be all-consuming, women religious themselves have not always paused to articulate how their ministries make sense in light of new calls and new needs, especially to generations whose memories of sisters were confined to the hospital or the school. To what extent do the previous rhetorics of decline reflect the true situation of religious institutes today, as compared to the sisters' more optimistic view?

The multiple definitions of the health and future of Catholic religious institutes of women therefore constitute an issue of significant import, with great consequences for the institutions of the Church in the United States and beyond, and especially for the poor and vulnerable of the world who are served by religious.

Multiple definitions also hinder the work of leaders as well as vocation and formation personnel, sometimes affecting their ability to move their institutes forward. One such issue is the retention rate of new sisters. The 2009 study found that both LCWR and CMSWR institutes had the same retention rate of 50 percent. The leadership of religious institutes must take these obstacles, real and perceived, into consideration. Without an accurate definition of their current situation, suggested remedies will fall short. What is needed is a thorough answer to some basic sociological questions about the complexity of religious life and its varied organizations.

Asking the Questions

As social scientists, we have to ask: Are the definitions of the situation— by researchers, the media, and the sisters themselves—accurate? Can these hypotheses be proven? Are the projections for the future true? Are alternate futures possible? These questions are more than an exercise in splitting sociological hairs. They raise significant concerns in light of W. I. Thomas's warning: When one describes a situation as real, it becomes real in its consequences.

One level of answer is statistical and demographic. What are the actual and current numbers of women religious? How does the number of sisters compare to the number of religious priests and brothers? How do women religious entering institutes in the two conferences compare by age? How do women in perpetual vows compare with women in formation? How do religious sisters, in general, compare with the rest of the Catholic population of the United States?

To answer these questions, we analyzed data from two studies of newer religious, conducted ten years apart. The first study, completed in 1999, comprised three surveys: one of the leaders of 818 religious institutes of women in the United States, one of 4,381 women who had entered those institutes since 1965, and one of 2,082 women who had entered after 1965 but later left their institutes. The present book concentrates primarily on the study's responses from the sisters who had entered their institutes between 1965 and 1980 and remained, in order to draw a clearer comparison with the respondents in the second study. This second study, which was commissioned by the National Religious Vocation Conference and published in 2009, surveyed both female and male religious institutes and the men and women who had entered them between 1993 and 2008. The present book focuses only on the women's institutes in this second study: 725 institutes of women religious and 2,244 women who entered them after 1993. Both studies attempted to gain information from the entire identified population of sisters, not merely from a sample of it. More detail about the studies is available in appendix 1.

It must be noted that, because of the present segmentation in U.S. Catholicism, the respondents in these two studies come from somewhat different populations of Catholics. The 1965–1980 entrants came from a wide spectrum of U.S. Catholics, many of whom became acquainted with sisters as their teachers in school. Some of the 1993–2008 entrants in the second study may have come primarily from the smaller segment of more traditionalist Catholic youth, whom scholars estimate form only 10–15 percent of Catholic young adults in the United States today (Pearson and Denton 2011, 6; Smith 2009, 167). Although the views and attitudes of the respondents in the 2009 survey may not reflect the views of the majority of Catholic young adults (Zagano 2011), they do accurately represent the views and attitudes of all the women who have entered CMSWR and LCWR institutes since 1993.

The present book, then, compares how women who entered religious institutes in two different time periods (1965–1980 and 1993–2008) viewed religious life. What attracted them to their particular religious institutes? What messages of encouragement or disapproval did they receive from their families and friends concerning their choice? What particular aspects of religious life most appealed to them? What aspects have they found most challenging? What are their preferences for ministry and community living?

In addition to comparing the responses to these questions across time, the book also compares them *across generations*. Are the answers of the women who entered their institutes at the age of nineteen or twenty different from those who entered at the age of thirty-nine or forty? How do the answers of two women born in 1950 compare if one entered her institute in 1970 at the age of twenty and the other entered hers in 1995 at the age of forty-five? What type(s) of institute will each prefer at the various stages of her life? What types of religious institutes will they have to choose from in their search?

Demographic Background

According to data from CARA at Georgetown University, the Vatican counted 1,004,304 sisters, 79,408 brothers, and 148,804 religious priests worldwide in 1975. By 2009, each of these numbers had fallen: to 729,371 sisters, 54,229 brothers, and 135,051 religious priests. But these overall figures mask a wide variation: Some countries experienced a much steeper decline, while in other areas the number of religious actually increased.

CARA statistics for the United States show that in 1965 there were 179,954 sisters, 12,271 brothers, and 22,707 religious priests. By 2010, the United States had 55,944 sisters, 4,606 brothers, and 12,629 religious priests: a decline of 69 percent, 63 percent, and 44 percent, respectively. These figures are stark, and from them one could infer that they do, indeed, portend the impending demise of Catholic religious institutes in the United States, especially institutes of Catholic sisters, whose decline has been the steepest. But does this drop in numbers reflect a linear or a cyclical pattern? A longer view (see figure 1.2) across the entire twentieth century shows a steady rise in the number of sisters until the 1960s. In 1900, the United States had almost 50,000 sisters (Stewart 1994, 564), and, according to the *Official Catholic Directory*, the number of sisters reached its peak at about 180,000 in 1965. This was

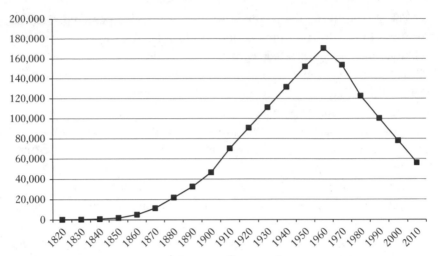

FIGURE I.2 Women religious in the United States, 1820–2010

Sources: Stewart (1820–1900), Official Catholic Directory (1910–2010)

an astonishing increase of 265 percent in just 65 years. Since then, the number of sisters has fallen to approximately the level of 1905. But their demographic characteristics are very different from those of the earlier population, while the total population of U.S. Catholics has grown more than 500 percent.[6]

Largely because of the extraordinary numbers of women entering religious life up to the 1950s and 1960s and the drop in religious vocations since that time, religious sisters today tend to be much older than the average Catholic. Only 9 percent of religious sisters are younger than sixty. Even though "retirement" is a term that is less commonly used in religious institutes—after all, religious life is a lifelong commitment rather than a career—the fact remains that more than two-thirds of men and women vowed religious in the United States today are older than sixty-five (see figure 1.3).[7] Although most sisters continue in some form of service ministry after this age—"re-phasing" from teaching to running the school library, for example, or from directing the parish religious education program to visiting the elderly and sick—and they typically experience a longer and more active old age than the typical American woman (Belluck 2001), age and illness eventually dictate their movement to a "ministry of prayer" in their institute's retirement homes.

As a result, the numbers of new members entering most religious institutes today are not at replacement level. There are not nearly enough

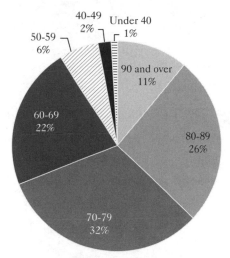

FIGURE 1.3 Age distribution of women religious, 2009
Source: 2009 NRVC/CARA Study of Recent Vocations to Religious life

new members in initial formation to compensate for the numbers that are dying or retiring from active ministry each year. Moreover, CARA research on institutes of religious sisters indicates that the number of new members in formation has continued to decline (see figure 1.4). Although there are a number of international sisters from institutes outside the United States who are in this country to work or study, they are not sufficient to make up the shortfall.

In addition to the overall number of religious sisters of varying ages, one must also consider their ethnic composition. In the past, there were very few women of color in most religious institutes (see figure 1.5), apart from a few specifically founded for particular ethnic groups. Most institutes were offshoots of existing European religious institutes in the nineteenth and early twentieth centuries, and ministered to the needs of the U.S. immigrant populations of their own ethnicities. Although many of their apostolates later broadened to include ministry to the poor and vulnerable of all racial and ethnic backgrounds and all faiths, they still continued to attract or recruit members largely from white European-American Catholics. As a result, more than nine out of ten religious sisters in the United States today are white and non-Hispanic/Latina.

In contrast, the newer members of religious congregations today are more diverse than the older members. Of those in initial formation,

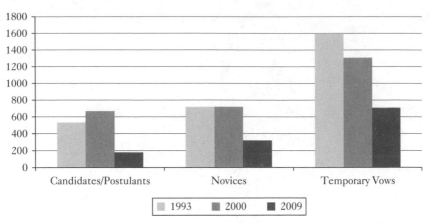

FIGURE 1.4 Estimated numbers in initial formation in institutes of women religious

Source: CARA Research on Institutes of Women Religious

42 percent are women of color. In ethnicity, the younger members of religious institutes look more like the younger generations of Catholics in the United States (see Chapter 4).

As we can see from Maria's story, the new generations of Catholic women bring with them to the sisters' communities all that shaped them from their families, their ethnicities, and their educations, as well as their experiences of Church, religion, and spirituality. Their choice of a religious institute, as we shall see in the following chapters, is anything but simple to analyze. Some commentators, for ideological purposes, attempt to create generalized typologies that mask the complexity of the religious reality, arguing that all new entrants go to traditionalist (CMSWR) institutes and few or none go to LCWR institutes. As this book shows, such stereotypes are not only inaccurate but dangerous, because they contribute to the increasing polarization of Catholics in the United States and hinder attempts to address the real challenges faced by religious sisters in this country. The decline and revitalization of women's religious institutes is one of the most serious issues facing the Church. A discussion of it demands the greatest precision and sensitivity for the sake of the future of the charism and mission that these institutes offer to the Church at large.

The reality of the situation is that an almost equal percentage of LCWR and CMSWR institutes have no one at all in formation at the present time (32 percent and 27 percent, respectively). One of the most striking findings regarding new entrants is that almost equal numbers

Women Religious in Perpetual Vows 2009

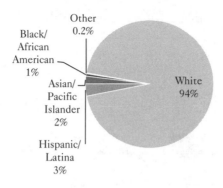

Women in Initial Formation 2009

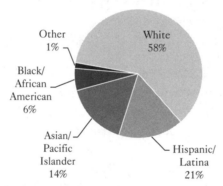

FIGURE 1.5 Race/ethnicity of women religious

Source: 2009 NRVC/CARA Study of Recent Vocations to Religious Life

of women have been attracted to institutes in both conferences in recent years. In 2009, LCWR institutes had 73 candidates/postulants, 117 novices, and 317 sisters in temporary vows/commitment, while CMSWR institutes had 73 candidates/postulants, 158 novices, and 304 sisters in temporary vows/commitment. Since over four times as many LCWR institutes as CMSWR institutes responded to the survey, however, the LCWR postulants, novices, and temporarily professed sisters are "spread out" over a larger base. According to the research that CARA conducted for NRVC on new vocations to religious life, the average number of new entrants to LCWR institutes is one; for CMSWR institutes, it is four (see figure 1.6).

The majority of institutes do not have large numbers of new entrants. Only 1 percent of the 274 responding LCWR institutes and 28 percent of

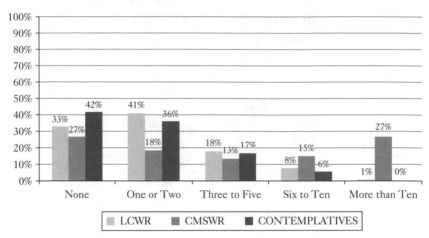

FIGURE 1.6 Numbers in formation in institutes of women religious by conference
Source: 2009 NRVC/CARA Study of Recent Vocations to Religious Life

the 61 responding CMSWR institutes have more than ten members in formation.[8] Media reports have focused on these outliers and generalized from them, inaccurately, to religious institutes as a whole. Instead, it is essential to probe what is happening across the spectrum of all the institutes to understand the complexity of these demographics.

One of the deeper implications of the demographics is that, although equal numbers of women are entering both LCWR and CMSWR institutes, the *ages* of these women differ radically. As chapter 4 shows, CMSWR institutes tend to attract younger women, while LCWR institutes tend to attract women who are over forty. This generational disparity may become self-reinforcing, causing the institutes to become less attractive to potential entrants who are not in the same generational cohort as the current members.

Another implication of the demographics is the comparatively large proportion (between one-fourth and one-third) of the institutes in both conferences with no new entrants at all. The majority of U.S. Catholic women appear far less interested in joining a Catholic sisterhood—of whatever ideology or style of life—than women were in the 1950s or earlier, if indeed they are interested in remaining Catholic at all (Wittberg 2012; D'Antonio, Dillon, and Gautier 2013). To the extent that only a small and atypical minority of the youngest age cohort of Catholic women are entering a limited number of Catholic religious institutes, the danger is that these few institutes will be out of step with the desires and concerns of the majority of younger Catholic women and less able to reach out to them. This possibility is further discussed in chapter 4.

Conclusions

The data in this chapter confirm a decline in the total number of women religious since the peak in 1965, a decline that commentators have been talking about for decades. Obviously, the decline will continue for some time to come, given the advanced age of a large number of religious today. But what we find most interesting are those aspects of the generational data that are not mentioned by the commentators.

First of all, the ethnic composition of the youngest generation of religious women resembles that of the youngest generation in the Church. This reality poses new questions: Will a more multicultural and multiracial generation bring new growth to religious life in this country? Has a demographic turn taken place that puts religious life on a new trajectory? What will religious life and the institutes that comprise it have to do in order to build and sustain multicultural communities and institutes that look more like the youth and young adults of the Church in this country? What structural and cultural changes will have to take place to insure a future for new generations of women religious whose cultural mix will look very different from the dominant generations in religious life today?

Second, evidence from various studies of young Catholics indicates that, although most have not abandoned Catholicism altogether, they are much less committed to the faith of their childhood than older generations are. Only a small minority of 10 to 15 percent can be classified as strongly orthodox (Pearson and Denton 2011, 64; Smith 2009, 167). A recent study of the ordained priesthood has found that the most recently ordained are more traditional than older priests (Gautier, Fichter, and Perl 2012). Is the same true for the youngest age cohort of Catholic women entering religious institutes? What implications does this recruitment pattern have for both CMSWR and LCWR institutes, and for the U.S. Catholic Church as a whole?

The ecology of religious life in the United States, with over 1,200 women in formation programs in religious institutes and monasteries, deserves a scholarly and sustained analysis devoid of both ideology and fatalism. The Church as a whole and the broader public deserve an accurate picture of the issues within and outside of religious institutes because the contributions of women religious continue to shape both Church and society.

Father Pierre Teilhard de Chardin, S.J. said, "The future belongs to those who give the next generation reason to hope." These data indicate that at least some of the institutes of women religious in the United States may be doing just that.

We turn now to the complex backdrop that both shapes and is shaped by religious life. Chapter 2 focuses on the array of structures that exist for people who wish to live and share committed lives of service and spirituality within the Catholic Church.

Chapter 2

Navigating the Contemporary Religious Landscape

DISCERNING DISTINCTIONS WITH A DIFFERENCE

Maria did not even notice the jostling on the subway as she stood in the crowded train on her way home. Her head was spinning after her conversation with the campus minister. She had liked the woman very much and felt very comfortable speaking with her, but she had left feeling even more confused.

The campus minister had been very encouraging of Maria's pursuit and mentioned that a couple of other students had asked the same questions. The campus minister had given them booklets from various religious institutes. She offered the same booklets to Maria, who glanced quickly at them. They were even more numerous than the posters on the bulletin board, and they struck her in the same way. The brochures all portrayed the sisters as happy, but they did not answer the questions she had.

The campus minister had told Maria that religious life must still be a valid and vibrant life choice, based on the numerous vocation booklets and DVDs on her bookshelf, and the number of media clips about sisters and their work that had appeared in the press over the last couple of years.

The campus minister remarked that some students had taken the vocation brochures home and had not returned to speak with her about religious life. She presumed that they had either made contact with sisters listed in the brochures or had lost interest.

Maria had looked up from the brochures and started to raise the many questions that she had. She had asked the campus minister what the difference was between the religious institutes, apart from a few obvious externals such as the religious habit. She wanted to know what the difference was between these religious institutes and the groups she had met in Italy—the Focolare and Sant'Egidio. Then she had asked: "What is religious life anyway?" since there had been many committed laywomen involved in her childhood parish who seemed happily fulfilled as they performed many of the necessary tasks of parish life. Maria also recalled that she had once met a married woman who was a canon lawyer, serving her diocese while also raising two children.

Maria knew that Vatican II had opened up new ministries for women, but she wasn't sure that it was just ministry alone that she wanted. So she asked the campus minister, with some frustration, "How do women even go about making a decision to enter a religious institute in the midst of all these choices?"

The campus minister had responded honestly that she had no idea how to answer Maria's questions because she had never worked with women religious. However, she would be happy to call a couple of her colleagues who might know how to find a sister with whom Maria could speak.

WHEN MARIA ASKED the campus minister about religious life, she was really asking about its identity. According to sociologists, institutions rise and fall based upon the clarity of their identity, or lack thereof, in the eyes of their members and the larger public. The focus of the Post-Vatican II Church on marriage and, to a much lesser extent, the single life, as valued and faith-filled vocations in the Church and society, has produced an unintended consequence: Other choices for young adults who wish to pursue alternate ways of life are sometimes obscured. And there is no easy and systematic way for young people to find and learn about the variety of ways of life in the Church.

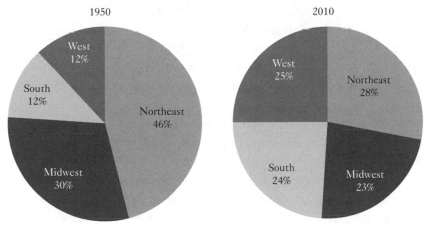

FIGURE 2.1 Shift in Catholic population, 1950–2010
Source: the official Catholic Directory, respective years

In reality, young adults like Maria navigate a very different Catholic landscape in pursuing a religious vocation today than people in previous generations did. This Catholic geography includes some new and obvious features, such as information channels via social media sites in cyberspace, especially Catholic websites and blogs. It also includes the less obvious plethora of newly established ecclesial movements and religious institutes, existing along with and partially supplanting the older Church structures of parishes and established religious institutes. Some melding of old and new structures and forms is also evident in various places.

Another feature of the Catholic landscape has to do with regional differentiation as seen in figure 2.1, with a significant loss of the Catholic population in the Northeast and Midwest between 1950 and 2010. The loss of population in those regions left an old infrastructure behind, too large for its new and smaller demographic. But the shift also produced a large increase in the Catholic population of the Western and Southern regions, resulting, for the first time, in equal proportions of Catholics across U.S. census regions.

Maria grew up on the West Coast during a time of significant growth in the Catholic population there. Maria's peers in the Northeast and upper Midwest experienced a very different reality. They came of age at a time of closing and merger of beloved institutions like parishes and schools, which produced great conflict and consternation in some areas. The loss of the old infrastructure produced feelings of loss and ambivalence. More painful and disorienting, however, was the clergy sex-abuse scandal that swept over Maria's generation leaving anger and outrage in its wake.

The multiple and complex features of the new Catholic landscape are profoundly unlike the geography that Maria's mother and grandmother traversed when they were coming of age as women of faith. Today, the pathways to learning about and finding a vocational choice are not as clearly marked; indeed, they are often hidden. As a result, not only have few young people been exposed to the wide variety of vocational choices in the Church; most have not been encouraged to pursue them.

In regard to religious life and priesthood, for example, two national studies of young adult Catholics, one published in 2001 and the other in 2012, found that only 15 percent had been encouraged to consider a religious or priestly vocation (Hoge et al. 2001; Gray and Gautier 2012). This was the case in spite of the fact that the 2001 study found that 48 percent of young adults (ages twenty to thirty-nine) considered religious orders of priests, sisters, brothers, and monks as "essential to the faith," a percentage equal to those who considered having a pope as essential (Hoge et al. 2001, 203).[1]

The authors of the 2001 study felt that the small percentage of young adults who were encouraged to consider a religious or priestly vocation was "a cause of concern" (Hoge et al. 2001, 236). They refuted the notion, prevalent in some quarters of the Church, that to encourage religious vocations was somehow to devalue the laity: "We believe that efforts to empower the laity to take their rightful place in the Church do not preclude the invitation of some young adults to consider religious life and priesthood" (Hoge et al. 2001, 236). This admonition suggests the existence of a false dichotomy in the thinking of some in the Church.

The authors also expressed their concern that few young adults were becoming lay ministers, and suggested that the Church should educate "all young adults about the various ways of life in the Church" (Hoge et al. 2001, 236). This would demand that individuals and organizations of the Church give structural and cultural support to education about and discernment of vocational choices. The newest generations' lack of familiarity with the wide variety of ways to live a vocation has obvious implications for the Church's ability to serve its members, and the global society, in the not-too-distant future. But lack of education alone does not explain the problem.

Many external challenges exist to discourage women from seeking entrance to religious life. One challenge is family. Data suggest that less than 30 percent of newer entrants indicated that their parents encouraged their vocational choice (Gautier and Saunders 2013). Other challenges come from issues of educational debt, immigration, and educational prerequisites. These challenges serve as structural stumbling blocks impeding the entrance of potential new members. A CARA/NRVC 2012 survey tells us that, in the last ten years, seven out of ten institutes have turned away someone because of educational debt (Gautier and Cidade 2012). Other external challenges include immigration issues for some women who are interested in entering, and also educational prerequisites that dissuade some immigrants and the poor from seeking entrance. Another challenge has to do with the significant number of young adult Catholic women in the United States who have fallen away from practicing their faith (Wittberg 2012; D'Antonio, Dillon, and Gautier 2013). Their ambivalence about the Church certainly has an effect on the discernment of a religious vocation (Johnson and Wittberg 2012).

Any attempt to map some of the factors affecting vocation discernment today reveals anything but a static picture and requires multiple responses on several levels. One such response is that the wider Church needs to support more structured outreach to younger people to ensure their integration into a Catholic culture. There is a correlation between seriously considering a vocation to religious life and attending some level of Catholic education, participating in parish youth groups, knowing a religious, or being invited to consider a religious vocation (Gray and Gautier 2012).

Today, the use of the Internet and the ability to compare and contrast websites of the available choices has brought vocational discernment to another level. Theologian Tom Beaudoin first described "virtual faith" (Beaudoin 1998); today, we observe "virtual vocation discernment." And with a more mobile society, more people are willing to move to find what they are seeking. All of these external issues point to a dynamic and complex picture, one that will not become simpler at any time in the near future. And the kinds of responses that are demanded to adequately address these issues will require new ways of thinking and new resources.

Another dimension of the vocation issue is embedded in the wider society, that is, the existence of a "spiritual marketplace" (Roof 1999). The array of religious and spiritual choices and the melding of some and the creation or re-creation of others provide a plethora of alternatives. In some areas of the country, there is a large marketplace, with more choice and variety of expression. In other areas, choice is more limited.

These choices illuminate another landscape, that is, the one that is internal to younger people. A religious and spiritual seeking was first identified among the baby boomer generation (Roof et al. 1993). Today, that seeking continues in the younger generations, generation X and the millennials. Some find what they are seeking in parishes or diocesan or campus ministries across the United States. Others search while exploring retreats, devotional practices, and prayer forms that are sometimes linked to and sometimes separate from service opportunities in this country and abroad. Some of this exploration takes place in communal settings, some alone. Some explore all of these forms within the Catholic tradition, some outside of it. And with a new religious pluralism in the United States, some take the spiritual practices of other religions and weave them into their own (Johnson 2006a). A few young people search for an "orthodox Catholicism" in a variety of Catholic organizations (Carroll 2002). These disparate journeys testify to a deep yearning for meaning and connection on the part of those who believe.

In response to these yearnings, Roof describes a variety of structures and forms that exist to support and provide a home for those who seek. He calls these structures and forms "religious subcultures" or "socio-religious" communities, and he states that they function simultaneously as communities, associations, and symbolic orders (1999, 181). Types of membership and commitment may vary. "People may *belong to them in a deep communal sense* or *simply associate with them* as they would with any other voluntary organization" (emphases added) (1999, 181).

Membership in these subcultures has the potential to affect the identity and emotional life of individuals, again along a typology of level of engagement: "They may identify with them symbolically and form moral and religious judgments about them, positively or negatively. Emotionally they involve attachments with varying degrees of intensity" (1999, 181).

These subcultures also fulfill the function of providing new social locations for people and adding new definition to their individual and collective identities: "Far more than just theology, or doctrine, or institution, socio-religious communities locate people in social space, defining them over against religious others" (1999, 181).

Using the image of a toolbox, Roof delineates the variety of resources that subcultures provide in the building of identity at a time of flux: "...subcultures provide resources for people to engage the world and to define themselves creatively in an ongoing, changing religious and cultural milieu. Symbols, customs, rituals, behavioral styles, theologies, and moral codes are all cultural tools for shaping a distinctive identity. Religious leaders and entrepreneurs engage such resources, of course, so too do ordinary people" (1999, 181).

Roof finds the locus of authority for this creation of religious identity and religious meaning within individuals themselves: "More than relying just on theologians and professional meaning-makers, people themselves are now playing a more active role in interpreting to themselves and to others who they are religiously" (1999, 181). And Roof concludes, "Increasingly, they are aware of the choices before them" (1999, 181).

We would argue that Catholic young adults are increasingly aware of "the culture of choice" in which they come of age (Hoge et al. 2001). Some are made aware of the religious choices that exist within the Church and outside of it. Some have explored new social locations and new identities, sometimes weaving those identities in a multilayered way. Some have taken old and new tools from the Catholic toolbox and have used traditional prayer styles, devotional practices, and rituals along with innovative ones, even to the point of imbuing old symbols with new meanings. Eucharistic adoration is one example of this. These are responses "to the fundamental need to find paths to contemplation in new, and sometimes inhospitable, social contexts" (Johnson 1998, 139).

The issues of identity, meaning, and social location are also of great importance to religious institutes, since they also exist within a wider context of religious choice today. In years past, the question was: How do people distinguish between institutes? Today, people discerning religious vocations also ask: How do we distinguish between religious institutes and other ways of life in the Church that are becoming more visible in some parts of the country and the world?

Although no perfect map exists of the variety of choices that are available for young people in the Church, we attempt here to create a framework that gives a sense of the breadth of choice that theoretically exists for discerning adults. We use the categories in the Code of Canon Law (1983) to note what characteristics distinguish between and among the ways of life in the Church. Some point to Roof's description of "religious subcultures." Some also suggest the possibility of the creation of multiple religious identities. One such example is priests and laypeople who are members of secular institutes. We use distinctions from the Code, when possible, to serve as sociological identity markers: for example, types of commitment, whether the commitment is made publicly or privately, types of community, and the type of work that members do.

Consecrated Life

Consecrated life refers to several ways of life in the Church, all of which presume a special dedication to God marked by attempting to conform oneself to the life of Jesus Christ. *Religious life* is one option among several in the wider Church category of consecrated life. Women and men in religious life express their dedication through the profession of the public vows of poverty, chastity, and obedience within a canonically established religious institute.[2] The charism and spirituality of each institute and the needs of its apostolate determine its particular practices regarding community, prayer, and ministry.

In addition to religious life, consecrated life also includes members of *secular institutes* and *hermits*. Members of *secular institutes* can be laywomen, laymen, or diocesan priests. This form of consecrated life was first recognized in 1947 by Pope Pius XII. Members live lives of poverty, chastity, and obedience. Unlike members of religious institutes, however, they make a private, not public, profession of these vows. They engage in a variety of works and are not required to live together, but they may gather periodically for meetings, retreats, etc. According to the U.S. Conference of Secular Institutes, there are thirty-two recognized secular institutes in the United States, with five more aspiring to ecclesiastical recognition (www.secularinstitutes.org).

Hermits profess the evangelical counsels by vows or other sacred bonds publicly before their diocesan bishop. They live lives of solitude, prayer, and penance in accord with a written rule that the bishop has approved. Hermits live alone in hermitages, sometimes, but not always, on the grounds of a monastery. They may share in liturgy and have some limited interaction with others for spiritual direction or spiritual works.

Consecrated Virgins

Consecrated virgins are women who resolve to follow Christ more closely by living celibate lives of dedicated service in the Church. They publicly express this intent and are consecrated by the diocesan bishop in the approved liturgical rite. They do not have to take vows of poverty or obedience, nor do they live communally, although they may form associations (Can. 604.2). While the Eastern Churches also have a provision in their canon law for *consecrated widows*, the Latin Church does not.

Societies of Apostolic Life

In addition to the forms of consecrated life mentioned above, another form of religious dedication is *societies of apostolic life*. Members of societies of apostolic life need not profess religious vows, but they engage in the apostolic purpose of their society while living the common life. Some societies of apostolic life may profess sacred bonds (vows, promises, oaths, etc.) privately for a limited time, as defined in their constitutions. Initially, societies of apostolic life were founded to address the poverty and misery of persons in local populations. Later, some societies trained missionaries for evangelization abroad. There are fewer than two dozen of these societies in the United States. One of the largest is the Daughters of Charity (Froehle and Gautier 2000).

Other Types of Association

Associations of the faithful are not forms of consecrated life; rather, they are groups of baptized persons devoted to pious causes or service. Associations for works such as burying the dead and addressing the needs of the poor have existed since the beginning of the Church. Some associations of the faithful are established as the preliminary step toward becoming a full-fledged religious institute or a society of apostolic life. Others always intend to remain simple associations. Associations of the faithful can contain ordained members, lay members, or both. Some associations are attached to a particular religious institute and share in its spirituality and apostolate. Some members of associations may make private vows and live a deeply committed spiritual life.

Another category, *lay ecclesial movements*, includes movements such as Focolare, Sant'Egidio, Communion and Liberation, and the Neocatechumenal Way. Members typically do not make the vows of poverty, chastity, and obedience, but some do live communally. Many of these movements were founded in Europe in the twentieth century and are now international in scope, with tens of thousands of members in dozens of countries. Each has a distinct mission: For example, Sant'Egidio, has a particular commitment to peace and conflict resolution (www.Santegidio.org).

Another category is *non-canonical communities*. These are communities that do not desire any formal recognition by the Church. Some, like the Immaculate Heart community, have a previous history as an institute of women religious (Caspary 2003) and are now ecumenical groups with both male and female membership. Others, like the Sisters for Christian Community, were initially organized to be non-canonical and continue to be solely female in membership.

This is not an exhaustive list, and new initiatives will continue to grow and develop, succeed, or fail. Further research and analysis are needed on these varied efforts, particularly on the design of new structures of governance and membership in some groups. One example of a group designing new structures of governance is Maryknoll. The Maryknoll Lay Missioners, along with the Maryknoll Sisters and the Maryknoll Fathers and Brothers, share aspects of mission, but maintain separate governance, finance, and membership structures (www.Maryknoll.org).

Emerging Religious Communities

Another phenomenon at work in the Church in the United States at the present time is the growth of *emerging religious communities*. A 1999 CARA study found that 136 such communities had been founded since 1965 in dioceses across the United States, with an additional twenty-one head-quartered elsewhere but having local houses in this country. A follow-up CARA study in 2006 found that one-third of the emerging communities in the 1999 directory had already vanished, but that many more communities had been founded, resulting in a new total of 165 such communities in the United States. Most of these communities are quite small, however, having fewer than one dozen members (CARA 2006).

This fluidity points to a historic phenomenon in Catholicism: the foundation and rapid dissolution of many new communities but the persistence of some, resulting in their eventual establishment as religious institutes. Because many of today's emerging communities are still developing, some have not yet decided what type of community they will become or what kind of status they will eventually seek within the Church.

As can be seen, there is much individual and communal variation in the forms of consecrated life, as well as in the other forms of Church service. Over time, some forms become more distinct from each other, while others lose their distinctiveness. Like patterns in American religion more generally, there has been a melding together of some forms and a breaking apart of others. Immigration and globalization continue to bring a variety of new forms to these shores, as has been the case with secular institutes, for instance. In the midst of all these shifts, how do religious institutes define themselves?

Religious Life: Internal Distinctions

In addition to the distinctions found in the Code of Canon Law between religious life in the Church and all of the other institutes, associations, and movements, there are also multiple internal characteristics that distinguish religious institutes from one other. First are the two prime classifications: contemplative versus active.

Contemplative religious life is lived within a monastery where the seven prayer periods of the Liturgy of the Hours form the core of the day. Silence, solitude, communal recreation, and work to support the monastery financially are included in the daily rhythm of the monastic lifestyle. Contemplative religious rarely leave their monasteries, and the limitations of cloister are often placed on their contact with the outside world. Individual monasteries vary in their spiritual heritage and interpretation of cloister. Contemplative women religious are usually called nuns; contemplative men, monks.

Active religious life engages with the needs of the world outside of the cloister. Some active institutes are *monastic*, in that the members reside in a monastery and share common prayer periods, but unlike contemplative monastics, they usually work outside of the monastery. For example, many Benedictines are active monastics. Other active institutes are *evangelical* institutes. In the spirit of medieval founders like St. Francis of Assisi and St. Dominic, they evangelize, that is, they preach and spread the Gospel using a variety of means. Many Franciscans and Dominicans consider themselves evangelical. Some of these and others are *mendicants* in that they beg for food and alms to provide for part of the sustenance of their communities. The Little Sisters of the Poor are an example of mendicants.

Still other active institutes are considered *apostolic*. Service to the needs of God's people belongs to the very nature of these institutes and often influences their practice of prayer and community. Each institute's apostolate is ordinarily described in its constitutions and ratified in the periodic decisions of its general chapters. Some apostolic institutes have a *missionary* dimension, that is, their members may spend all or some of their religious lives as missionaries, or missioners, outside their home country. A few institutes are solely missionary, such as the Maryknoll Sisters.

Table 2.1 presents the types of religious institutes found in our studies, as identified by the institutes themselves. Among responding religious institutes, about two-thirds considered themselves to be apostolic in both studies.

Table 2.1 Type of religious institute

	1999	2009
Apostolic	68%	69%
Contemplative	12	28
Monastic	11	18
Evangelical	7	12
Other	2	6

The 1999 study required institutes to select just one category to describe themselves, while the 2009 study allowed them to select all categories that apply to them. Thus, the percentages in the 2009 study add up to more than 100 percent to account for the groups that placed themselves in more than one category. Interestingly, a significant minority of the institutes in 2009 identified themselves as both apostolic *and* contemplative. As chapter 7 will show, this combination of identities reflects the members' desire to balance apostolic work and contemplative prayer in their daily lives.

This mixing of terminology highlights a continuing tension between the categories the Church creates to identify religious institutes and the self-definitions the institutes apply to themselves. These tensions may lead to either frustration or a creative adaptation of future forms by the institutes involved.

Further Distinctions

Religious institutes can be further distinguished by whether they are of *diocesan* or *pontifical* right. Diocesan institutes often exist in one or a few dioceses, sometimes, but not always, in neighboring dioceses. A diocesan institute has a particular accountability to the bishop of the diocese where its motherhouse or leadership offices are located. The accountability to the bishop involves matters of import, for example, the election of new leaders or the disposal of institute property. Pontifical institutes, on the other hand, may be located in several dioceses, or even in several or many countries, and are accountable to the Vatican. The comparative percentages of diocesan and pontifical institutes in the United States are listed in table 2.2.

Sometimes laywomen, laymen, and priests have sought to be associated with a religious institute whose spirituality and mission are attractive to them. These persons are known as *associates, oblates,* or members of

Table 2.2 Diocesan or pontifical right

	1999	2009
Pontifical	85%	87%
Diocesan	15	13

Third Orders. The terms and parameters of the associate relationship vary according to each institute. Although a few institutes have had associates since their founding, all religious institutes are now permitted to do so by the 1983 Code of Canon Law. According to a CARA study commissioned by the North American Conference of Associates and Religious and conducted in 1999 and 2000, women's religious institutes reported approximately 20,000 associates. The study revealed at that time that, relative to race and age, the majority of associates are white and middle-aged or older (Bendyna and Gautier 2000).

There is new evidence of successful efforts to recruit a younger cohort of associates (ages eighteen to forty) in at least one congregation (Garcia 2011).[3]

Figure 2.2 displays the establishment of associate programs in 429 religious institutes by decade. Before 1970, only 5 percent of the associate programs had been established. The 1970s saw the establishment of another 18 percent. The largest growth in programs occurred in the 1980s, with more than half (53 percent) of the programs being established in that decade. The 1990s saw almost one-quarter (24 percent) of programs established during that decade (Bendyna and Gautier 2000).

On an inter-organizational level, institutes with a similar charism— for example, various institutes of Sisters of Charity, Sisters of St. Joseph, Franciscans, etc.—collaborate in various types of *federations*. Other organizations of sisters are based on race or ethnicity. The National Black Sisters' Conference was established in 1968 (www.nbsc68.com). The Hispanic Sisters Conference was established in 2011 and is organized more informally. An organization of Vietnamese sisters has also been established in the United States. Some of these organizations exist to provide a voice for sisters of color in religious institutes whose members are primarily white.

There are also several *conferences* to which the members filling particular roles in religious institutes may belong (Johnson 2006b). Vocation directors, for example, may join the National Religious Vocation Conference (NRVC), which was founded in 1988, and formation directors may join

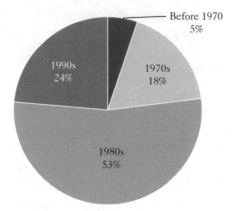

FIGURE 2.2 Establishment of associates in women's religious institutes
Source: 2000 NACAR/CARA Study of Associates

the Religious Formation Conference (RFC), founded in the 1950s. As previously mentioned in chapter 1, the leaders of women's apostolic institutes may belong to one or both of two canonically approved organizations: the Leadership Conference of Women Religious (LCWR) and the Council of Major Superiors of Women Religious (CMSWR). The United States is the only nation in the world with two different conferences for the leaders of women religious.

The LCWR was first established in 1956 as the Conference of Major Superiors of Women, at the request of the Vatican office responsible for religious institutes. Its beginning followed the First General Congress of the States of Perfection in Rome in 1950, when Pope Pius XII called upon the leaders of all the religious institutes of the world to meet. The Pope believed that national conferences of religious would aid in the updating of religious life.

In 1971, the Conference of Major Superiors of Women revised its bylaws and changed its name to the Leadership Conference of Women Religious. A small number of leaders broke with LCWR at that time, due to disagreements over what they considered to be essential to religious life. This small group became known as *Consortium Perfectae Caritatis*. In 1992, the Consortium was officially founded as the Council of Major Superiors of Women Religious (CMSWR), and in 1995, it received Vatican approval.

The percentages of institutes that belong to LCWR, CMSWR, both, or neither are shown in table 2.3. The table also shows how this affiliation has changed over time.

Sixty-five percent of religious institutes surveyed in the 2009 study belong to LCWR; 14 percent belong to CMSWR; 20 percent to neither; and

Table 2.3 **Leadership conference membership**

	1999	2009
LCWR	80%	65%
CMSWR	7	14
Neither	11	20
Both	2	1

1 percent to both. The number of institutes that belong to LCWR decreased by 15 percent from 1999 to 2009. Much of this can be explained by mergers of institutes and provinces. The percentage of institutes that belong to CMSWR has doubled during that time to 14 percent, and the percentage of institutes that belong to neither conference has increased to 20 percent. Many of the institutes that belong to neither conference are contemplative monasteries, which are not eligible for membership. Other institutes feel that neither conference fully represents who they are. In some of these latter institutes, this may be because a majority of their members were born outside of the United States.

The unit of analysis in the above paragraph is the institute. When focus is shifted to the individual as the unit of analysis, the majority of sisters (more than 80 percent) in the United States belong to LCWR institutes.

Some contemplative nuns had hoped after the Second Vatican Council that a conference for contemplative religious could be organized similar to the LCWR, or that contemplative institutes could be part of LCWR itself. In 1968, however, the Vatican's Sacred Congregation for Religious forbade the nuns to organize such a conference; thus no umbrella organization exists for contemplative monasteries today. Although contemplative monasteries do not have their own conference and do not belong to one of the two already-established conferences, some individual nuns belong to the Association of Contemplative Sisters, which was founded in 1969 and opened to laywomen in 1986. Today, the membership of this group is more lay than religious (Denham and Wilkinson 2009).

Conclusions

We have seen in this chapter that the path to entrance into a religious institute is sometimes obscured by multiple roadblocks, and that mapping the changing landscape of religious institutes and similar ways of life is more complicated than one might initially imagine. While we know that there was a total of 721,935 sisters in religious institutes located in almost every nation of the world in 2010,[4] the size and social locations of the other forms of commitment are harder to quantify. The assortment of forms—consecrated life, secular institutes, associations of the faithful, new ecclesial movements, and non-canonical and emerging communities—theoretically provides a wide and flexible set of options for commitment and service in the life of the Church. In practice, a tension has always existed between the efflorescence of new forms to meet the changes of time and place, and the need of Church authorities to monitor and codify their development. Over time, previously clear distinctions merge and blur, causing inevitable problems of identity. After a few decades or centuries, it may not be clear which of the formal distinctions in Canon Law actually point to real-life differences between the forms and which do not.

Today, questions about religious life like the ones that Maria posed are being asked of campus ministers, spiritual directors, and vocation directors, as multiple forms of consecrated life and other forms and movements become more visible. Less visible and less available are places where people learn to discern, analyze, and weigh the distinctions as they attempt to answer their call. Paradoxically, retreat houses, which are natural sites for vocation exploration, continue to close due to financial constraints, even as the need for the creation of a culture of discernment increases. Websites and blogs provide some venues where interested searchers are attempting to sift through the many and varied forms of commitment in the Church, but they provide an opportunity for a comparative analysis that is superficial at best. This suggests that the real work of defining and articulating the identity of each of the old and new forms mentioned in this chapter will take place within the structures themselves. This presents challenges.

If religious institutes do not do the hard work of defining themselves, they will be defined by others, and the definitions of others may not adequately capture their distinctive identities. Further, the institutes' own expressions of their identities may have become overly diffuse and vague, making definitions on websites and in periodicals difficult to articulate and harder to understand. What can be observed at the micro level is apparent at the macro level as well. Chapter 3 examines and critiques some recent attempts to give definition to religious life in and by the Church.

Chapter 3

Priest and Prophet

TENSIONS IN THE THEORIES AND PRACTICES OF RELIGIOUS LIFE

Maria glanced at the door of the hospital coffee shop, waiting impatiently for her cousin to appear. Anna was Maria's first cousin and was like a sister to her. They had been close since childhood, sharing confidences and seeking each other's advice. Anna was also a woman of faith, a practicing Catholic who shared many of Maria's values. She had worked hard in school and was now an executive vice president in a hospital on the other side of the city.

When Maria called Anna to share the news that she was looking into religious life, she had not been ready for Anna's reaction. Anna had tried to dissuade her, arguing that the Catholic Church was too conflicted, too male-dominated, and too unappreciative of women. Most importantly, she thought that Maria would be constrained and would not be free to use her many talents if she were to become a sister.

Maria had been stunned by the response and asked if they could meet for coffee to talk further. As she waited for Anna to appear, she thought, "I know there are great tensions in the Church that are becoming more apparent every day, but if a committed Catholic like my cousin has such concerns, would I be making a mistake?"

BENEATH THE FORMAL distinctions outlined in the previous chapter are deeper and more foundational layers whose interpretations influence the development and direction of Catholic religious life. One layer can be found in the documents of the popes and the Second Vatican Council concerning religious life; another can be found in the various initiatives of Vatican offices to codify and implement these statements. Still another layer is in the experience of sisters themselves, and in their reflections on this experience. Over the last half-century, there has been a veritable river of reflection from theologians, psychologists, and sociologists, all coursing through the experiences of religious institutes and having profound implications for religious life itself, the Church, and the larger society.

But there have also been tensions and clashes regarding the meaning(s) of religious life found in these various layers, which sometimes result in serious conflict. One indication of these tensions is the three major investigations of U.S. women religious conducted by the Vatican since the 1980s.

Vatican Interventions

Tensions between the hierarchy and religious institutes are not new. The long history of religious life in the Church reveals many past clashes between local bishops and leaders and/or members of religious institutes (Wittberg 1994, 78–97). It is highly unusual, however, for the Vatican to investigate religious life in an entire country, much less do so three times in thirty years.[1]

The first recent intervention occurred in 1984, when Pope John Paul II appointed a three-member pontifical commission, chaired by Archbishop John Quinn of San Francisco, to study the decline of vocations to religious life and to assist the U.S. bishops in providing "pastoral service to the religious communities in their dioceses." In October 1986, after extensive study, the commission submitted a largely positive 152-page report of their work to Pope John Paul II, as well as a summary to the U.S. bishops (United States Catholic Conference 1986).

The Quinn Commission report's favorable view represented the opinion of many U.S. bishops.[2] However, during their later *ad limina* visits to the Vatican, some bishops found that the Vatican officials had been surprised by the positive tone of the report. Many Vatican officials expressed negative criticisms of U.S. religious, which the U.S. bishops attempted to refute. For example, during his 1983 visit, Archbishop Hurley of Anchorage tried to speak to the pope about "the positive things religious were doing in his diocese ... he felt that religious women were being unfairly criticized." And Archbishop O'Meara of Indianapolis, when asked by the pope how he got along with the religious in his arch-diocese replied, "I think I get along with them pretty well, Holy Father. Better you should ask them that question, because their view of it is more meaningful" (Reese 1989, 319–320).

A second Vatican initiative was announced in 2009. This was an apostolic visitation of all women's religious institutes in the United States, initiated by the Vatican's Congregation for Institutes of Consecrated Life and Societies of Apostolic Life (CICLSAL). The visitation collected various materials from superiors general and leaders of the U.S. institutes and conducted selected onsite visits to various institutes across the United States (www.apostolicvisitation.org). It culminated in the compilation and delivery of a comprehensive report to the head of CICLSAL.[3]

The third Vatican initiative was announced by the Congregation for the Doctrine of the Faith (CDF), also in 2009. This initiative, conducted by a different curial office, was independent of the apostolic visitation being held at the same time. The CDF conducted a lengthy doctrinal assessment of the Leadership Conference of Women Religious (LCWR) and, on April 18, 2012, announced its results in an eight-page denunciation of certain LCWR statements and practices (www.usccb.org/news/2012/12-062e. cfm). In this document, the CDF mandated a reform of the LCWR, appointing an archbishop and two bishops as overseers.[4]

These last two initiatives caused great consternation among many women religious, as well as among significant groups of laity. Some of the consternation was summed up by one lay board member of a Catholic foundation who remarked, "...as church-related crises unfold in Europe, the image of the church is being harmed by the perception that serious abuses among the clergy have been ignored while committed religious women who have faithfully served the Gospel are under Vatican scrutiny" (FADICA 2010b, 42).

The outpouring of public support for sisters by groups of laity and by some priests and brothers, both within and outside the United States, was well-documented by multiple media outlets across the United States and the world. At the June 2012 annual spring meeting of the U.S. Catholic bishops, Cardinal Sean O'Malley, O.F.M., Cap., archbishop of Boston, characterized the media coverage of the LCWR doctrinal assessment and several other recent Church controversies[5] as a public relations "debacle" for the Church (Gibson 2012).

Priests and Prophets

The German sociologist Max Weber offered a distinction that is useful in interpreting this ongoing tension between the hierarchy of the Church and the members of religious institutes. In his *The Sociology of Religion*, Weber made a distinction between priests and prophets within religious traditions. The role of priests, as Weber saw it, is to systematize and routinize religious law and ritual. The role of prophets is to stand apart from the religious bureaucracy and, through their charismatic qualities, call humanity to an ethical meaning system based on religious reality. Weber believed that these two contrasting roles are interconnected and mutually reinforcing:

> Prophets systematized religion with a view to simplifying the relationship of man [sic] to the world, by reference to an ultimate and integrated value position. On the other hand, priests systematized the content of prophecy or of the sacred traditions by supplying them with a casuistical, rationalistic framework of analysis, and by adapting them to the customs of life and thought of their own class and of the laity whom they controlled (Weber 1963, 69).

Sister Pat Farrell, O.S.F., in her 2012 presidential address to the annual assembly of the Leadership Conference of Women Religious, pointed to this role distinction and to its possibilities for the life of the Church:

> There is an inherent existential tension between the complementary roles of hierarchy and religious which is not likely to change. In an ideal ecclesial world, the different roles are held in creative tension, with mutual respect and appreciation, in an environment of open dialogue, for the building up of the whole Church. The doctrinal assessment suggests that we are not currently living in an ideal ecclesial world (Farrell 2012).

Many of the official statements of the Church hierarchy on consecrated life do assign a prophetic role to women and men religious. The 1994 Bishops' World Synod on Consecrated Life remarked upon the "prophetic quality of consecrated persons," stating that "detachment from wealth, power and family ties invites those in consecrated life, from the depth of their being, to give themselves to the mission which strengthens God's kingdom and extends its borders." But while the synod's statement captures the social location of a prophet as defined by Weber, *it also locates them in relation to the Church*: "Obedience to the Father leads consecrated men and women to unite themselves with Christ's own mission to save the world *and to make themselves one with the Church*, giving a witness of love to all…" (emphasis added) (Synod of Bishops 1994, 6). Contained in the synod document, therefore, is a dual call that is sometimes in tension: the call of religious life to live its prophetic character, and the call to "make themselves one with the church."

Confusion in the very definition of Church leads to differing interpretations, attitudes, and behaviors. To some, "Church" suggests the hierarchy, whereas many in the post-Vatican II period stressed the conciliar definition that the Church is the "people of God." With which "Church" are religious to "make themselves one?" In which should they exercise Max Weber's prophetic role?

Still another example of the tension is manifested in the question of what role, if any, religious should play in the "priestly" governance activities of the Church. The 1994 synod's statement makes it clear that there should be more of a role for women religious in consultation and decision-making:

> We especially thank consecrated women. Their total giving of themselves to Christ, their life of adoration and of intercession for the world bear witness to the church's holiness. Their service to God's people and to society in various fields of evangelizing—pastoral activity, education, care of the sick, the poor and the abandoned—make visible the motherly face of the church. *Consecrated women should participate more in the church's consultations and decision-making as situations require* [emphasis added]. Their active participation in the synod has enriched our reflection on consecrated life and in particular on the dignity of consecrated women and their collaboration in the mission of the church (Synod of Bishops 1994, 2).

This historic and ongoing tension between the priestly and the prophetic functions of religious, as well as a lack of clarity in the terms used to define their role,[6] deserve more space than this chapter allows. The focus here is simply to summarize some of the significant Church documents from the last half-century that reflect these tensions. Echoing historians, however, we caution that the documents of Vatican II are all of a piece, and each must be read in relation to the whole (O'Malley 2012).[7]

Church Documents on Religious Life

Religious life was discussed in three documents of Vatican II: *Lumen Gentium: Dogmatic Constitution of the Church* (LG), which places religious life within the larger mission of the Church; *Perfectae Caritatis* (PC), which focuses on the renewal of religious life; and *Ad Gentes* (AG), which discusses the role of religious life in the Church's missionary activity. Also significant is the document *Ecclesiae Sanctae* (ES), a papal decree issued immediately after the close of Vatican II with guidelines for the renewal process. Here we examine *Lumen Gentium, Perfectae Caritatis,* and *Ecclesiae Sanctae.*

Lumen Gentium

In *Lumen Gentium* (1964), religious life is put in the larger context of the structure and mission of the Church. Table 3.1 lists the key elements of religious life as described in *Lumen Gentium*: the vows, the mission of religious within the salvific mission of the Church, the spirit or charism of religious institutes, and the role of religious life within the Church.

Table 3.1 Key elements of religious life in *Lumen Gentium*

Evangelical Counsels (Vows)	Mission	Spirit/Charism	Role in the Church
"The evangelical counsels of chastity dedicated to God, poverty and obedience are based upon the words and examples of the Lord." (LG 43)	"...the religious state of life is not an intermediate state between the clerical and lay states. But, rather, the faithful of Christ are called by God from both these states of life so that they might enjoy this particular gift in the life of the Church and thus each in ones' own way, may be of some advantage to the salvific mission of the Church." (LG 43)	"Thus it has come about,...various forms of solidarity and community life, as well as various religious families...." (LG 43)	"Thus, the state which is constituted by the profession of the evangelical counsels, though it is not the hierarchical structure of the Church, nevertheless, undeniably belongs to its life and holiness." (LG 44)

Table 3.2 Key elements of religious life in *Perfectae Caritatis*

Evangelical Counsels (Vows)	Mission	Spirit/Charism	Role in the Church
"The purpose of the religious life is to help the members follow Christ and be united to God through the profession of the evangelical counsels." (PC 2e)	"Institutes should promote among their members an adequate knowledge of the social conditions of the times they live in and of the needs of the Church. In such a way, judging current events wisely in the light of faith and burning with apostolic zeal, they may be able to assist men [sic] more effectively." (PC 2d)	"It redounds to the good of the Church that institutes have their own particular characteristics and work. Therefore let their founders' spirit and special aims they set before them as well as their sound traditions— all of which make up the patrimony of each institute— be faithfully held in honor." (PC 2b)	"All institutes should share in the life of the Church, adapting as their own and implementing in accordance with their own characteristics the Church's undertakings and aims in matters biblical, liturgical, dogmatic, pastoral, ecumenical, missionary and social." (PC 2c)

Perfectae Caritatis

Perfectae Caritatis, the Council's Decree on the Adaptation and Renewal of Religious Life, was promulgated by Pope Paul VI on October 28, 1965. The decree mandated that the renewal of religious institutes must be based on three sources: "the *constant return to the sources of all Christian life* and to *the original spirit of the institutes* and *their adaptation to the changed conditions of our time*" (emphases added) (PC, 2). The key elements of religious life according to *Perfectae Caritatis* are listed in table 3.2.

Ecclesiae Sanctae

Ecclesiae Sanctae is Pope Paul VI's 1966 apostolic letter that includes directives on the implementation of the Second Vatican Council's decrees on bishops, priests, religious, and missionaries. We focus here only on the directives regarding the renewal of religious life.

According to *Ecclesiae Sanctae*, "The most important role in the adaptation and renewal of the Religious life belongs to the institutes themselves, which will accomplish it especially through general chapters....The task of the chapters is not completed by merely making laws, but especially by promoting spiritual and apostolic vitality" (ES I, 1).

Five criteria were listed for renewal and adaptation. The first stated that the norms and spirit for renewal should come not only from *Perfectae Caritatis*, "but also from other documents of the Second Vatican Council," especially from chapters 5 and 6 of *Lumen Gentium*.

The second criterion stated that religious institutes should take care that the principles established in *Perfectae Caritatis* actually do pervade the renewal of their religious life. Toward that end, the document stated, true renewal should flow from the following sources:

- The Gospels and Sacred Scripture: "Study and meditation on the Gospels and the whole of Sacred Scripture should be more earnestly fostered by all members from the beginning of their novitiate. Likewise, care should be taken that they share in the mystery and life of the Church in more suitable ways" (ES I, 16[1]).
- Church Doctrines on Religious Life: "The various aspects (theological, historical, canonical, etc.) of the doctrine of the religious life should be investigated and explained" (ES I, 16[2]).
- The Original Spirit of the Founder: "To achieve the good of the Church, the institutes should strive for a genuine knowledge of their original spirit, so that faithfully preserving this spirit in determining adaptations, their religious life may thus be purified of alien elements and freed from those which are obsolete" (ES I, 16[3]).

The third criterion stated that certain elements of religious life should be considered obsolete if they no longer "constitute the nature and purpose of the institute," have lost their "meaning and power," and "are no longer a help to religious life" (ES I, 17).

The fourth criterion mandated that members of religious institutes should have a "really effective part" in selecting members of chapters and councils, and it stated that the exercise of authority should be made "more effective and unhindered according to modern needs" (ES I, 18).

Finally, the last criterion notes that the renewal of religious institutes is never finished: "Suitable renewal cannot be made once and for all but should be encouraged in a continuing way, with the help of the zeal of the members and the solicitude of the chapters and superiors" (ES I, 19).

It is important to note that the voice of women religious was not included in these Church documents. This absence was regrettable, according to Bishop Huyghe, a member of the commission charged with the writing of *Perfectae Caritatis*, who felt that "[t]he commission should consult superiors general of women's orders, especially those who have been invited to the council as auditors," instead of having the legislation drawn up solely by men. "It was a matter of concern to him that no woman religious had been consulted by the Commission on Religious Life, even to the extent that male lay auditors and experts had been consulted on the document on the apostolate of the laity" (Confoy 2008, 202–203).

The Role of the Charism

How might the renewal of religious institutes mandated by *Perfectae Caritatis* and *Ecclesiae Sanctae* be carried out? Jesuit canonist Father Ladislas Orsy gives a key role to each institute's charism:

> The ways and means of a renewed form of life ought to be created by the communities themselves. The potential for it is contained in the original charism, which ought to be a source of living water and not a set of rules carved into a lifeless rock. The Spirit who inspired the founders is not dead or absent. The Spirit's creative generosity is ever present. Excessive attachment to the ways and means of a remote past is a deadly apostasy from the life-giving present (Orsy 2009, 13).

According to Orsy, relying on the charism of religious institutes is the one recommendation that is found throughout papal, conciliar, and post-Vatican II Church documents. But what exactly is a religious institute's "charism"? On a basic level, it might be defined as the spirit or purpose of a religious institute. However, the Church documents do not give any guidance on how an institute might best discern and articulate this "spirit" in a clear and distinctive way. More broadly, the term also refers to the spirit or prophetic role of religious life itself in the life of the Church. But, as we have seen, the prophetic function of religious in the Church has sometimes been at variance with the priestly function in the Church.

So what constitutes an institute's charism? When does a charism or vision become so expansive that it becomes unattainable? And when do concepts like charism, community, mission, or the vows mean so many things to so many people that they become meaningless?

Still other questions flow from this lack of specificity: When do efforts to be inclusive lead to a situation where the center cannot hold and the particular mission can no longer be achieved? How can identifiers like "charism" be specified concretely enough to distinguish vowed commitment from the kind of life expected of all Christians and distinguish one religious institute from another? How can the prophetic role of religious life be kept in tension with the priestly (i.e., clergy and hierarchy) role, while each performs its vitally necessary function of challenging the other, for the sake of the mission of the whole Church?

Despite the conceptual vagueness of the term, the Church documents continue to emphasize that it is an institute's particular charism that gives it its uniqueness and spirit. As the 1994 Bishops' Synod on Consecrated Life put it, "The charism to found an institute of consecrated life is a grace given by God to founders and foundresses for the sake of fostering holiness in the church and of responding, through their mission, to the challenges of the times. A particular way of following Christ with total generosity becomes visible in each institute" (Synod of Bishops 1994, 5).

Such charisms were believed to be many and distinct from each other. According to the 1994 Synod of Bishops, "The diversity of charisms among consecrated persons and groups in the church is therefore a sign of God's infinite love and a cause of joy for the church...." But the synod also struck a cautionary note: "The charism should not be a source of tension between the hierarchy and consecrated persons. Among several difficulties to which we have given our fraternal attention is the need for communities of consecrated persons and their members to integrate themselves into their particular churches" (Synod of Bishops 1994, 5).

Here again we find the tension between the priestly and prophetic functions in the Church. How can the integration advocated by the 1994 synod be achieved? Prophets and priests typically engage each other in productive dialogue and collaboration only with difficulty, since their stances and social locations within the larger Church are so different. But, according to Weber, both roles are necessary. Having priests without prophets would result in a Church whose laws and rituals would be sterile, losing its ability to engage its members and the wider world; having prophets without priests would result in an unstable Church, with no way to discern true from false prophecy or to articulate and execute a coherent response to the prophetic message.

Later Papal Writings

Vita Consecrata (1996), the Consecrated Life, is an apostolic exhortation of Pope John Paul II, written after the 1994 Bishops' Synod on Consecrated Life. In it, he described the distinctiveness of religious life. The vows, he said, are a "gift not given to everyone"; the mission of religious life is a "particular duty... bearing striking testimony"; the fidelity to the charism of the founders provides inspiration for the practice of the "essential elements." Finally, he maintained that a "Church made up only of sacred ministers and lay people does not conform to the intentions of her divine Founder" (see table 3.3).

In *Vita Consecrata*, Pope John Paul II emphasized the distinctive identity markers of religious life. Such boundary markers are essential for the very existence of all human organizations and the preservation of their missions. Posing questions about boundary maintenance is sometimes seen as "conservative," but in reality, such questions are absolutely necessary in order to clarify an organization's reason for existence and thus its institutional vitality.

Numerous other documents about religious life have been promulgated by the pope and other Church officials since Vatican II.[8] Again illustrating the wariness that, according to Weber, the priestly role has always held toward its prophetic counterpart, the documents attempted to codify the "Essential Elements" of religious life and to place the institutes firmly under the authority of priestly officials:

> ...each religious institute depends for the authentic discernment
> of its founding charism on the God-given ministry of the hierarchy.
> This relationship obtains not only for the first recognition of a reli-
> gious institute but also for its ongoing development. The Church
> does more than bring an institute into being. She accompanies,
> guides, corrects, and encourages it in its fidelity to its founding
> gift... (Essential Elements 7, 41–42).

As with previous papal and council documents, subsequent Church decrees also emphasized the importance of the vows, mission, and public witness of religious. We note again, as in previous documents, that the voice of actual members of religious institutes, especially of sisters, was not included in these formulations.

Table 3.3 Key elements of religious life in *Vita Consecrata*

Evangelical Counsels (Vows)	Mission	Spirit/Charism	Role in the Church
"The profession of the evangelical counsels thus presupposes a particular gift of God not given to everyone, as Jesus himself emphasizes with respect to voluntary celibacy. This call is accompanied, moreover, by *a specific gift of the Holy Spirit.*" (emphasis in original text) 30	"A particular duty of the consecrated life is to *remind the fundamental values of the Gospel,*" by bearing "splendid and striking testimony that the world cannot be transfigured and offered to God without the spirit of the Beatitudes." (emphasis in original text) 33	"It is precisely in this fidelity to the inspiration of the founders and foundresses, an inspiration which is itself a gift of the Holy Spirit, that the essential elements of the consecrated life can be more readily discerned and more fervently put into practice." 36	"…the profession of the evangelical counsels *indisputably belongs to the life and holiness of the Church.*… The idea of a Church made up only of sacred ministers and lay people does not therefore conform to the intentions of her divine Founder, as revealed to us by the Gospels and the other writings of the New Testament." (emphasis in original text) 29

A Voice of Religious

In this section, we present an example of the collective voice of religious, which is less readily available than official Church documents. The example we choose is the final statement of the first World Congress on Religious Life. Held in Rome in November 2004, the congress was sponsored by the two international Unions of Superiors General for women and men religious, and was attended by the leaders of over 800 religious institutes from six continents, as well as theologians, directors of publications on religious life, and young religious. Bishops and members of the Vatican's Congregation for Institutes of Consecrated Life and for Societies of Apostolic Life (CICLSAL) and the Congregation for the Evangelization of Peoples also attended (World Congress on Religious Life Final Document 2004).[9]

In using this particular case, we do not suggest that the concepts necessarily represent the thinking of the unions or those members and guests gathered at the congress. We do use the following schema to demonstrate the differences in language, tone, and emphasis used by one international gathering of religious men and women, as compared to that used by the hierarchy in their pronouncements on religious life. The language of the final eight-page summary of the congress's deliberations captures the participants' apostolic zeal and their passion for religious life and its prophetic mission (see table 3.4). The document uses concepts that are notably different in expression from the key elements of religious life listed in the Vatican documents.

In contrast to the Vatican documents, these statements deemphasize formal structures in favor of cultural values when discussing *Lumen Gentium's* key elements of the vows, mission, charism, and Church role. A key difference is the lack of treatment of the vows as such. Chastity (consecrated celibacy) is mentioned simply as one of the convictions for a new praxis, not as a vow; poverty is mentioned only in parentheses; and the vow of obedience is not mentioned at all.

The document concludes: "The responsibility is ours—UISG, USG, national conferences of religious, communities and consecrated persons—to translate the Congress implications into attitudes, initiatives, decisions and projects." This statement points to the distinction between the sociological concepts of conceptualization and operationalization. Although the document contains many fine concepts, *it does not include operations to make those concepts real.* As in many other cases, the creation

Table 3.4 Key elements of religious life, World Congress on Religious Life (2004)

Evangelical Counsels (Vows)	Mission	Spirit/Charism	Role in the Church
"*Consecrated celibacy* brings one into a deeper relationship with Christ and helps to share the love of others. Celibacy for us is a free choice, it is our call, it is for us a healthy and balanced way of living our sexuality. Today we feel more at home with our bodies, with our feelings, and with our emotions. We believe, as the old Nicodemus did, that we were born again. The choice of our chastity is mostly resplendent when we make visible that ours is a journey towards the reign of God." (emphasis in original text) (III.2.7)	"The fundamental importance of our mission realized in accord with our particular and shared charisms, a mission that excites our imagination and impels us to undertake bold and prophetic new initiatives; to go beyond our frontiers to proclaim Jesus Christ through inculturation, inter-religious and inter-confessional dialogue; to express our option for the lowly and excluded ones in society; to explore new means of communication: a mission and an option for the poor (poverty)." (I.1.b.2)	"We affirm that we are a gift for the whole Church (*Vita Consecrata* 1): . . . We recognize that our different charisms and ecclesial ministries are a great gift for us." (I.1.b)	"We seek our place in the Church, the People of God, home and school of communion: • It is not easy to re-situate ourselves within the Church as men and women, as brothers, sisters, and ordained. • We thirst for a new level of 'mutual relations' with our pastors, with other groups and movements in the Church, animated by equality, sisterhood and brotherhood, and a greater mutual trust and openness to one another." (I.1.b)

of structures is left to the local level. But efforts on the local level sometimes fail to create structures that will support and sustain the concepts that have been identified as meaningful to groups on the national and international levels. While it is impossible to measure the myriad influences for the good that may come from these concepts, there is also the need for structures to undergird and sustain the cultural values that are vital to a group.

A cautionary note needs to be struck here, concerning another structural form that contains and supports essential religious values: namely, the vows or evangelical counsels. From the perspective of social science, the vows are *the* identifying norms and identity markers that bond sisters to their institute and to its other members. And theologians have written extensively on their scriptural and theological meanings. For example, theologian Sister Sandra Schneiders, I.H.M., has produced an expansive multivolume work on the significance of the vows to religious life (2000, 2001, 2013).

Sociologists recognize the vows as the glue that holds the common life of the institute together and as the prophetic vision that inspires and energizes both individual religious and their institutes in their daily lives. While all Christians are called to live the *values* of the evangelical counsels, the specificity of the religious vows operationalizes these values in a radical way, in transcending the basic human tendencies to make decisions based upon one's own desires, to have a spouse and create a family, and to own property. Many people may also share in the charism, spirituality, and mission of a religious institute, but only vowed religious share its way of life.

When the personal and social operationalization of the vows is not clearly articulated by religious themselves, a dangerous vacuum is created. If the vows are defined so broadly that most Christians could be said to be living them, the distinctive identity of Catholic religious life is blurred. If the vows are so rigidly defined that no Catholic either desires or is able to live them, religious institutes will come to be seen as irrelevant or even psychologically harmful. In either case, the future of religious institutes would be threatened.

Our example of the disparity between the Vatican documents and those of the World Congress in articulating these fundamental characteristics of religious life is striking. And the inability of either to address the tension between the priestly and prophetic roles in the Church makes it difficult to negotiate how to proceed. On the one hand, a liberty of spirit has to flourish in the lives of individual religious and their institutes so that their institutes' distinctive charisms, and the overall charism of religious life, can adapt to the changing needs of the Church and world. On the other hand, Church authorities must question and evaluate these adaptations, truly listening to the experience and perspective of religious, in order to challenge any unintended consequences that could result in the demise of religious life in certain parts of the world where religious are still very much needed.

But at this time, no mediating structure exists to ensure this kind of constructive engagement between these two key roles in the Church. Because of this vacuum, an authoritarianism can develop on the part of the hierarchy when they presume they alone know what the charism of religious life is, and a parochialism can develop on the part of religious when they presume that the charism of religious life is the concern of religious alone.

One path forward to address this structural void may be contained in the final document of the 2004 World Congress. In it, the participants said, "Twenty-five years after the proclamation of *Mutuae Relationes*, we must continue the dialogue at all levels in the Church ... *consecrated life has to be an experience of communion*" (emphasis added) (III, 2, 15).

The document to which the congress refers, *Mutuae Relationes, Directives for the Mutual Relations between Bishops and Religious in the Church*, was released in 1978 by two Vatican offices: the Sacred Congregation for Religious and for Secular Institutes and the Sacred Congregation for Bishops. *Mutuae Relationes* says in its conclusion: "Dialog and collaboration [between bishops and religious] are already a reality on various levels. There is no doubt, however, that they have to be developed further, so that they produce more abundant fruit." The conclusion continues by asserting the need in the relations between bishops and religious for cooperation, mutual trust, respect for the role of each individual, and "mutual consultation in determining and organizing undertakings on every level" (diocesan, national, and international) (1978).

It would seem that, given the concerns expressed in this chapter by members of the hierarchy, religious institutes, and the laity, the participants in the World Congress were religiously prophetic and sociologically astute when they called for further dialogue between bishops and religious. They were also resourceful in citing *Mutuae Relationes* as a foundation for this dialogue, in the service of what the document itself describes as the Church's "mission of salvation."

Decisions and Their Consequences

Religious institutes are not the only organizations that must be alert to the unintended consequences of their decisions and choices. But religious institutes must remain especially vigilant since some of these consequences can affect their organizational vitality and long-term mission. One challenge along this front today regards membership. The sociological distinction between core and peripheral elements of identity may be helpful in this discussion.

All organizations, either explicitly or implicitly, struggle to define the core elements of their identity that, if they were changed, would fundamentally alter the organization and its mission. Conversely, organizations must also acknowledge which elements are peripheral and can be altered without changing the organization's basic identity. One key clarifying question for religious institutes is: "Who are the members of the institute?" Or, to put it another way: "Who is one *of* us and who is one *with* us?" A false or naïve sense of inclusivity can lead to serious unintended consequences.

An example that illustrates the danger of failing to ask (and answer) these questions is the Association of Contemplative Sisters (A.C.S.), which was mentioned in chapter 2. Although it is not a religious institute, it does illustrate the consequences of changing an organization's basic identity. Founded in 1969 with the express purpose of serving as a forum for contemplative communities, the A.C.S. decided in 1986 to allow contemplatively minded laywomen to join as full members. Later, A.C.S. membership was also opened to apostolic sisters, men, other Christians, and finally to people from non-Christian traditions. Personal accounts of these latter members testify to the positive influence that the A.C.S. had in their spiritual lives (Denham and Wilkinson 2009).

But the structural transformation of the A.C.S. from an association specifically for vowed contemplative nuns to one that admitted persons with a contemplative interest from any religion or state of life led to an unforeseen problem. According to Sister Constance FitzGerald, OCD, while the admission of laywomen initially seemed consistent with the organization's goal of helping all people realize the contemplative dimension of their lives, their inclusion "as full members decisively changed the direction, purpose and vision of A.C.S., though perhaps unintentionally" (Denham and Wilkinson 2009, 86). Today, the majority of the membership of the organization is lay, and at least one of its founders has said that this new A.C.S. represents "a change in function fundamentally different from what we had first dreamed" (Denham and Wilkinson 2009, 86). The A.C.S. "lost much of its ability to serve as a forum for contemplative communities to collaborate and to speak and act in the Church" (Denham and Wilkinson 2009, 86). No other forum now exists to bring contemplative religious communities together as the A.C.S. founders had originally intended.

This case illustrates the serious concern sociologists have about the necessity of boundaries to protect and undergird any group's identity and mission. It is especially relevant at a time when many new initiatives are underway to widen the understanding of what religious life is today and what it could be in the future. Some institutes are currently deliberating whether to expand full membership to their associates or to others, and questioning which identity markers distinguish their boundaries.

There is a constant tension in all religious groups over how closely to embrace the larger culture, lest they one day awaken to the realization that they have *become* the larger culture—that the boundaries have melted away. The effort to be countercultural demands a critical ability to gauge when distinctions really point to a difference, and what difference that difference makes to the Church and world. Institutes have to honestly assess when their individual and collective lifestyles have become too domesticated, thereby losing their power to attract and retain a new generation.

Conclusions

As we have seen, most Church documents do not contain the voices and experiences of religious themselves. At least one bishop at the Second Vatican Council commented on this, as did the bishops in the 1994 Synod on Consecrated Life. Possibly as a result, many of the writings of religious, including those of the religious leaders at the World Congress, exhibit somewhat different emphases from those of the official Vatican documents. Differences in emphases have resulted in tensions between Vatican officials and religious institutes of women, especially in the United States. The unaddressed Weberian dilemma of how to mediate the prophetic role of religious institutes and the priestly functions of the hierarchy adds to the difficulty.

The conceptual vagueness of some key terms such as "charism" also poses a difficulty. Without a clear articulation of its charism, the members of an institute would be simply individual laborers doing good within individual ministries, and not collective members holding together the distinctive guiding mission entrusted to them by the Holy Spirit. Another disturbing vagueness involves the role of the vows, which were barely mentioned in the document of the World Congress.

Words are important, but words alone will not suffice. Prophetic words that are not undergirded by strong and life-giving structures with clear boundaries will exist only on the pages of documents. But structures that are not enveloped in the flesh of rich values, charisms, and visions will be like skeletons, just piles of dry bones.

Subsequent chapters shed further light on these tensions by exploring another layer of interpretation, that is, generational differences. We analyze how different generations of women in religious institutes view various elements of their institutes' identities.

Chapter 4

Generations and Their Cultures

CHALLENGES AND POSSIBILITIES

Maria hurried down the escalator toward her train. She always hated being late when invited to someone's home, and this was not the usual dinner invitation. Maria was on her way to visit a community of sisters, to pray with them, eat with them, and talk about her journey toward religious life.

When she first received the invitation, Maria had hesitated because she had never been to a religious community before. She asked what the community was like and was told that there were five sisters ranging in age from their forties to their eighties, that they were involved in several ministries, and that the three oldest sisters came from the local area, the fourth was from India, and the youngest had come from Africa to study. "Why are there so few young American sisters now?" Maria wondered. "What drew the older sisters to enter the convent when they were young, and what is different today?"

WHEN SOCIOLOGISTS SPEAK of a "generation," they mean more than simply a given age range of siblings and cousins in a family. According to Karl Mannheim, the German sociologist whose writings form the basis for all subsequent studies of generations (Mannheim 1952), a generation is a social location (as are one's class, gender, and hometown) that determines the kind of experiences one will have growing up. These experiences, in turn, fundamentally shape the kind of person each of us becomes as an adult: our attitudes and values, the amount and type of schooling we desire to attain, our hopes and expectations for the future, and so on. A wealthy white female growing to adulthood on Manhattan's Upper East Side in the 1990s will, for the most part, think and act quite differently than a migrant farm worker who began helping his parents pick tomatoes in California after dropping out of high school in 1955. We are all, Mannheim said, profoundly influenced by the social locations that shaped our childhood and adolescence. And the decades in which we were born and grew up are a key aspect of that social location. Whether a generation passed its childhood and adolescence in the Great Depression of the 1930s, in the early television and Cold War era of the 1950s, or in the ever-expanding electronic world of the 1990s will forever shape how that age cohort sees the world. In a fundamental and basic way, we are products of the eras in which we grew up.

The awareness of individuals that they have been formed into a generation occurs subtly. The members of a generation usually do not notice any differences in attitudes or beliefs between themselves and their elders until they come of age. Sociologist Wade Clark Roof quotes psychologist Daniel J. Callahan about what this awareness involves:

> All of us in the process of growing up, sooner or later come to notice that we are part of a generation. The first hints of this often steal upon us by surprise. We may observe in a dim fashion that we do not seem to respond to things the way our elders do, even though we may think we share the same general values and talk the same language. Or we may find that those writers and ideas that enthralled our parents and teachers leave us unmoved...at the same time we may gradually come to realize that we are not alone. What seemed a very private response turns out to be a common one (quoted in Roof 2009, 616).

Mannheim believed that, around the age of eighteen, our mental capacity matures so that we are able to evaluate, for the first time, the beliefs and customs we had unreflectively absorbed in childhood, and we discard or alter those that no longer make sense to us. The generational mindset we adopt when we first reach adulthood, Mannheim thought, becomes our "native" culture for the rest of our lives. It colors forever the way we think about the "foreign" generational cultures that preceded and will follow us. The farther removed these generations are from us in time, the more difficult it is for us truly to understand their mental and emotional worldview—and for them to understand us.

Generational differences, of course, interact with the other social locations. There are generational differences within the working class, among African Americans and Latinos, and so forth. To date, sociologists who study generational cultures in North America have primarily studied generations among middle-class whites. Within this group, they have delineated the following generational cohorts[1] :

- **The "greatest generation": born 1915–1929.** Members of this generation were shaped by the hardships of the Great Depression in their childhood. They learned at an early age to sacrifice their own plans for the greater good of their families and society. As they grew up, the United States entered World War II, in which many of them fought. The members of this generation are rapidly decreasing in number, since the youngest among them are in their mid-80s.
- **The "silent generation": born 1930–1945.** Members of this generation were too young to fight in World War II. They were also fewer in number than the generations that preceded and followed them. As they came of age in the 1950s, social critics accused them of passivity and lack of civic commitment, even though it was the silent generation that precipitated and participated in the modern Civil Rights movement and the antiwar protests of the early 1960s.
- **The "baby boomers": born 1946–1961.** The oldest members of this generational cohort were born nine months after the end of World War II, and birth rates did not fall to pre-1946 levels again until 1961. The sheer size of the boomer generation tended to overwhelm the experiences of the generations before and after them. Dr. Benjamin Spock had taught many of the boomers' middle-class parents to raise them permissively and to foster their individuality. They were the first TV and transistor radio generation and the first to be targeted by mass marketers selling them hula hoops, Davy Crockett caps, and 45 rpm rock-and-roll records.
- **"Generation X": born 1962–1981.** This much smaller generation passed its childhood in less optimistic decades than the baby boomers had experienced. Their earliest memories were of corruption in government, gasoline shortages, economic stagnation, and gloomy predictions of a coming environmental catastrophe. They were the first generation in which a large number of their parents were divorced, and many were "latchkey children," returning after school to an empty house. Gen Xers have been stereotyped as cynical and extremely reluctant to trust any institution, whether government, religion, or business.

As they entered their twenties and thirties, many were reluctant to commit themselves to a spouse or career, leading older generations to accuse them of having a "Peter Pan" complex and failing to assume their adult responsibilities.

- **The "millennials": born since 1982.** In sheer size, this is the largest and most ethnically diverse generation the United States has ever had. They are the first true Internet generation: accustomed to computers and cell phones from childhood, they spend more time online than they do watching TV. They are more team-oriented and more likely to trust institutions, including the Church. The recession of 2008 hit millennials especially hard: More than 20 percent are unemployed or underemployed. Many have huge college debts and therefore continue to live with their parents well into their late twenties, postponing marriage and children. In spite of this, they remain basically optimistic about their future, reflecting the formative influence of the relatively prosperous environment in which they had passed their childhood and adolescence (Pew Research Center 2012, 29–34).

- **The "next generation": born after 1996?** No one knows what this generation will be like as adults, since they are still in elementary and high school. All we can say is that, since they passed their childhoods in the turbulent post-9/11 world and their teen years during the stock market collapse and the 2008 recession, they will *not* be like the millennials, who grew up in a much more optimistic decade (Brooks 2013).

How are these generational differences displayed in the U.S. Catholic Church? In addition to the events experienced by all members of their generation, U.S. Catholics have experienced additional formative influences that shaped their cohort's worldview, including, most especially, the changes following Vatican II. Catholics who experienced these changes after they became adults, Catholics who experienced them as they were entering adulthood, and Catholics who do not remember the pre-Vatican II Church at all will have different attitudes about the beliefs and practices involved in being "Catholic" today. In this book, we use CARA research categories, which are similar to those used by previous Catholic researchers (e.g., D'Antonio et al. 2007, 98–101) in mapping the following generational cohorts of U.S. Catholics:

- **The pre-Vatican II generation: born before 1943.** This generation includes most of the silent generation, plus the remaining members of the greatest generation. These Catholics reached Mannheim's key age of eighteen to twenty prior to the Second Vatican Council. Many had grown up in solidly Catholic subcultures: They attended parish schools, were taught by sisters, and had little contact with non-Catholics. Throughout their childhood and young adulthood, as in the lifetimes of their parents and grandparents before them, the Church had been an unchanging anchor, and they assumed that it would always remain so. For some, the Council's reforms brought about a welcome liberation and a deepening of their spirituality; for others, the Council was a threatening disruption of the way things had always been.

- **The Vatican II generation: born 1943–1960.** Members of this generation experienced the changes of Vatican II as teens or children, prior to the age of twenty. While the oldest Vatican II Catholics have some early memories of the pre-Vatican II Church, the Latin Mass, and the Baltimore Catechism, most of those born after 1955 do not. For Vatican II Catholics, the Church of their youth and young adulthood was in constant and invigorating flux. They welcomed its changes.

- **The post-Vatican II generation: born 1961–1981.** These Catholics received their religious formation in the early post-Vatican II era. The Baltimore Catechism had been discarded in favor of more experiential religious education. Few, if any, sisters taught them in parochial schools. Distinctively Catholic devotions such as May Crowning, Forty Hours, and Benediction were being de-emphasized. The post-Vatican II generation's experience of the Church was often of an institution in constant and *disorienting* flux, unable to articulate anything worth believing in. Most remain relatively uninformed about religious history and Church teachings, preferring an eclectic, do-it-yourself spirituality. As they age and begin their families, they do not appear to be returning to regular religious practice, contrary to the pattern of previous generations (Silk 2012; D'Antonio, Dillon, and Gautier 2013).

- **The millennials: born since 1982.** Millennials are two or more generations removed from pre-Vatican II Catholicism. Not only they, but also their parents and sometimes even their grandparents, have had little or no experience with the traditional Catholic practices and catechesis that had formed the previous generations. Although they are more trusting of the Church than either the post-Vatican II or the Vatican II generations, they are also the least knowledgeable about Catholicism. White, middle-class millennial Catholics therefore have less to attach them to Church membership, and many are drifting away. Millennial

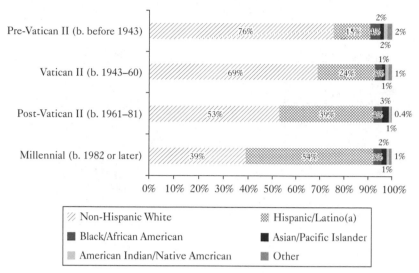

FIGURE 4.1 Race and ethnicity of the U.S. adult Catholic population by generation
Source: compilation from CARA Catholic Polls

Catholics today are the most ethnically diverse generation of Catholics in the United States. As figure 4.1 shows, for the first time, fewer than one-half of millennial Catholics in the United States are non-Hispanic whites.

All generations, of course, blur into each other, and there are no hard and fast attitudinal boundaries between them. A Vatican II Catholic born in 1960 probably feels closer to a post-Vatican II Catholic born in 1964 than he or she does to Vatican II Catholics born in the late 1940s. The important thing to remember, however, is that wherever a social scientist arbitrarily draws the boundaries of these generations, Catholics born twenty or thirty years apart will have very different experiences shaping the views of both the Church and the larger society.

Can we ever really see through another generation's eyes? Karl Mannheim did not think so:

Any two generations following one another always fight different opponents, both within and without. While the older people may still be fighting one battle, in such a fashion that all their feelings and efforts and even their concepts and categories of thought are determined by that adversary, for the younger people, this adversary may be simply non-existent: their primary orientation is an entirely different one (Mannheim 1952, 298–299).

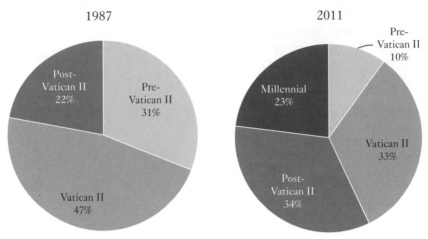

FIGURE 4.2 Generations of Catholics in the United States

Source: D'Antonio, Dillon, and Gautier 2013, 30

Staying mentally flexible enough to communicate across any cultural boundary—whether of ethnicity, class, or generation—is hard work. As a result, most people do not bother to do it very often. We tend to choose our friends from those like us, which in this case means that we associate mostly with persons our own age. The older we get, therefore, the more twenty-somethings seem foreign to us, and we to them, unless we make concerted attempts to bridge the gap.

Over the years, each generation grows older and ultimately fades from the scene, to be replaced by new and younger age cohorts. This can be seen when comparing the generational composition of the Church in 1987 with its counterpart twenty-five years later, as we show in figure 4.2. The pre-Vatican II and Vatican II cohorts, which comprised 78 percent of U.S. Catholics in 1987, had shrunk to only 43 percent by 2011. In other words, the majority of adults in the Church in 2011 were in their twenties, thirties, and forties.

We have already noted that the youngest Catholic age cohorts are more racially and ethnically diverse. They are also better educated and more likely to postpone marriage and children (Pew Research Center 2012, 16, 20). All of these factors—marital status, family, school, etc.—influence a person's attitudes, *but one's generation intersects with and colors them all.* How have generational experiences shaped the attitudes of U.S. Catholics?

The religious landscape of the country has indeed shifted considerably for young Catholics, a large percentage of whom resemble other young adults in saying that they no longer belong to a particular religion. One recent study found that twenty-somethings today are much more likely to reject all religious affiliation than their parents and grandparents had been when they were young—33 percent today, as compared with 12 percent in the 1970s (Putnam and Campbell 2010, 41–42). Another study found that while 20 percent of college-age millennials say they are Catholic, another 8 percent say they *used* to be Catholic in childhood but no longer are, "indicating a significant drop-off of Catholic affiliation by adulthood" (Jones, Cox, and Banchoff 2012, 7). Nevertheless, CARA analysis of the Pew Religious Landscape Survey data demonstrate that seven in ten Catholics remain affiliated with their faith as adults, a higher proportion than any other Christian faith group except Greek Orthodox (Gray 2012).

The attitudes of the 70 percent of young adults who remain Catholic, however, also present challenges to the leadership of the Church. Fewer than a quarter of U.S. Catholics in their twenties and thirties accept the Church's teaching authority on moral issues such as divorce, contraception, abortion, homosexuality, and nonmarital sex (D'Antonio et al. 2007, 98–101). Only 11 percent of millennial Catholics feel that having a celibate male clergy is important (as compared to 38 percent of pre-Vatican II Catholics), and only 26 percent say that the teaching authority of the Vatican is important (as compared to 52 percent of pre-Vatican II Catholics). More recent research shows that although four in ten pre-Vatican II Catholics remain highly committed to the Church, only 16 percent of post-Vatican II and millennial Catholics are this committed (D'Antonio et al. 2013, 58). Although young Catholics do pray regularly and believe in the core tenets of the faith (the Resurrection, the divinity of Christ, the significance of the role of Mary, the preferential option for the poor), they do not attend Mass weekly in large numbers and do not participate in parish life to a great degree (Gray 2012).

There is also a gender difference among young adult Catholics that has ominous implications for the future of the Church if it is not addressed. In the past, the women in every U.S. Christian denomination have prayed and attended religious services more often and have held more orthodox beliefs than the men *But this is no longer true for the youngest generation of Catholic women*. General Social Survey data from 2002–2008 indicate that, while both genders of millennial and post-Vatican II Catholics are much less devout and much less orthodox than their elders, "the decline is steeper among women. Millennial Catholic women are slightly more likely than Catholic men their age to say that they never attend Mass (the first generation of U.S. Catholic women for whom this is so), and the women are significantly more likely to hold heterodox positions on whether the pope is infallible and whether homosexual activity is always wrong. None of the millennial Catholic women in the survey expressed complete confidence in churches and religious organizations" (Wittberg 2012, 14). This greater disaffection does not occur among millennial Protestant women, who remain more devout and orthodox than Protestant males their age.

Generations and Religious Life

The disaffiliation from religion of the millennial age cohort in general—to say nothing of the even greater alienation of millennial Catholic women— makes it likely that fewer women will be interested in entering a religious institute of sisters or nuns than was the case for previous generations. This does not, however, mean that *no* young women are interested in a religious vocation. As chapter 1 pointed out, a recent CARA study found that more than 250,000 never-married Catholic women in the United States have "very seriously" considered becoming a religious sister at some time in their lives (Gray and Gautier 2012, 7). Millennial women who are interested in religious life today, however, may face cultural differences that make many religious institutes less attractive than they had been to older generations. Of course, absorbing members from a different culture is very difficult for any organization, for it means welcoming—and being changed by—persons whose beliefs, priorities, and values may differ from those of the current members. This is one reason why so many religious institutes were ethnically homogeneous in the past. A solidly Irish, German, or Polish institute was often unwilling or unable to change the ethnic aspects of its identity sufficiently to make other groups welcome. Attracting different generational cultures may pose an even greater challenge. Members of an older generational culture may resist making the necessary cultural changes in their institute to make it attractive to a potential millennial entrant.

Although it is possible for a religious institute to survive for centuries composed of only one ethnic group, *it is not possible for it to do so if it is composed of only one generational cohort.* Whether they want to or not, members of religious institutes must eventually attract members from younger age cohorts if their institute is to survive. But in order to adapt to the culture of a new generation, the institute's practices and its very identity must change, in both subtle and profound ways. All this assumes, of course,

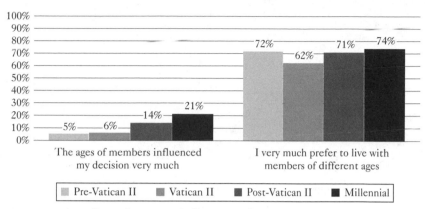

FIGURE 4.3 Age of members as an influence on discernment (percentage responding "Very Much")

Source: 2009 CARA/NRVC Study of Recent Vocations to Religious Life

that anyone from the next generation will even want to join. Many religious institutes are becoming increasingly mono-generational: They have not attracted a sufficient number of young recruits for there to be continuity between their largely middle-aged and elderly current members and any twenty-somethings who may wish to enter. The responses to the 2009 survey show that the age of an institute's current members does matter to potential entrants—especially for millennials, fully a fifth of whom said that the age composition of their institute was an important factor in their decision (figures 4.3 and 4.4). Millennial respondents were also the least likely to say that the age of current members was not important at all. New entrants from every age group preferred to live with members of different ages rather than in mono-generational communities, especially mono-generational communities where most members were in their sixties or seventies.

In their open-ended responses to the 2009 survey, strong percentages of both the millennial and post-Vatican II sisters in largely mono-generational institutes expressed this generational isolation as one of their greatest challenges. This was especially true for new entrants to LCWR institutes:

What do you find most challenging about religious life?

> The isolation experienced at times by a young woman going through formation without peers in her community or sisters that can really relate to her experience (millennial respondent, LCWR).
> I find it most challenging to live with sisters much older than I. I love them dearly and learn a lot from them, but we come

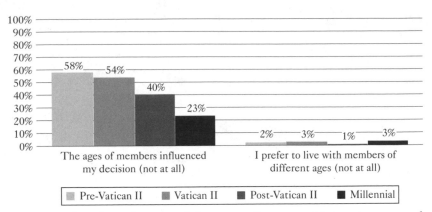

FIGURE 4.4 Age of members as an influence on discernment (percentage responding "Not at All")

Source: 2009 CARA/NRVC Study of Recent Vocations to Religious Life

> from two different time "eras" and so sometimes our ways of
> thinking or completing a task will clash (post-Vatican II respondent, LCWR).
>
> I'm one of the few younger ones, so we don't have a collective
> voice. In other words, I'm usually outnumbered (post-Vatican II
> respondent, LCWR).

Another challenging aspect of religious vocations today is the lack of support a potential member receives from the larger society. For older religious, the call to religious life was often mediated by a family member, teacher, etc. In contrast, as was mentioned in chapters 1 and 2, only 15 percent of young adult Catholics in 2001 were ever invited to consider religious life or priesthood (Hoge et al. 2001, 236). More recent research from CARA finds that those who were encouraged to consider religious life are twice as likely as those who were not encouraged to have seriously considered a vocation (Gray and Gautier 2012, 4). In contrast to the encouragement potential entrants received in previous generations, figure 4.5 shows that a significant percentage of the 2009 respondents received no support at all from their families, diocesan priests, or friends prior to entering their institute. Older respondents were more likely to say they received no support, but even among the young, fully 20 percent reported that their families were not supportive.

Another important factor is prior acquaintance with sisters. Our 1999 survey found a steady decrease between 1965 and 1980 in the percentage

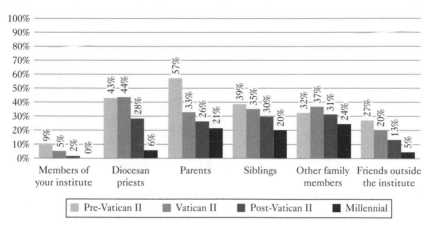

FIGURE 4.5 How much encouragement from these when entering (percentage responding "None At All")

Source: 2009 CARA/NRVC Study of Recent Vocations to Religious Life

of respondents saying they had entered their institutes because they had relatives who were sisters there, or because they had been acquainted with sisters from their institute in their childhood parish or school.

Reasons for Entering a Particular Religious Institute

The Prayer Life of the Institute

Generational experiences strongly impact the reasons our respondents gave for why they chose to enter one religious institute rather than another. Although all of the generations in the 2009 survey were equally likely to say that they had been attracted to their institute by a sense of God's call, a desire for prayer and spiritual growth, and the general spirituality of the institute, millennial respondents were more likely to say that they were attracted by the prayer life of the institute. The Vatican II generation respondents were the least likely to say that the prayer life of their institute was important in attracting them to enter—although, even among this generation, over 50 percent did so. In contrast, the millennial respondents were the least likely to say they had been attracted to their institute by a desire to be of service, by the mission of the institute, or by the ministry the sisters performed—characteristics that pre-Vatican II and Vatican II respondents were more likely to emphasize, possibly because many millennials had already performed service. These are true generational differences, not a result of the year in which the respondents entered—since

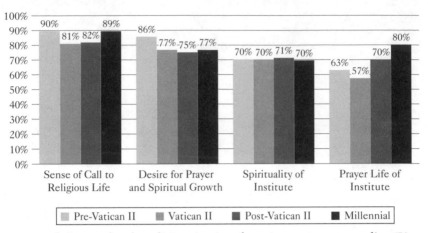

FIGURE 4.6 Attracted to the religious institute by...(percentage responding "Very Much")

Source: 2009 CARA/NRVC Study of Recent Vocations to Religious Life

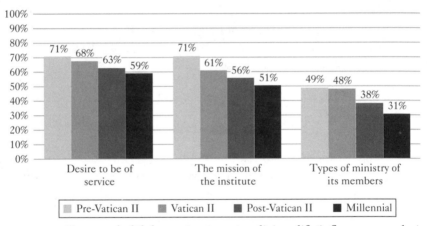

FIGURE 4.7 How much did these attract you to religious life/influence your decision? (percentage responding "Very Much")

Source: 2009 CARA/NRVC Study of Recent Vocations to Religious Life

even the Vatican II and pre-Vatican II respondents in the 2009 survey had entered their institutes since 1993. Because the two surveys are of an entire population, not a random sampling of it, the differences in percentages reported here reflect actual differences (figures 4.6 and 4.7).

The Ministry Settings of the Institute

Clear generational differences also exist in the respondents' preferences regarding where they would like to minister (see figure 4.8). Millennial

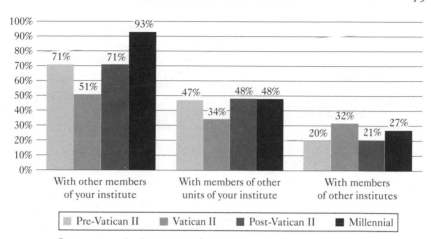

FIGURE 4.8 How much do you prefer ministry in these settings? (percentage responding "Very Much")

Source: 2009 CARA/NRVC Study of Recent Vocations to Religious Life

respondents strongly prefer working in an institute-sponsored ministry with other members of their own institute. Respondents from the Vatican II generation were the least likely to express these preferences. In contrast, respondents from the Vatican II generation were the most likely to say that they preferred working with members of other institutes, although no generation expressed very high support for this latter option. Again, these are generational differences, since all the respondents had entered their institutes since 1993.

The Community Life of the Institute

While pre-Vatican II respondents were the most likely to say that they had entered because of a simple desire to be part of a community, it was the youngest generation of new members who cited the community life of the institute as being very important to them (see figure 4.9). As we will see in chapter 7, millennial respondents were the most likely and Vatican II respondents least likely to consider living and socializing with other members of their own institutes to be very important.

Evaluating One's Religious Institute

When asked to evaluate various aspects of their religious institutes, millennial respondents gave their institutes higher marks than the other generations did for welcoming and supporting new members, for the quality

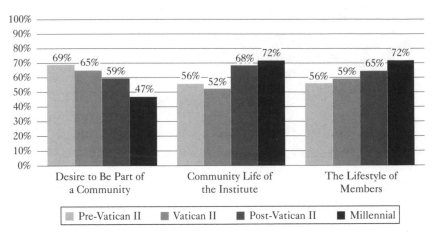

FIGURE 4.9 How much did these attract you to religious life/influence your decision? (percentage responding "Very Much")

Source: 2009 CARA/NRVC Study of Recent Vocations to Religious Life

of community life, and for fostering good relations among members. This may reflect the tendency of millennials in general to express a more positive view of institutions. In contrast, the Vatican II respondents consistently gave their institutes the lowest marks for each of these aspects. In a like manner, the millennial respondents were the most positive and the Vatican II respondents the least positive about how well their institutes had prepared them for ministry, and about how focused on and committed to mission and ministry their institutes were. This, of course, may be due to the fact that older entrants were already professionally prepared for ministry prior to entering. In contrast, the Vatican II and pre-Vatican II respondents were more positive than the millennial and post-Vatican II respondents about their institutes' efforts to promote social justice (figures 4.10 and 4.11).

In all of these answers, we can see a generational pattern: When looking for a religious institute, the millennial and post-Vatican II respondents who entered between 1993 and 2008 were more likely to search for institutes with a strong and evident prayer life, common living, and common ministry, and they were less likely to be attracted to an institute because of its mission or its focus on ministry. For the older Vatican II respondents who entered during the same period, the opposite was true. Millennial respondents were usually more positive in evaluating most dimensions of their institutes; Vatican II respondents were usually more critical. Millennial and post-Vatican II respondents were less likely to have been

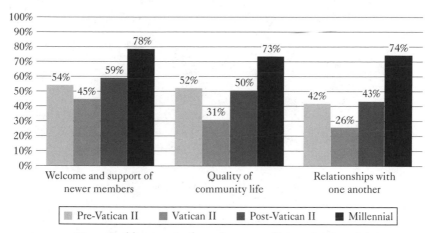

FIGURE 4.10 How would you rate these in your religious institute? (percentage responding "Excellent")

Source: 2009 CARA/NRVC Study of Recent Vocations to Religious Life

intimately acquainted with their institute prior to entering it—whether through having had the sisters in their childhood parish or school or by having a relative in the institute. Without these prior attachments to a given institute, young potential members may find it easier to search for one that has a larger percentage of persons their own age, and they may be deterred from entering any in which they would be the sole person of their generation. This tendency may be self-reinforcing, channeling the young people currently contemplating a religious vocation to institutes that are already relatively youthful. The 2009 survey indicates that this is already occurring: As table 4.1 shows, while equal numbers of women are in initial formation in LCWR and in CMSWR institutes, over 50 percent of the new entrants to CMSWR institutes are in their twenties (another 34 percent are in their thirties), and only 15 percent are older than forty. In LCWR institutes, the percentages are reversed: Over 50 percent of the new entrants are over forty and only 15 percent are in their twenties, with 28 percent in their thirties.

Conclusions

Previous data on generational differences paint a challenging picture for the Church since they show a gap between Church teaching, on the one hand, and the beliefs and practices of most young Catholics, on the other. The data also point to a troubling lack of young adult involvement

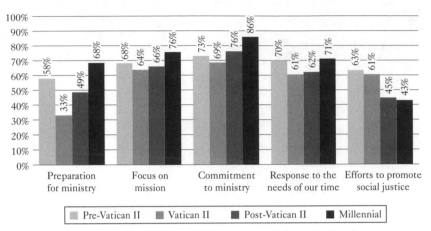

FIGURE 4.11 How would you rate these in your religious institute? (percentage responding "Excellent")

Source: 2009 CARA/NRVC Study of Recent Vocations to Religious Life

in parish and diocesan structures, or even regular prayer and attendance at Mass (Smith 2009, 167). *Although most young people who were raised Catholic still consider themselves to be so, they are less likely to be strongly committed Catholics.*

Since vocations to the religious life do not occur in a vacuum, the Church must grapple with the challenge this disaffection presents for recruitment to all forms of religious life, and to the diocesan priesthood as well. To the extent that only an anomalous minority of Catholic young adults is sufficiently involved in their religion to be attracted to religious life or the priesthood, future priests and religious may become increasingly removed from the beliefs and interests of the majority of their generational cohort—which, in a vicious circle, may further deter the rest of young Catholics from joining them. Recent studies of young diocesan priests indicate that this may already be happening (Gautier, Fichter, and Perl 2012; Hoge and Wenger 2003, 132–133). Is it also happening for religious sisters?

Our data also present multiple challenges for the leadership and membership of religious institutes of women in the United States. There are real generational differences in perception and attitude between millennial or post-Vatican II entrants and older entrants, differences that manifest themselves most readily to vocation and formation personnel. But they soon become apparent in community living, communal prayer, and ministry settings as well, and must be faced. Without some willingness

Table 4.1 Age distribution: initial formation
(percentage in each category)

	All Women	LCWR	CMSWR
Under 20	2%	1%	<1%
20–29	33	15	51
30–39	29	28	34
40–49	17	25	10
50–59	13	23	4
60 and over	6	8	1

Source: 2009 NRVC/CARA Study of Recent Vocations to Religious Life

to adapt to the desires of the post-Vatican II, millennial, and subsequent generations of Catholic women, an institute will not attract them, and its older members will become increasingly isolated from the changing culture. This will obviously impact an institute's witness to the Church and the larger society and, indeed, its ultimate survival. A limited number of institutes will be able to avoid this fate by attracting the anomalous minority of millennials who are still strongly attached to the Church, but studies estimate that these account for only 10–15 percent of all millennial Catholics (Smith 2009, 167). The rest will seek their call elsewhere. As one commentator recently noted, CARA's 2009 NRVC study necessarily reflects only *the interests and preferences of those currently entering LCWR and CMSWR religious institutes*:

> It did not (nor could it) track the interests of women not attracted to religious life as defined by the Vatican, especially those who find the institutes receiving the bulk of new vocations too constraining.... How many young Catholic people are attending universities for study in theology and ministry? How many of these are in non-Catholic institutions? How many are choosing non-Catholic ordained Christian ministry?
>
> ... proportionately, there are probably no fewer women seeking to serve the church, but they are seeking to serve in a manner free of the constraints of traditional religious life for women.... The two missing parts of the syllogism are, first, there are several other places women—especially young women—can obtain qualifications for

ministry, and, second, some young women simply move to other Christian denominations so as to be able to serve as fully certified ministers (Zagano 2011).

If these other millennial Catholic women Zagano cites follow their desire for prayer, ministry, and community elsewhere, religious life will be poorer as a result.

The data from the two surveys point to a significant challenge for vocations to religious life in many institutes. Those institutes currently attracting millennial and post-Vatican II entrants may be drawing them only from a small and non-representative minority of all young Catholic women. The majority of that age cohort remains less involved in Catholicism, or may even leave to follow their spiritual call in another religious tradition. Those institutes that have failed to attract the younger generations (although they may, indeed, be receiving entrants from older generations) will eventually need to appeal to younger Catholic women as well. The following three chapters consider aspects of this dilemma in more detail.

Chapter 5

Identity

DISTINGUISHING ELEMENTS

Maria's visits to several local groups of sisters had left her more confused than ever. On the one hand, she was attracted by their joy and their commitment to their various ministries, and she was deeply moved by their evening prayer. On the other hand, however, she had a hard time figuring out what differences, if any, there were between their religious congregations. None of the sisters wore habits, their lifestyles appeared similar, and their descriptions of their "charisms" seemed somewhat general. "Those words could apply to any good Christian," Maria thought. "We are all supposed to 'follow the call of Jesus' and 'stand with the poor.' Why is being a sister any different from being a group of Catholic laywomen who live together?"

ANY GROUP COMPOSED of voluntary members will continue to exist only as long as it maintains a discernible identity. Without a strong group identity, potential recruits will have no incentive to join it, and existing members will not be motivated to continue any meaningful participation in it. But while a clear identity is necessary for a group's survival, it is not sufficient. This identity must also be congruent with the interests, fears, and desires of some culture or subculture within the larger society in order to entice new members to join.

Most sisters are accustomed to considering how attractive their institute's identity and practices might be to persons from different racial and/or ethnic cultures. A predominantly German-American or Irish-American institute may not necessarily appeal to Hispanics or African Americans. A North American institute with a thriving new province in Korea, Nigeria, or Brazil may struggle with divergent expectations among its members as to what it should be and do. In previous centuries, cultural differences such as these were sometimes so severe that several religious institutes eventually split along ethnic lines.

As chapter 4 pointed out, however, *generations are also subcultures*, each with its own distinctive preoccupations, memories, and expectations that will render a given religious institute more or less attractive to that generation. The appeal of membership in a given institute will wax and wane as the desires and preoccupations of succeeding generations of Catholics change. Chapter 4 noted that younger entrants to both CMSWR and LCWR institutes were more likely in the 2009 survey to cite their institute's prayer life as being a very important attraction, and its mission and ministries as *less* important. Conversely, the survey's older Vatican II respondents, who had also entered between 1993 and 2008, rated the desire to be of service and the institute's mission as more important. In answering the open-ended questions, the Vatican II respondents in both surveys were the least likely to mention spontaneously the attraction of prayer, no matter whether they had entered their institutes as young adults prior to 1980 or in middle age after 1993. In other words, *one's generational cohort—the years in which one was born and grew up—has a strong effect on whether a particular aspect of a religious institute's identity will be attractive to the members of that generation, an effect that is visible throughout their life.* Institutes whose identity was quite attractive to young Catholics of one generation may need to consider how to rearticulate this identity in order to attract the next one. Otherwise, the differential appeal of this or that aspect of their institute may result in the predominance of one generational cohort and the underrepresentation of other age groups. To the extent that the two umbrella conferences to which religious institutes belong—LCWR and CMSWR—tend to have member institutes with differing identifying characteristics, we might expect the institutes in these two conferences to be differentially attractive to different generational cohorts. This appears to be the case: As chapter 4 showed, institutes in LCWR tend to attract women who are older than those attracted to CMSWR institutes. Do these disparities reflect the differential attractiveness of the various institutes to different generations? Do differences in generational composition, in turn, affect the identity of the institutes?

Elements of Group Identity

Demographic Characteristics

What elements make up a religious institute's identity? In a secular organization, the most obvious would be its various demographic

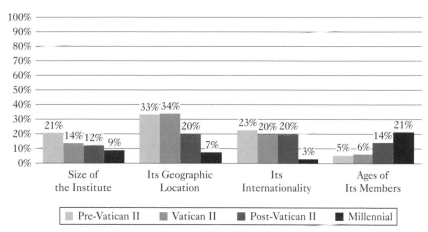

FIGURE 5.1 How much did these influence your decision to enter your religious institute? (percentage responding "Very Much")

characteristics: whether it is large or small, concentrated in one (rural or urban) locality or spread internationally, ethnically homogeneous or heterogeneous, recently established or celebrating its 200th anniversary. However, as figures 5.1 and 5.2 show, relatively few respondents in the 2009 survey said that the size, geographic location, or internationality of their institute's identity had attracted them "very much." These characteristics were the least important to the youngest members, and the respondents in CMSWR institutes typically were less attracted by these identifying characteristics than the respondents in LCWR institutes. The one exception to all of this was the age composition of the institute, which was more important to younger and CMSWR respondents.

The 2009 survey shows that, while the demographic composition of a religious institute may strongly impact its identity and mission— a religious institute with 100 members concentrated in a single area is obviously different from an international institute with several thousand members—it was *not* the major attraction cited by the survey respondents. Respondents of all ages in the 2009 survey were more than twice as likely to cite their institute's spirituality as being very attractive than they were to cite its size, location, or international character. But these preferences were uniformly expressed; they did not reveal many differences either between the generations or between the two conferences. For example, in their answers to the limited choice question, "How much did the spirituality of your institute attract you to enter? (Not at all, Only a little, Somewhat, Very much)," all age groups in both LCWR and CMSWR institutes expressed

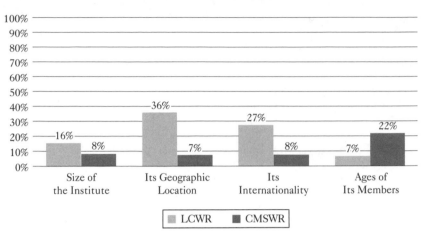

FIGURE 5.2 How much did these influence your decision to enter your religious institute? (percentage responding "Very Much")

equal attraction—with about 70 percent saying that their institute's spirituality had attracted them "Very much."

A similar lack of variation occurred in the answers to whether "A sense of call to religious life" had been an attraction: Between 75 percent and 90 percent of respondents in all generations and both conferences answered "Very much." To discover some of the finer distinctions, therefore, it is necessary to examine the open-ended questions at the end of each survey—the questions where the respondents were asked to write their own answers instead of picking from a limited selection of options (see below). The spontaneously volunteered information gleaned from these answers shows some surprising patterns in which characteristics are, or are not, attractive elements of the institutes' identities, as seen from the varying perspectives of newly entered respondents from different generations.

> 2009 Survey: "What most attracted you to your religious institute?"
> "What do you find most challenging about religious life?
> 1999 Survey: "Why did you enter your particular institute?"

It should be noted that answers to open-ended questions always vary widely. It is noteworthy if even 10 percent of the respondents spontaneously volunteer a similar response. In both the 1999 and 2009 surveys, the percentages of respondents giving a common answer to the open-ended questions rarely rose above 40 percent. Percentages in the single digits were much more typical. This should be kept in mind when considering the open-ended responses discussed below.

Charism

Every religious institute is considered to have an identifying "charism," the particular spirit or collective personality developed and passed on by its founder. Taken from the same Greek root as "Eucharist," a religious charism is considered to be a particular gift of the Holy Spirit for the benefit of the entire Church. But as chapter 3 pointed out, the exact definition and contents of a charism are not precisely specified, even in Church documents. As a result, it was difficult to know what respondents meant by this term when they used it to delineate the identities of their institutes. The percentage of respondents in the open-ended sections of both surveys who spontaneously cited their institute's charism as a key attraction of their community varied widely (from 9 percent to 58 percent across the various age groups and conferences). There was no discernible generational pattern in this variation, but there was a slight tendency for LCWR respondents to mention charism more frequently than CMSWR respondents (14–57 percent of the various LCWR age cohorts as compared to 14–24 percent of the CMSWR cohorts). For the most part, however, the respondents did not indicate what their institute's charism was; they tended simply to say that "The charism" or "The charism of our founder" had attracted them. Only a minority attempted to specify their institute's charism in more detail, and even these usually did so in relatively general terms:

What attracted you to your religious institute?

Charism: Eucharistic and Marian (millennial, CMSWR).

Our charism of reparation to the Sacred Heart really drew me (millennial, LCWR).

Charism—making Christ's merciful love visible (post-Vatican II, CMSWR).

Their charism of unity and reconciliation (post-Vatican II, LCWR).

I was delighted to learn that the charism is the offering of ourselves as victims to the Justice of God for the sanctification of the world (Vatican II, CMSWR).

Charism of peace through justice (Vatican II, LCWR).

In a similar manner, the "spirituality" of the institute was often cited in general rather than specific terms, such as "The sisters' spirituality" or "Carmelite spirituality."

Specific Distinguishing Features

While "charism" and "spirituality" were rarely mentioned in a way that could give any clear idea of how these identifying features attracted the various age cohorts to a specific religious institute, other, more specific features did differentiate the respondents. The most striking feature—drawing a sharp distinguishing line both between CMSWR and LCWR communities and between generational cohorts as well—was the wearing of a religious habit. In the limited-choice question, "How much did your religious institute's practices regarding the habit influence your decision to enter?" 91 percent of the youngest respondents answered "Very much." The different generations of CMSWR respondents were uniformly likely to attach a great importance to the habit: In all four age cohorts, over 90 percent said their institute's practices regarding the habit had strongly influenced their decision. Among the LCWR respondents of the three oldest generations, only 24 percent to 30 percent attached this level of importance to the habit—but close to twice as many (56 percent) of the millennial cohort did. While a "habit" can mean a variety of things—a simple cross, a common color of clothing, a short veil—in the open-ended questions of the 2009 survey, a third of all CMSWR respondents, of every generation except the very oldest, volunteered that they had been attracted to their institute precisely because its members wore a full, traditional habit. Recall that this is an unusually high percentage for an open-ended question. Few respondents (usually fewer than 5 percent) from LCWR institutes volunteered this response in 2009, and even fewer (1 percent) of the respondents did so in the 1999 survey.

An interesting age pattern appeared in the answers of the LCWR respondents to the open-ended questions: Almost all of the millennial and post-Vatican II respondents in the 2009 survey who mentioned the habit (admittedly a small number—only twenty-one women) stated that they had been attracted to their community *because* the sisters wore a habit. In contrast, half of the Vatican II and pre-Vatican II respondents who mentioned the habit (again, a very small number) said that they had entered their institute precisely because the sisters did *not* wear one. In the 1999 survey among respondents who had entered prior to

1980, the cutoff was at a slightly different point: Half of the respondents born in the 1940s who mentioned the habit in the open-ended questions entered their institute because its members did *not* wear one, while all of the respondents born after 1950 who mentioned the habit stated that they had entered their institute because the sisters *did* wear a habit. In either case, however, the older the respondent in an LCWR community was, the more negative she considered the habit as a sign of religious identity to be. This generational pattern held whether the respondent had entered her institute before 1980 or after 1993: The younger respondents were more positive and the older ones more negative regarding the religious habit.

What attracted you to your religious institute? (LCWR institutes only)

Wearing the habit, their love for one another, the charism of our foundress, the Blessed Sacrament (millennial, 2009 survey, born 1984).

A community that still wears a habit, values community life, common prayer life, and authentic to the Church (post-Vatican II, 2009 survey, born 1974).

The sisters were joyful! Our sisters wore a habit when I entered, but I came in spite of the habit (post-Vatican II, 2009 survey, born 1961).

The "down to earth" lifestyle and spirituality of my community. Lack of habit. Strong collaboration with the laity, love for the Eucharist, a variety of ministries (Vatican II, 2009 survey, born 1954).

I saw how happy the Sisters were. I also was attracted by the full habit. Many communities had recently removed the habit (Vatican II, 1999 survey, born 1951).

My community taught me through grade school and high school. However, it was the changes—the moving out of the habit into lay clothes that made them seem more human (Vatican II, 1999 survey, born 1949).

The sisters' hospitality and joyful spirit. They were also updated— no habit. The sisters reflected the mentality of Vatican II (Vatican II, 1999 survey, born 1946).

I was looking for a group that did not wear a habit and allowed members to live in apartments—basically, I wanted a group that allowed for individuality and personal needs (Vatican II, 2009 survey, born 1946).

An even more striking generational difference was evident in the use of "spousal" or "bride of Christ" images in the open-ended questions, when articulating the identity of a religious community. This occurred only among CMSWR respondents:

What attracted you to your religious institute? (CMSWR institutes only)

Their realization that they are brides of Christ, first and foremost (millennial, 2009 survey, born 1986).
How the community preserved being a bride of Christ through prayer and their daily life (millennial, 2009 survey, born 1985).
Above all, their love for Jesus as Spouse (millennial, 2009 survey, born 1982).
I fell in love with the Lord and realized he was calling me to be His spouse (post-Vatican II, 2009 survey, born 1972).

Among millennial respondents in CMSWR communities, 14 percent spontaneously mentioned this spousal identity when responding to the 2009 open-ended question about what had attracted them to their religious institutes; 6 percent of the post-Vatican II cohort of entrants also did so. No older respondent in the CMSWR institutes mentioned spousal identity in the open-ended questions of either the 2009 or 1999 survey. Thus, just as the LCWR respondents displayed diversity across the generations with regard to their opinions on the habit, the CMSWR respondents displayed a similar generational diversity in their use of the "bride of Christ" image.

A final striking difference could be seen in the respondents' attraction to their institutes' loyalty/obedience to the Church's official magisterium. As figures 5.3 and 5.4 show, almost 90 percent of the CMSWR respondents said that their institute's fidelity to the Church was very important in influencing their decision to enter it, while only 21 percent of the LCWR respondents said this. The attraction of fidelity to the Church was highest among the youngest respondents in both conferences: 93 percent in CMSWR and 44 percent in LCWR rated this as very important, while only 36 percent of the pre-Vatican II and 20 percent of the Vatican II LCWR respondents did. The youngest LCWR respondents were also almost twice

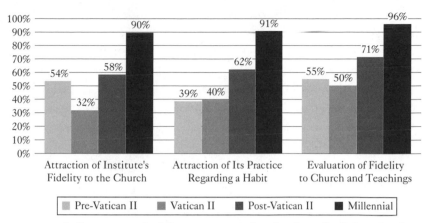

FIGURE 5.3 Influences on decision to enter and evaluation of religious institute (percentage responding "Very Much" or "Excellent")

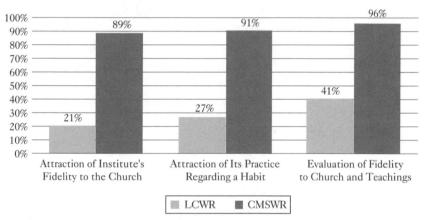

FIGURE 5.4 Influences on decision to enter and evaluation of religious institute (percentage responding "Very Much" or "Excellent")

as likely as the older generations to evaluate their institute's fidelity to the magisterium as "excellent"; among CMSWR respondents, all generations were equally likely to evaluate their institute highly on this question.

The responses to the open-ended questions reflected similar differences between the conferences. In the 2009 survey, 35 percent or more of each age cohort in the CMSWR institutes spontaneously mentioned fidelity to the Church, the pope, or the magisterium as very important in attracting them to their institute. This is a very high rate for an answer to be volunteered without prompting and was among the highest of all the responses. In contrast, fewer than 1 percent of the respondents from

LCWR communities in 2009, from any generational cohort, and fewer than 1 percent of the 1999 respondents who had entered before 1980 included this in the list of their institute's attractive aspects. A related, if subtle, difference occurred in the open-ended responses about the institutes' charism: Only CMSWR respondents stressed that their institute was *faithful* to the original charism of its founder—which may imply that, in the minds of these respondents, other institutes were not as faithful as their own had been.

What attracted you to your religious institute?

Love for the Church and the Holy Father. Fidelity to living authentic religious life according to the heart and mind of the Church (millennial, CMSWR).

Fidelity to the Church's teachings, monastic customs, contemplative-apostolic life (post-Vatican II, CMSWR).

Fidelity to the Church and Pope. Devotion to the Holy Eucharist and Mary. Community life. Religious habit and name. Monastic customs. Faithfulness to founder (post-Vatican II, CMSWR).

Community life, faithfulness to the Church, spirit of sacrifice, faithfulness to the original spirit of the founder (Vatican II, CMSWR).

Traditional versus Progressive

In the larger U.S. society, a group's reputation as traditional or progressive, or conservative or liberal places it on one side or the other of an increasingly widening ideological divide (Bishop 2008). The same split occurs in the open-ended questions: Only the LCWR respondents in both the 1999 and 2009 surveys mentioned that they were attracted to their community because of its progressive reputation, while the CMSWR respondents were the most likely to cite the traditional character of their institutes as attractive. But the percentages in all of these cases are quite small: Fewer than 5 percent of LCWR respondents, of any generational cohort, cited their institute's progressive reputation as attracting them to enter, and fewer than 8 percent of the CMSWR respondents cited their institute's traditional reputation. There are also two interesting generational cohort effects on these answers: *Millennial* respondents in CMSWR were the most likely to name the traditional reputation of their institute as an attractive aspect of its identity; *Vatican II and pre-Vatican II* respondents in LCWR orders were the most likely to be drawn to institutes they identified as progressive.

Intangibles

In addition to readily grasped characteristics—whether visible like a religious habit or conceptual like "bride of Christ" or "traditional"—a group's identity will also be formed from less easily articulated elements: small daily customs, the sum of the personalities of the sisters, and even the physical features of the motherhouse buildings and grounds. These intangibles were not measured by the limited-choice questions in either the 1999 or 2009 survey. The open-ended questions, however, elicited many such intangibles. For example, all groups of respondents named "joy" as the characteristic of the sisters that had most attracted them, with the millennial and post-Vatican II CMSWR respondents the most likely to do so (44 percent as compared to 7–33 percent among LCWR or older CMSWR respondents). Similarly, all groups were equally likely to mention that the sisters were "normal" people. With regard to the other personal characteristics volunteered by the respondents—characteristics that imparted an intangible distinctiveness to the institute's identity in the eyes of its newest members—the following patterns emerged:

- LCWR respondents were more likely to say that the sisters were
    - *Welcoming* (9–20 percent of the various LCWR generations mentioned this, as compared to 2–3 percent of the CMSWR respondents);
    - *Loving* to each other (10–17 percent among the various LCWR generations, compared to 8 percent among young CMSWR respondents and 0 percent among the older ones); and
    - *Kind* to those to whom they ministered (2–8 percent among the LCWR generations compared to 1–2 percent of the CMSWR respondents).
- CMSWR respondents were more likely to say that the sisters were clear about their institute's identity and mission (5–15 percent of the various CMSWR generations compared to 1–2 percent of the LCWR respondents).

Boundary Drawing

A common way of reinforcing the identity of a group is to construct strong boundaries distinguishing it from outsiders. Other researchers (e.g., Smith 1998) have noted that a sense of being beleaguered by hostile outside forces or of being a "true remnant" among a faithless majority can unite a religious group—so much so, in fact, that its members often retain this image of themselves even if outside observers cannot find any basis for it in fact.

This appears to be the case for both ends of the ideological spectrum among the new entrants who responded to the surveys' open-ended questions. The tendency of CMSWR respondents to cite their institute's fidelity to the magisterium and to its charism has already been mentioned. Such a response might lead an outside observer to infer that these respondents thought other religious institutes had not been as faithful. But the perceived unfaithfulness of other religious institutes, however, might not be grounded in reality, at least according to the responses in our survey. Only three individuals in all of the open-ended responses in both the 1999 and 2009 surveys mentioned that they had been attracted to their institutes because the sisters there were willing to question the magisterium: two from LCWR institutes and one from a CMSWR institute. But whether or not other institutes really *were* more or less faithful to the Church, if some of the CMSWR respondents *thought* that they were, this could be a strong boundary marker between them.

CMSWR respondents were also the most likely to volunteer the information that the outside world in general opposes religious life. The younger respondents from both conferences were also equally likely to mention the danger of secular values infecting religious institutes. Such comments were, however, relatively rare—given by only 2–9 percent of the various generations of CMSWR respondents and by 3–4 percent of the LCWR respondents.

What do you find most challenging about religious life?

The opposition of the current culture/society (millennial, CMSWR).

Religious life is so countercultural that it's hard to be living in a different lifestyle than most of mainstream America. This is especially true when religious values are being replaced with secularism (millennial, from an institute belonging to both LCWR and CMSWR).

We need to be firm in our faith and our calling. The world and its views are all over, and we need to be careful in keeping the Church's teaching and living our charism to the fullness. Sometimes all the world's thinking infiltrates our religious communities, making life harder and more superficial (post-Vatican II, CMSWR).

Meeting the challenges of a Culture of Death society (Vatican II, CMSWR).

The open-ended comments of some older LCWR respondents sometimes reflected a sense of being beleaguered or persecuted by the Church itself. It was primarily the Vatican II and pre-Vatican II respondents in LCWR communities who expressed dissatisfaction with the policies of the Church hierarchy, its teachings about women, and the perceived preference of bishops for conservative, habited religious orders. Few post-Vatican II LCWR respondents—and *no* millennial LCWR respondents—mentioned these concerns, and the percentages even of the Vatican II and pre-Vatican II respondents who did so were quite small (4–8 percent). It is worth noting, however, that the data in our surveys were collected prior to the 2009 apostolic visitation of U.S. religious and prior to the 2012 release of the doctrinal assessment of LCWR. A more recent survey might elicit different responses.

What do you find most challenging about religious life?

As a religious woman, I often feel like a second-class citizen. Prayers for vocations seem to center around priests only. It is hard to believe in "the Church" when it fails to recognize the giftedness of at least half its members—because we are female rather than male (post-Vatican II, LCWR).

The judgmentalism of the Religious Right. The support given to the "more conservative" newer religious communities in our diocese by our bishops after our sisters' years of free service to the Church as parish teachers (post-Vatican II, LCWR).

The absolutism within the institutional Church in general (Vatican II, LCWR).

Belonging to the Institutional Church which is oppressive and yet I love (Vatican II, LCWR).

The institutional Church, i.e., the hierarchy (pre-Vatican II, LCWR).

Overall, the LCWR respondents expressed less concern with drawing a boundary against the outside world than the CMSWR respondents did. Although this lack of boundary-drawing may help them become closer to those they serve, it may also mean a loss of their distinctive identity. The post-Vatican II LCWR respondents, especially, worried about the seductions of a middle-class lifestyle in their institutes and wondered if the distinctiveness of religious life was being obscured:

What do you find most challenging about religious life?

I find it challenging to identify or be aware of the relevance of religious life in the world today when what I do isn't any different from others. To keep in the forefront my relationship with God is challenging in a culture of so much material goods, activities, etc. (post-Vatican II, LCWR).

I find giving witness to the values I hold to be challenging—it is so easy to let the world influence me! Living a middle-class lifestyle doesn't always give the witness I desire (post-Vatican II, LCWR).

I have found that while some are claiming a vow of poverty, they are living middle-class and even upper-middle-class lives. . . . I find this hard because we could be leading lives radically committed to the Gospel, but too often we are choosing consumerism and individualism (post-Vatican II, LCWR).

The Importance of Visible Identity Markers

The elements of identity are manifold. Some are subtle; others are readily visible, both to the members themselves and to those outside of the institutes. A religious institute with visible and/or easily articulated identity markers—wearing a habit, emphasizing its loyalty to the magisterium on its website—will find it easier to attract entrants with similar preferences, even though, as we saw in chapter 4, these entrants are only a small percentage of all young adult Catholics. In contrast, religious institutes with less visible or not easily expressed identities—a charism expressed in relatively vague terms, or an institutional spirit based on personal qualities of their "welcoming" or "down-to-earth" sisters—will find it harder to attract potential entrants who have not had a chance to meet them in person. The 2009 and 1999 surveys both show that the younger respondents were less likely to have had prior contact with the sisters of their institute through being taught by them in school, working with them, or having relatives who were also members. But they were *more* likely to have learned of their institute from a media story—precisely the mode in which visible identifiers like the religious habit or easily summarized traits like loyalty to the

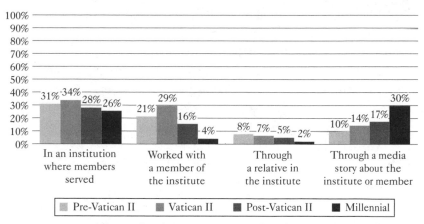

FIGURE 5.5 How did you first become acquainted with your religious institute? (percentage selecting each response)

pope are most easily presented, and in which more subtle cultural differences might easily be missed. Figure 5.5 reports the generational variations from the 2009 survey.

The responses in the 1999 survey show the same pattern. As many as two-thirds of the Vatican II respondents who entered prior to 1980 had been educated by the sisters in their institute, as had almost half of the post-Vatican II respondents and 38 percent of the pre-Vatican respondents. In the open-ended questions of the 1999 survey, between 21 and 28 percent of the Vatican II and pre-Vatican II respondents who had entered before 1980 mentioned having had extensive prior contact with the sisters in their institute. Regular interaction with the sisters allowed these respondents to "pick up" on the subtle, less easily articulated intangibles that distinguished their institute's identity and made it attractive to them:

> Before I entered my community, I was privileged to work as a nurse's aide, taking care of our sisters at our infirmary. Although I could not have put into words then how they influenced me, now I can say that the faithful witness of their lives—in joy and suffering—communicated our charism (millennial, 2009 survey, LCWR).
> While participating in a lay volunteer program, living with the sisters, I realized that their lifestyle attracted me, and that by becoming a religious I could live out my calling to mission, justice, and be who God created me to be (post-Vatican II, 2009 survey, LCWR).
> I knew the sisters because they served in the schools I attended. They were not my teachers, but were principals and taught

religion or other grades. I liked the sisters and the way they served people (post-Vatican II, 2009 survey, LCWR).

I have aunts and other, more distant relatives in my community and I had the sisters in my community as teachers from the first through the twelfth grade (Vatican II, 1999 survey, LCWR).

The sisters were my college professors. The novices and postulants were my classmates. The spirit of the order was evident everywhere (Vatican II, 1999 survey, LCWR).

I had [sisters from my institute] in high school and remained friends with two of my high school teachers from the time I graduated high school until I entered nine years later (pre-Vatican II, 1999 survey, LCWR).

In contrast, fewer than 2 percent of millennial and post-Vatican II CMSWR respondents in the 2009 survey mentioned similar experiences, and *no* older CMSWR respondents did so. For most, just seeing or hearing about the visible identity markers of their institute was sufficient. An institute's habit and its explicit profession of loyalty to the Church can easily be ascertained by reading a news article or looking at a website; the sisters' welcoming spirit, their kindness, or their love for each other require personal contact to be experienced. This renders it easier for CMSWR institutes to recruit new members from the specific subculture of young Catholics who are attracted to their distinctive identity markers.

The differences in clarity of identity persist after entrance (see figure 5.6). CMSWR respondents in the 2009 survey were twice as likely to evaluate their institute's sense of identity, both generally and specifically, as "Excellent." And it was primarily the LCWR respondents who stated in their open-ended responses that one of the things they found challenging was that there were diverse opinions among the sisters about their institute's identity—although, again, this was only a small percentage (3 percent in LCWR as compared to less than 1 percent in CMSWR communities). It is also notable that none of the youngest entrants in either conference mentioned these difficulties with identity.

What do you find most challenging about religious life?

I find the conversations, processes...about identity, purpose, and mission of religious life the most challenging, because of the

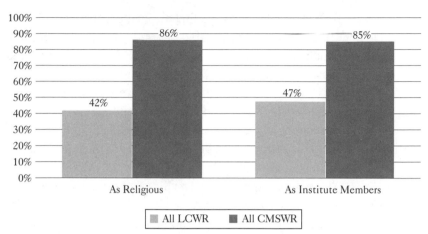

FIGURE 5.6 Evaluation of religious institute's sense of identity (percentage responding "Excellent")

diverse attitudes, experiences, perspectives (ecclesial and theological) among our members (post-Vatican II, LCWR).

The lack of a unified vision and purpose...the challenge of diversity (post-Vatican II, LCWR).

Individuals who are prophets of doom or question the identity and charism of the congregation (Vatican II, LCWR).

Conclusions

As generational cohorts succeed each other in Catholicism, the identities of its various religious institutes may become more or less attractive to them. Or it may be that Catholics of a particular generational cohort will be attracted to one aspect of a particular religious institute (its spirituality, for example, or its service to the poor), but alienated by another aspect (the vow of chastity or some teachings of the magisterium). In any case, institutes that have built an identity around, for example, ministry and social justice (reflecting the priorities of the generational cohort that predominates among their current membership) may need to explore ways of emphasizing other aspects of their charism—their founder's devotion to the Eucharist, for example, or radical service to the poor—in order to appeal to a subsequent generation. Institutes that languished in more activist or ecumenical times may find that their insistence on traditional prayer styles and orthodoxy have come back into fashion among some young adult Catholics. And to the extent that the institutes clustered in one or the other of the two conferences are able to attract younger entrants, the institutes in that conference will display strikingly different identifying elements than those in the other—as we have seen in this chapter.

U.S.Catholicism, however, is not monolithic—even within its generations. Although the majority of a given generational cohort's members may prioritize the identifying elements of one style of religious life over another, not all of the members will do so. Even in the most progressive and activist age cohort, there will be some who desire the stability and permanence of traditionalist forms of religious life. And even within generations stereotyped as conservative or traditionalist, there will be some who wish to work for social justice and systemic change.

The important thing is for an institute to have a clear identity, preferably one that can be portrayed or articulated in the media outlets that today's youngest generation of Catholic adults most commonly use. The characteristics described in this chapter are some of the elements that might comprise such an identity. Others—prayer styles, community living practices, and ministry—will be covered in chapters 6 and 7.

Chapter 6

Prayer, Spirituality, and the Vows

THE COMMON CORE

Maria knelt before the image of Our Lady of Guadalupe in the side chapel of the church where she attended Sunday Mass. The many lit candles flickered on the familiar image as she fingered her rosary. "O Santissima Virgen Maria,"—she always prayed to Our Lady of Guadalupe in Spanish—"help me decide what to do."

In her visits to several different religious communities, Maria had always been invited to pray with the sisters. She had never prayed the Divine Office used by some of the communities, and was still trying to find her way among all of the various ribbon markers. It seemed much more natural to pray to Mary as she had always done since she was a child. She also liked sitting quietly before the Blessed Sacrament during the weekly Eucharistic Adoration offered at the university. More and more, she felt a pull toward religious life with its focus on prayer. But many of the sisters were also very active in their apostolates—as much or more so than many laypeople Maria knew. How could they find the time to pray as much and as deeply as she was beginning to desire to do?

IN ITS ESSENCE, religious life is a response to a call from God: 78 percent of the 2009 survey's respondents cited this as "very important" in their decision to enter their institutes—the highest percentage of all the potential attractions listed. But what exactly is God calling one *to*? In former times, the call may have been to serve the poor, to evangelize nonbelievers, or to nurse the sick; indeed, the "desire to be of service" was still considered "very important" by 65 percent of the 2009 survey's respondents. But

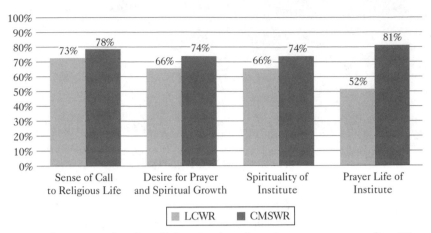

FIGURE 6.1 Attracted to the religious institute by...(percentage responding "Very Much")

"a desire for prayer and spiritual growth" (74 percent "very important") and "the spirituality of the institute" (66 percent "very important") were even more important to them. As in all the previous official and popular articulations of the goal of religious life (Wittberg 1994, 110–116), its primary purpose according to the 2009 respondents was still responding to God's call for personal spiritual growth. Reflecting this primacy, there were few significant differences between the generations in the importance they attached to a sense of God's call, in their desire for prayer/spiritual growth, or in their institute's spirituality. The youngest generation in LCWR institutes, however, did place somewhat greater importance than the older LCWR generations on the specific prayer life of their institutes. Even though the number of LCWR millennial respondents is quite small, because the survey was of the entire population and not a sample, the difference in their answers from those of the other LCWR generations is important. In contrast, CMSWR respondents attached equally high importance to this feature across all generations except the very oldest. (See figures 6.1 and 6.2.)

The respondents in the 2009 survey were also equally likely to mention a sense of divine call in the open-ended questions, across all generations and both conferences:

What most attracted you to your religious institute?

The inexplicable sense that this is where God wants me (millennial, CMSWR).

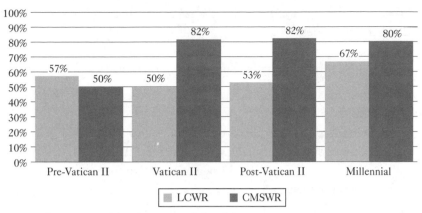

FIGURE 6.2 Attracted by the prayer life of the institute (percentage responding "Very Much")

God kept pushing me, directing me here (millennial, CMSWR).

An unwavering hunger for God. The "more." A sense of call out of an experience of contemplative prayer (post-Vatican II, LCWR).

Deep in my heart, I knew that this was where God wanted me to be (post-Vatican II, CMSWR).

The hand of God and a desire to fully serve God and His people in the manner of the growing seed God planted within, to serve God in a fuller manner (Vatican II, LCWR).

Before I even knew about the . . . Sisters, I felt called to offer myself to God as a victim for priestly holiness (Vatican II, CMSWR).

At the death of my husband, I drew closer to God and Jesus. I asked God in prayer to invite me if he wanted me to be a sister. I was invited three days later to dinner and knew this was the community (pre-Vatican II, LCWR).

To be honest, God wanted me in this one and no other (pre-Vatican II, CMSWR).

In their open-ended responses, the youngest respondents of both conferences were more likely than the older ones to volunteer the information that the sisters' prayerfulness was what had attracted them to their institute. Between 16 percent (CMSWR) and 25 percent (LCWR) of the millennial respondents in both conferences named this one of the sisters' attractive qualities, as compared to 7 percent of the Vatican II and pre-Vatican II respondents. Indeed, the prayerfulness or holiness of the sisters was their second most-frequently mentioned attractive quality (after the sisters' joy) for the millennial respondents in both CMSWR and LCWR communities.

What most attracted you to your religious institute?

The deep spirituality and radiant JOY of the members (millennial, LCWR).

The holiness of the members (millennial, CMSWR).

I was attracted to the Sisters' joy and I thought their joy was related to the way they prayed. So I began to desire that sort of prayer life (post-Vatican II, CMSWR).

A call and a feel of being home. I found women who were prayerful, wacky, and down home, deeply rooted in God (post-Vatican II, LCWR).

The sisters—very authentic, committed, absolutely support the Church, totally given in prayer, community life, habit (Vatican II, CMSWR).

They could enjoy each other, laugh, but were also very prayerful (Vatican II, LCWR).

The tendency to value prayerfulness seems to have increased in recent decades: The Vatican II and pre-Vatican II respondents in the 2009 survey were more likely than the respondents from the same age cohort who had entered prior to 1980 to list the sisters' prayerfulness and spirituality as something that had attracted them to their institute.

Specific Prayer Types

When it came to specific *kinds* of prayer, however, there were sharper differences, by both age cohort and conference (see figure 6.3). Eucharistic Adoration was rated as "very important" by almost three times as many millennial (93 percent) as Vatican II (34 percent) respondents in the 2009 survey, and was the most spontaneously cited attraction of all prayer types in the open-ended questions. Daily Mass was highly valued by all age cohorts, although the Vatican II cohort, at 60 percent, was the least likely to value it "very much." Praying the Liturgy of the Hours in common was also highly valued—again, more by the millennial respondents (94 percent) than by the Vatican II respondents (55 percent), and more by CMSWR respondents (95 percent) than LCWR respondents

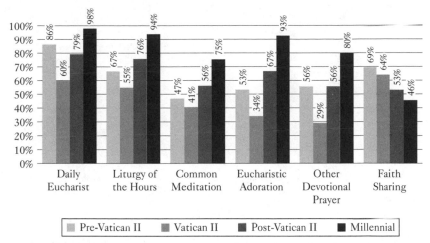

FIGURE 6.3 How important to you are these types of prayer...(percentage responding "Very")

(47 percent).[1] Similar patterns occur with other devotional prayers such as the rosary: The youngest respondents were the most likely (80 percent) and the Vatican II respondents the least likely (29 percent) to value these types of prayer. In contrast, the older respondents were more likely than the younger respondents to value faith-sharing.

Since CMSWR institutes attract more millennial entrants than LCWR institutes, these generational differences are reflected in the proportion of respondents from these two conferences who valued the various types of prayer. CMSWR respondents were more likely than LCWR respondents to value daily Eucharist, Eucharistic Adoration, Liturgy of the Hours, common meditation, and devotional prayers such as the rosary; LCWR respondents were more likely to value faith-sharing (see figure 6.4).

However, the same generational distinctiveness appears even when looking solely at LCWR respondents: The youngest entrants to LCWR institutes were three times as likely as Vatican II respondents to say that they valued Eucharistic Adoration and devotional prayer very much, almost twice as likely to say they valued daily Mass very much, and significantly more likely to value the Liturgy of the Hours as well (see figure 6.5). In CMSWR institutes, in contrast, there were few generational differences in attaching a high value to these types of prayer.

The responses to the open-ended questions showed the same patterns. In general, CMSWR respondents were more likely than LCWR respondents spontaneously to mention Eucharistic spirituality and Eucharistic

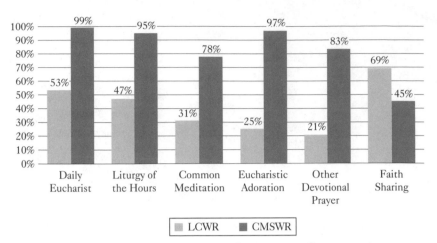

FIGURE 6.4 How important to you are these types of prayer...(percentage responding "Very")

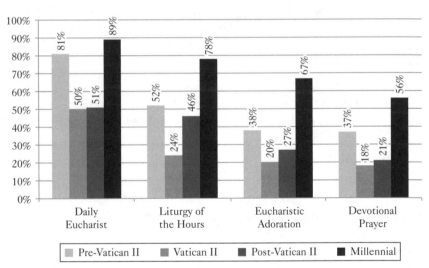

FIGURE 6.5 How important to you is...(percentage among LCWR responding "Very Much")

Adoration as practices that had attracted them to their religious institutes, with the millennial CMSWR respondents the most likely to do so. Almost a quarter of the millennial CMSWR respondents (24 percent) in the 2009 survey spontaneously mentioned Eucharistic Adoration as something that had attracted them, far higher than the post-Vatican II (16 percent) and Vatican II (14 percent) CMSWR respondents. This tendency seems to be increasing over time: Less than 1 percent of the pre-Vatican II and Vatican II respondents who had entered prior to 1980 had mentioned the attraction of Eucharistic Adoration in the 1999 survey.

Interesting variations occurred in the open-ended responses regarding common prayer. The youngest respondents in LCWR institutes were more likely than other age cohorts to list common prayer as an attraction, while it was the older Vatican II respondents who were more likely to do so in CMSWR institutes. Marian devotion was much more likely to be spontaneously mentioned by younger than older respondents, and by CMSWR more than LCWR respondents. As with Eucharistic Adoration, the attraction to prayer in common and Marian devotion appears to be increasing over time; few if any of the 1999 survey's respondents had mentioned either type of prayer as something that had attracted them to their institutes when they entered prior to 1980. Other types of prayer were mentioned only rarely or not at all in the survey.

What most attracted you to your religious institute?

Eucharistic devotion, fidelity to the Church, devotion to Our Lady, joy of the sisters and desire for holiness obvious in the sisters (millennial, CMSWR).

I was attracted by the faithfulness to our primary charism of perpetual adoration. In adoring Our Lord exposed in the Blessed Sacrament, we aid the Church in a special way by always interceding for those in need (millennial, CMSWR).

The devotion to Mary and daily Eucharist and community life (post-Vatican II, LCWR).

Prayer life—Mass daily, rosary, adoration all daily. Liturgy of the Hours (post-Vatican II, CMSWR).

The prayer life in daily Mass, Eucharistic adoration, Rosary, community prayers, Liturgy of the Hours, and meditation (post-Vatican II, CMSWR).

I knew I wanted a monastic community with the practice of the Liturgy of the Hours prayed communally, of daily Eucharist, and time for personal prayer. My community does all of these (post-Vatican II, LCWR).

That they would consider a fifty-five-year old transfer who had been a United Methodist Pastor who joined the Church in 1987. Perpetual Adoration, non-habit, on the cutting edge (Vatican II, LCWR).

My community has maintained perpetual adoration, around the clock, since 1878. Eucharist has continually been my support and total gift (Vatican II, LCWR).

Evaluating Opportunities for Spiritual Growth

The purpose of all prayer, of course, is to grow closer to God. "A desire for prayer and spiritual growth" was ranked as very important by 73 percent of the 2009 survey's respondents and as somewhat important by another 23 percent. In general, the younger the respondent, the more positively she evaluated her religious institute in offering opportunities for spiritual growth, in faithfulness to prayer, and in the quality of its communal prayer experiences. Again, because of the larger number of younger members in CMSWR communities, the respondents from that conference rank their institutes higher than LCWR respondents do (see figures 6.6 and 6.7).

Within LCWR institutes, the youngest respondents are much more positive in evaluating their institute along these three spiritual growth and prayer dimensions (averaging a 67 percent or higher positive rating), and the Vatican II are the least positive (36–59 percent), with the other two generations somewhere in between. In CMSWR institutes, there were no generational differences in how respondents evaluated their institutes' faithfulness to prayer, but the youngest two CMSWR generations did rank their institutes' communal prayer experiences and opportunities for spiritual growth higher than the older generations did.

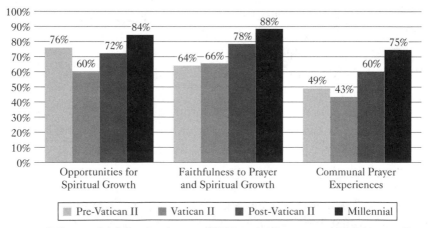

FIGURE 6.6 Rate the following in your religious institute (percentage responding "Excellent")

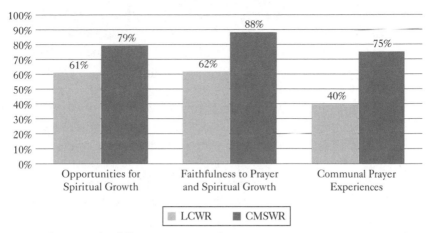

FIGURE 6.7 Rate the following in your religious institute (percentage responding "Excellent")

Spiritualizing Challenges

An interesting pattern occurs among respondents to the 2009 survey who were asked in an open-ended question to list the *challenges* they experienced in religious life. CMSWR respondents, of all age cohorts, showed a much greater tendency to spiritualize this question, citing personal, internal difficulties with spiritual growth as their primary challenge. Some listed the specific aspects of spiritual growth that they found most challenging: patience with self or others, self-knowledge, and perseverance. Uniformly, these spiritual difficulties were cited much more frequently by CMSWR respondents than by LCWR respondents: A full 25 percent of both the millennial and post-Vatican II CMSWR respondents and 12 percent of the Vatican II CMSWR respondents named such challenges, while fewer than 5 percent of the LCWR respondents in any generation did so. It is not certain whether this tendency has increased over time, as a similar open-ended question was not asked in the 1999 study.

What do you find most challenging about religious life?

The difficulties come from my own selfishness and weaknesses, in relating with those around me with charity, yet when I bring my failures and difficulties to Jesus, he bears them with me (millennial, CMSWR).

Most challenging is my personal weakness, which at times hinders the great work of God that He would do in and through me. The good thing is that when I surrender my weakness to Him, His power can be made even more manifest in me (millennial, CMSWR).

The most challenging thing about religious life for me is being able to attain holiness. Yes, it is a constant striving, but being holy and thinking about God without distractions is challenging (millennial, CMSWR).

To daily die to self so as not to take back the gift I offered to God— not to take back or desire the things I gave up for the love of God (post-Vatican II, CMSWR).

Rubbing off those rough edges is painful and constant. Takes a lot of work on my part. Mess up a lot along the way. God is patient and merciful. Can I be the same for myself? (post-Vatican II, LCWR).

To grow in holiness vs. personal weaknesses and vices and imperfections! (Vatican II, CMSWR).

The Vows

The three vows of poverty, chastity, and obedience have traditionally been considered a key identifying characteristic of religious life. Some institutes also added a fourth vow specific to them: to care for the poor, for example, or to tend the elderly sick without remuneration. Chapter 3 noted, however, that the 2004 World Congress on Religious Life did *not* list the vows as a specifically identifying element, however much the vows may continue to be emphasized in official Vatican documents. This is reflected in the responses to the open-ended questions in both the 1999 and 2009 surveys: Less than 1 percent of the respondents—of any age cohort or from either conference— listed the vows as something that had attracted them to their religious institute. Few mentioned their institute's special fourth vow either; the most likely age cohort to do so was the Vatican II CMSWR entrants in the 2009 survey. But even here, less than 3 percent mentioned this characteristic.

The CMSWR respondents, however, *did* find the vow of obedience especially difficult, with between 9 and 11 percent of the post-Vatican II and millennial respondents spontaneously mentioning this vow when describing what they found most challenging about religious life. Including potential synonyms for obedience such as "surrender," "abandonment," "renouncing self," and "sacrifice" would make the total percent of responses even higher (over 30 percent for the millennial CMSWR respondents and over 20 percent for the post-Vatican II CMSWR respondents). In contrast, far fewer respondents (less than 4 percent across all generations and both conferences) mentioned having difficulties with poverty or celibate chastity—or with the vows in general. This corresponds to the findings of Nygren and Ukeritis (1993, 183) in the early 1990s: that women religious found the vow of obedience to be the most difficult, while the male religious found the vow of celibate chastity the most difficult.

What do you find most challenging about religious life?

The vow of obedience—accepting all that is daily asked of me without questioning the other's motives and without complaining. I pray daily for docility to God's will (millennial, CMSWR).

Not being listened to by my higher superiors. I also find obedience hard at times, especially when I don't understand why I am being asked/told to do something (millennial, CMSWR).

Surrendering to the will of God in religious obedience. The separation from family. Patience with myself in conversion and growth and weaknesses that can only be overcome by grace. Dying to self (post-Vatican II, CMSWR).

Obeying one another without grumbling. Living in peace with decisions made by the community that I may not have agreed with (post-Vatican II, LCWR).

Obedience—I am a product of the culture I lived in—independent. I struggle not to take back my will which I have given to Jesus by my vows (post-Vatican II, CMSWR).

Our profession of stability (I love to travel) and poverty (I'm "Imeldific"—re: Imelda Marcos—on a monastic budget!) (post-Vatican II, LCWR).

Obedience is very challenging. I often feel very keenly that I am unable to make decisions on my own. I sometimes feel controlled and a lack of freedom. Chastity is very difficult. In spite of the difficulty, the Lord has always given me the necessary grace to be faithful and persevere (post-Vatican II, CMSWR).

The challenges vary over the years. In my 30s and 40s, the vow of chastity was the most challenging. As I enter my 50s, I'd say the most challenging aspect is the vow of obedience (Vatican II, LCWR).

I'm 62—yet I still find celibacy a challenge. I miss the absence of one special person whom I can love and who will love me (Vatican II, LCWR).

Balancing Prayer and Ministry

The 2009 survey responses have shown that prayer and spiritual growth were among the strongest attractions drawing respondents to their religious institutes. As a result, there was often a tension, especially in the "active" institutes focused on ministerial work, between the demands of the apostolate and the need for prayer. While few of the 1999 respondents (less than 2 percent) spontaneously mentioned their institute's attempts to balance action and contemplation as something that had attracted them to enter, between 4 and 5 percent of the 2009 respondents did so. The attraction of an "active-contemplative" lifestyle was mentioned by similar percentages of older and younger respondents from both CMSWR and LCWR communities.

What most attracted you to your religious institute?

I really liked how the Sisters had a balance between work and prayer (millennial, CMSWR).

Adoration of the Blessed Sacrament, combined with an apostolic outreach—the combination of contemplative prayer plus being "out in the world" (post-Vatican II, LCWR).

Prayer and community life. Evident joy and goodness of the sisters. Structure/horarium of their contemplative-apostolic life (post-Vatican II, CMSWR).

The lifestyle these sisters lived. I had volunteered at an active order and they worked or overworked too many hours a day. I had entered a cloistered community. With the community I am in now, I have a happy medium (Vatican II, LCWR).

Blend of prayer and ministry (pre-Vatican II, CMSWR).

The tension between these two pulls surfaced strikingly when the respondents were asked to name the challenges they faced. Again with only slight differences between old and young, or between CMSWR and LCWR institutes, respondents mentioned the challenge of balancing the demands of prayer and ministry and, to a somewhat lesser extent, prayer and community.

What do you find most challenging about religious life?

Balancing our interior life with our apostolate (millennial, LCWR).

The most challenging aspect of religious life is the activity. It is very difficult to maintain a balance between prayer and the apostolate (millennial, CMSWR).

It is sometimes difficult to remain prayerful or committed to spiritual practices when the rigors of ministry fill the day (post-Vatican II, LCWR).

Trying to balance work and prayer (post-Vatican II, CMSWR).

The demands of ministry and the constant effort to balance prayer and ministry (post-Vatican II, LCWR).

Balancing work and prayer (Vatican II, CMSWR).

Making time to always pray (Vatican II, LCWR).

Conclusions

Again, we find that generations matter. Our millennial respondents were more likely than respondents from previous generations to value Eucharistic Adoration, prayer in common, and Marian devotion. To the extent that a religious institute is seen by millennial searchers as offering these types of prayer, they will be more likely to attract this generation. In contrast, older entrants, especially the Vatican II generation, remain much less attached to these prayer types and are more interested in faith-sharing. These appear to be true generational differences, not dependent on whether a woman of the Vatican II age cohort entered her institute as a teenager in 1968 or as a middle-aged widow with grown children in 1998. It is thus likely that institutes emphasizing different types of prayer will attract different generations of entrants. This may be one reason why CMSWR institutes are attracting a younger demographic than LCWR institutes.

It may appear that, if LCWR institutes wish to attract more new members from the millennial generation, they will need to emphasize those aspects of their spirituality that millennials find attractive. As the responses quoted above show, Eucharistic Adoration, the rosary, and devotion to Mary are key components of our millennial respondents' attraction to LCWR institutes, as well as to CMSWR institutes. *But our respondents are not representative of all millennial Catholics*, the majority of whom have become less, rather than more, attached to Catholic beliefs and practices. Institutes may therefore wish to emphasize aspects of their spirituality that these other millennials might value: Ignatian or other types of discernment, for example, or centering prayer. Recent authors working with young adults have noted an intense desire for these types of prayer (Prejean-Sullivan 2009; Hayes 2007, 140–150). Institutes may also wish to experiment with various forms of online prayer experiences, such as the Jesuit site "Pray as You Go" (http:// www.pray-as-you-go.org). The population of traditionalist Catholics comprises less than 15 percent of the whole; the other 85 percent may be attracted by other types of prayer, with or without simultaneously valuing traditional practices.

Catholic religious life, like all forms of religious virtuosity, has as its primary goal to grow closer to the divine. The various prayer forms developed by religious orders through millennia of experience are ways to this end, and religious institutes have adopted and relinquished them, revived and adapted old forms, or created new ones to meet the needs of successive generations of their members and the spiritual hungers of the larger culture. The successful prayer forms developed by the religious orders—the Dominicans' rosary, the Jesuits' structured meditation points and discernment of spirits, the Benedictines' *lectio divina*, the centering prayer of the early monastics and hermits—spread to the laity as well, enriching the spiritual life of the entire Church in the process. Religious institutes are called to be a similar leaven in the Church today, developing and teaching the prayer forms most desired and needed by coming generations.

But an institute's prayer life, although central, is not its only attraction. Our increasingly individualistic society also generates a hunger for communal connection, and our unmet social needs, too, demand attention. Chapter 7 examines the differences among generations and institutes in how they address these issues.

Chapter 7

Community and Ministry

BALANCING LIFE AND WORK

Maria gnawed on her pen as she sat at her computer. Surfing the web pages of the various religious institutes had turned up numerous sites with pictures of happy-looking young sisters in habits—sites that emphasized that the sisters all lived, prayed, and worked together teaching school, nursing the sick, or conducting retreats. The common bonds these sisters obviously possessed were attractive, but "would they be interested in a budding immigration lawyer like me?" she wondered. "Would I fit in?" Other websites showed somewhat older sisters without habits, happily engaged in what was obviously a wide variety of ministries. "But what if the only legal job I could find was in El Paso—would there be any sisters from this institute there to live and pray with?" Maria sighed as she logged off her computer.

AT LEAST SINCE the time of St. Benedict, religious life has usually been lived in community with others. Serving in a common external ministry, however, is of more recent origin—especially for women. While the male Franciscans, Dominicans, and other evangelizing orders of the thirteenth century engaged in preaching and teaching outside of their convents,[1] their female counterparts remained strictly cloistered in monasteries. Only in the seventeenth century were women permitted to teach and nurse outside of their cloisters, and then only if their institutes were classified by Rome as "merely" pious societies and not as "real" religious orders.

When the earliest sisters first came to North America, they often had to live and minister alone or in very small groups in order to serve the people of the expanding frontier. By the late nineteenth and early twentieth centuries, however, most sisters lived together in convents attached to a school, hospital, or orphanage, and ministered in the same institutions where they lived. After their recognition as bona fide religious in the 1917 Code of Canon Law, a form of cloister adapted from the earlier monastic model was imposed on the sisters.

Cloistered isolation from the mainstream culture was beneficial in that it helped the sisters retain their distinctive worldview and spiritual focus, even as early-and-mid-twentieth- century U.S. society was moving farther and farther from the all-encompassing Catholic village milieu that the sisters' immigrant parents and grandparents had experienced. One historian notes that, in the first half of the twentieth century, the sisters' convents "were closed systems, islands of religious ideology...insuring the complete integration of life and work" (Byrne 1990, 112). The sisters comprised almost the entire faculty of their schools and a significant proportion of their hospitals' staffs, a circumstance that contributed greatly to maintaining their common belief system and esprit de corps. Secure in their common living and ministry, the sisters were "in the parish but not of it," rarely interacting with the rest of the parishioners outside of the classroom or hospital setting.

Sociologists who have studied other communal religious groups like the Shakers, the Amana colonies, or the Oneida community have found that their survival depended on whether they were able to erect boundaries against pernicious outside influences and engage their members completely in common activities (Kanter 1972; Veysey 1973; Zablocki 1980; Shenker 1986). Kanter put it this way: "The cement of solidarity must extend throughout the group" (1972, 86).[2] Without commitment mechanisms such as boundary maintenance and without common and exclusive mutual interaction, few communities were able to survive even a single generation (Zablocki 1980, 289).

Though useful and even necessary for the maintenance of religious worldview and commitment, cloistered isolation also had harmful effects. Commitment mechanisms such as boundary maintenance and interaction only with other community members limited the sisters' contact with the laypeople they served and, as time went on, also restricted their ability to obtain the professional certifications that were becoming increasingly necessary for their ministries. Even before the Second Vatican Council,

Pope Pius XII had urged sisters to obtain the professional credentials they needed. In his 1952 address to an international assembly of all the superiors of women's religious institutes, the Pope said:

> In the training of your sisters for the tasks that await them, be broad-minded and liberal and admit of no stinginess. Whether it be for teaching, the care of the sick, the study of art, or anything else, the sister should be able to say to herself, "My superior is giving me a training that will put me on an equality with my secular colleagues." Give them also the opportunity and the means to keep their professional knowledge up-to-date. This is important for your sisters' peace and for their work (quoted in Ewens 1989, 172).

But obtaining professional degrees often removed individual sisters from their communities for months or years, while exposing them to outside ideas, values, and friendships. At times, it also led to a sort of "class" system within the institutes, dividing the sisters with advanced degrees from those without (Wittberg 2006, 104–105). Both of these side effects could potentially weaken community life. An increased professional identification among the sisters, some feared, might also compete with their identity as religious (Wittberg 2006, 237).

As we saw in chapter 3, the Second Vatican Council had urged sisters to study the history of their institutes and to renew their communities according to the original spirit of their founders and foundresses. When the sisters did this, many discovered that their institutes had been founded to teach and care for the poor, that the first sisters had mingled relatively freely with laypeople without the cloister restrictions later imposed on them, and that their odd-looking habits were simply the usual dress of peasant women or widows in a bygone era. Many institutes, therefore, modified or eliminated their habits and cloister restrictions, and encouraged their members to search out new apostolates to serve the poor and marginalized.

While the sisters were renewing their institutes as they had been mandated to do by the Council, their traditional ministries were also changing. Hospitals were becoming larger and more professionalized; no longer was it possible to send an untrained sister there and expect her to learn on the job. Both parents and state educational officials were beginning to expect that sister-teachers would be credentialed like their lay colleagues. It became less and less likely that a sister could count on finding employment simply because she was a sister, even in the schools and hospitals that her institute had once completely staffed and administered. As the members of a focus group in one study put it:

> All these years, we had somebody tell us where to go and what to do when we got there; there was somebody in charge to guide us through and tell us what we're going to do. And we felt safe and secure with this. And now we have to go out and ask for a job and apply for a job like anybody else (Wittberg 2006, 217).

As a result of more limited opportunities in their former ministries on the one hand, and their new appreciation for their original charisms on the other, many sisters shifted to social service or advocacy ministries. This often meant accepting positions in other Catholic or even secular organizations separate from the members of their institute. Quite frequently, it also meant living apart from them as well. Initially, many sisters saw these options as freeing. Over time, however, cross-cutting responsibilities began to make it difficult for them to be present in their local communities or to participate adequately in the meetings of their larger institute (Gottemoeller 1997, 127–128). In addition, a lack of suitable housing became a serious issue. Convents were closed or repurposed by parishes or dioceses, and no provision was made for the sisters who had lived there. High costs and a dearth of housing in the mainstream market large enough to accommodate communities of more than three adults[3] resulted in sisters living individually or in groups of two or three.

What do the newest entrants feel about these issues? As chapter 4 noted, the millennial generation of sisters is by far the most likely to prefer living and ministering with other members of their institutes. Millennial and post-Vatican II respondents in the 2009 survey were also the most likely to say that the community life of their institute was something that had attracted them to enter it. The present chapter analyzes these responses in greater detail.

Community

The 2009 survey reveals that the youngest entrants to both LCWR and CMSWR institutes are the most likely to value living and interacting with other members (see figure 7.1). Millennial respondents in both conferences were more likely than any other age cohort to say that living together,

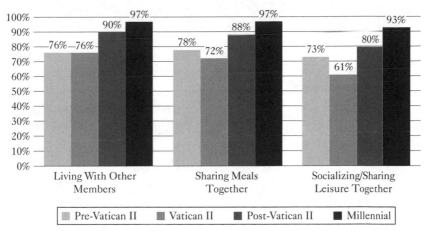

FIGURE 7.1 How important to you are these aspects of religious life? (percentage responding "Very")

sharing meals together, and socializing together with other members of their institutes were very important. LCWR entrants from the Vatican II and pre-Vatican II generations were the least likely to say this, but even among these older cohorts, close to three-fourths valued living and eating together.

When asked about what living arrangements they preferred (figure 7.2), few LCWR respondents (22 percent or less) of any age cohort preferred living alone "very much," and almost no CMSWR respondents did.[4] Living with only one or two other sisters also presented difficulties. As sociologists have long noted, there are special difficulties faced by groups of two (dyads) or three (triads). Dyads are dependent on the continued commitment of the two individuals involved: If either withdraws, the group ceases to exist.[5] As a result, a sister may feel "trapped" in a dyadic living situation, since her departure to a new ministry or to a retirement facility would also affect the other sister in the dyad. Triads, on the other hand, are prone to divisive coalitions.[6] The third member in a triad may also feel a sense of isolation from the other two.[7] Perhaps for these reasons, comparatively few survey respondents preferred living in small communities of two or three. In LCWR institutes, the largest percentage of respondents preferred to live in communities of between four and seven sisters or (for the pre-Vatican II cohort) in groups of eight or more. Most CMSWR respondents of all generations likewise preferred living in groups of eight or more. These findings replicate earlier findings that most sisters prefer living in communities of more than four persons (Gottemoeller 2005, 273; Johnson

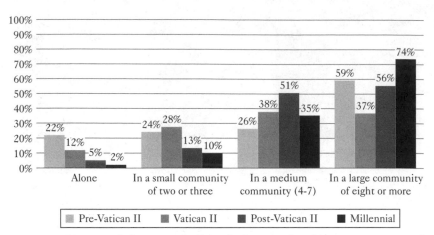

FIGURE 7.2 How much do you prefer living in these settings? (percentage responding "Very Much")

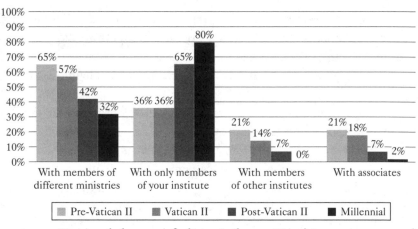

FIGURE 7.3 How much do you prefer living in these settings? (percentage responding "Very Much")

2001, 234), and they also echo a strong call from the 2004 World Congress on Religious Life for "more human and meaningful" community living.[8]

In addition to preferring to live in larger communities, the millennial respondents in the 2009 survey were also the most likely to prefer that these communities be composed only of members from their own institutes (figure 7.3). Almost none of the millennial respondents, in either LCWR or CMSWR, liked the idea of living with their associates or with members of other institutes. Millennial respondents of both conferences were also the least likely to prefer living with members who were all engaged in different ministries.

These different generational emphases on community living were also reflected in the answers to the open-ended questions. The youngest respondents were the most likely of all the generational cohorts in LCWR institutes to volunteer the information that their sisters' community lifestyle was something that had attracted them to enter (17 percent); the older generations entering LCWR institutes were progressively less likely to mention this. In contrast, it was the *older* Vatican II entrants in CMSWR institutes who were the most likely to cite common life as an attraction (27 percent), while the post-Vatican II (25 percent) and millennial (20 percent) CMSWR cohorts were less likely to do so. In every generational cohort, however, the CMSWR respondents were more likely than the LCWR respondents to mention the attraction of the common life in the open-ended questions (20–27 percent as compared to 10–17 percent).

Too much should not be made of these differences, however; common living was among the top attractions for every generation and in both conferences—at least in the 2009 survey. More telling is the fact that those respondents in the 1999 survey who had entered their institutes prior to 1980 were much *less* likely to mention the common life as an attraction when responding to their survey's open-ended question: Fewer than 4 percent of either generation did so.

What most attracted you to your religious institute?

Our charism of reparation to the Sacred Heart really drew me. I was also attracted by the order's community and prayer life. Our life in common is a lived reality, not simply words on paper (millennial, member of an institute belonging to both LCWR and CMSWR).

How real and alive the sisters are. They love being with one another at prayer, at leisure, or at work, and the love they have for one another and for God is so evident (millennial, CMSWR).

Common way of life: community prayer life; faith sharing through meals, etc. (eating and sharing God's words together as a community) (post-Vatican II, CMSWR).

The prayer life and the community aspect of a monastic community. Living, praying, eating all with the same women every day—stability (post-Vatican II, LCWR).

Fidelity to the Church, common prayer life. Strong and vibrant community life with the Eucharistic Christ as its center (Vatican II, CMSWR).

A desire to minister to the poor with other like-minded women. The idea of living in community was important as I ministered to others, and prayer life within community attracted me to religious life (Vatican II, LCWR).

The first time it was to save my soul and the souls of others as I was taught by some very cheerful, friendly, younger sisters. The second time, I wanted to participate in community life, especially in the Eucharistic and prayer life in this community (pre-Vatican II, LCWR).

While the common life was one of the greatest attractions mentioned by all of the respondents in the open-ended questions of the 2009 survey, they also found it to be the most difficult. Except for millennial respondents in LCWR institutes, respondents in every generation were far more likely to cite community living as their greatest challenge than they were to cite any other aspect of religious life—but it was also, some volunteered, their greatest joy and an opportunity for growth:

What do you find most challenging about religious life?

I find adjusting to the structure of religious life challenging, as well as learning to live well in and with community (millennial, LCWR).

I would never want to live outside of the community, but I must say that living with so many women can be a bit hard at times ☺ (millennial, CMSWR).

Learning to live in community after living alone for over 20 years— it's also one of the greatest joys! (post-Vatican II, LCWR).

Community life definitely. When you live with such a large variety of personalities and background, it is challenging to live the virtues day by day. Especially challenging for one who lived alone and has at times a preference for solitude. Each day I have to remind myself that religious life cannot be lived without community, and it is precisely there that I am to find Christ in my sisters and to serve Him (post-Vatican II, CMSWR).

Community living is by far the best and worst part of living this life. Living with personalities that you wouldn't naturally be drawn to is quite the challenge, and then figuring out who you are and what you're willing to give up in order to make life do-able! (Vatican II, LCWR).

The true labor of love in developing and seeking to maintain sisterly
relationships so as to remain a true "community" and so as to
give witness to the world of the work of unity which is the one
mission of the Church—the mission of Jesus Christ who came
to earth to draw all people to Himself (Vatican II, CMSWR).

Creating and enhancing community life (pre-Vatican, LCWR).

Living with 17 women—moods and irritability of the younger
ones—sometimes I feel I have my once teenagers back. Only
difference now, as then, is now I have the patience that comes
with age to ignore them (pre-Vatican CMSWR).

Some respondents listed specific aspects of common living that they
found challenging, such as dealing with personality conflicts, differences
of opinion, and difficult personalities:

What do you find the most challenging about religious life?

Living with people with whom I have very little in common or who
are poor communicators and base their impressions of me on
unverified judgments/opinions (post-Vatican II, CMSWR).

The differences of opinion that members of my congregation seem
to have about: attracting/inviting newer members, community living, lifestyle, our future as a congregation, relationship
with the Church, various social justice issues (post-Vatican II,
LCWR).

Community life. Newer members are looking for community liv-
ing/communal prayer. Older sisters are looking in some ways
for the opposite (post-Vatican II, LCWR).

I find there are many people in community in need of healing, that
either don't want to get help or can't admit they need help. And
others that feel there is nothing they can do about it. But what
we close our eyes to is eating away at a healthier environment
(post-Vatican II, LCWR).

Number of members with significant psychological baggage
(Vatican II, CMSWR).

Living in community with sisters who see community life very differently than I do (Vatican II, LCWR).

Other respondents mentioned various difficulties resulting from their
lack of age peers, the existence of pre-established friendship patterns,

loneliness, communication difficulties, and lack of acceptance. These difficulties were most often mentioned by LCWR respondents, but they also occurred, to some extent, in the CMSWR responses:

What do you find the most challenging about religious life?

Community life in general is harder than I thought it would be. Not feeling supported and/or heard is hard (millennial, CMSWR).

Not having more younger members to share the experience with. Perhaps this is only heightened because there are so many that are significantly older (post-Vatican II, LCWR).

Not having sisters around my age. Lack of support or encouragement from members. Older sisters being jealous of the "young sister" (post-Vatican II, CMSWR).

It is difficult trying to form relationships with other members when the others have been established with particular groups within the community (those who were in formation together have their stories and have maintained friendships) (post-Vatican II, LCWR).

Moving into a situation in which all the other sisters already know each other well and have their ways of doing things (Vatican II, LCWR).

Finding ways to belong to an established group not necessarily interested in welcoming newer members (Vatican II, LCWR).

Finally, several of the older LCWR respondents lamented the difficulty of finding a "good" community, and the fact that so many members were living alone.

What do you find the most challenging about religious life?

Finding others who want to live a more regular common life, especially in my peer group (Vatican II, LCWR).

Finding other religious who are committed to living common life in the community I live in/minister in. Many prefer to live alone (Vatican II, LCWR).

Finding others who want to live more radically among those who need us most, and to live with others who want to pray communally daily (Vatican II, LCWR).

Living with only one other person (Vatican II, LCWR).

That we no longer emphasize common life, living together, common good, common prayer (Vatican II, LCWR).

Individualism and Community

According to recent social critics, Americans are losing their sense of community connectedness. Compared to thirty years ago, they are less likely to participate in all kinds of groups, from labor unions to churches; they report having fewer friends; and they are more likely to live alone (Putnam 1995, 2000; McPherson, Smith-Lovin, and Brashears 2006). At least one sociologist notes that younger Americans are accustomed to having their own bedroom, with its own TV and Internet connection, from childhood (Klinenberg 2012, 50). These cultural trends are both an opportunity and a danger for religious institutes. On the one hand, they may mean that the community lifestyle lived by religious will be increasingly attractive, as secular life is less and less able to fulfill Americans' unmet needs for connectedness and belonging. The increased preference for common living among the millennial respondents to the 2009 survey may already be evidence of this. On the other hand, the danger exists that the rising individualism of U.S. society will infect the lifestyle of the religious institutes themselves. Several respondents to the open-ended questions mentioned that one of their challenges was individualism and lack of community among the sisters. This challenge tended to be listed primarily by post-Vatican II and Vatican II respondents in LCWR institutes, and by Vatican II respondents in CMSWR institutes.

What do you find the most challenging about religious life?

I find that among some members there is an overemphasis on "personal freedom," which often translates into individualism. We have too many sisters living alone and failing to participate in any but the most basic ways in the life of the province....I find this hard because we could be leading lives radically committed to the Gospel, but too often we are choosing consumerism and individualism (post-Vatican II, LCWR).

I find the progressive women's communities have become over-individualistic and have lost their group edge and voice. Due to demographics, there are a large number who can get very defensive and seem to have difficulty truly hearing anyone who came of age after Vatican II (post-Vatican II, LCWR).

Lack of personal commitment—we seem to be becoming more individualistic. "My needs are more important than the common good" (post-Vatican II, LCWR).

The "ME" attitude of the younger generation—young members who don't know how or want to work hard (Vatican II, CMSWR).

Another danger is that, with so little previous experience of community connection with others, new entrants to religious institutes will find it difficult to adjust to the give-and-take necessary for living together. Living a community lifestyle in the midst of an individualistic U.S. culture is likely to pose challenges to religious institutes for some time to come.

Ministry

As chapter 4 pointed out, there were also clear generational differences in the respondents' preferences regarding where they would like to minister. Millennial respondents strongly preferred working with members of their institutes in a common ministerial setting: 93 percent preferred this "very much." Respondents from the Vatican II generation were the least likely to express these preferences, although 51 percent still preferred "very much" to minister with members of their institutes. Vatican II respondents were the most likely (32 percent) to say they preferred working with members of other institutes, although no generation expressed very high

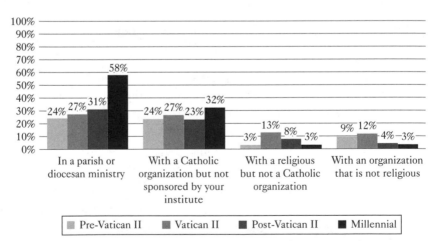

FIGURE 7.4 How much do you prefer ministry in these settings? (percentage responding "Very Much")

support for this option (see figure 4.8 in chapter 4). As figure 7.4 shows, millennial respondents were far more likely than respondents of other generational cohorts to say that they preferred to minister in a parish or diocesan ministry, and the least likely to say that they would be willing to work in non-Catholic or secular settings (although very few of any generation expressed the latter preference). No significant differences existed between the generations in whether they preferred ministering in other Catholic settings. Interestingly, as chapter 4 also noted, while the youngest respondents wished to minister together, the *type* of ministry seemed to be less important; millennial respondents were the least likely of any generation to say that the types of ministry their institute performed was one of the things that had attracted them to it (see figure 4.7 in chapter 4).

Most of the generational differences in these preferences were much more strongly evident among LCWR respondents than they were among CMSWR respondents. There was a steady increase from the oldest to the youngest generations entering LCWR institutes in the percentage who preferred "Somewhat" or "Very Much" to work only with other members of their institute, to work in ministries sponsored by their institute, or to work in parish or diocesan ministries. CMSWR respondents, in contrast, usually rated these ministry settings highly across all generations. In addition, millennial LCWR respondents were the least likely of all LCWR age cohorts to prefer ministries in non-Catholic or secular settings. CMSWR respondents showed no definite pattern in their preferences for ministry in these latter settings, except that they were uniformly lower than the LCWR responses.

In the open-ended questions, most generations, from both conferences and in both the 2009 and 1999 surveys, were approximately equally likely to volunteer the information that they had been attracted to their institute by its ministries. In the 2009 survey, there was a tendency for the Vatican II respondents in both LCWR and CMSWR to mention this more often than the other generations did (39–45 percent of the Vatican II respondents as compared to 21–25 percent of the millennial respondents and 26–37 percent of the post- and pre-Vatican respondents). In the 1999 survey, Vatican II and pre-Vatican II respondents who had entered their institute prior to 1980 were also highly likely to mention the sisters' ministries as an attraction (23 percent of the Vatican II respondents and 33 percent of the pre-Vatican II respondents).

When a *specific* ministry was named as an attraction, it was most often service to the poor (3–11 percent across all generations, both conferences.

and both surveys). Only LCWR respondents, in both 1999 and 2009, mentioned working for social justice as attracting them to their community, but
the percentages were usually quite small (between 1 and 8 percent across the
generations). Only among the 2009 Vatican II respondents in LCWR communities did this percentage reach higher: 13 percent. Similarly, Vatican II
LCWR respondents were several times more likely to mention its ministry
to women as something that had attracted them to their institute, but here
again, the percentages were small (3 percent for this age cohort as compared
to less than 1 percent for the others). No millennials of either conference
mentioned ministry to women as a particular attraction of their institutes.

There were no patterns across the generations or between the two conferences in which respondents mentioned education, missionary, or nursing ministries as something that had attracted them to their institutes,
except that few or no millennial respondents mentioned any of these
ministries. Millennial CMSWR respondents were the most likely to mention evangelizing ministries as an attraction (4 percent mentioned this as
compared to 2 percent or less of the other CMSWR age cohorts and less
than 1 percent of all LCWR age cohorts). LCWR respondents were more
likely than CMSWR respondents (4–8 percent across the various generations as compared to 2–3 percent) to say that they were attracted by the fact
that their institute engaged in a variety of ministries. On the other hand,
CMSWR respondents of the post-Vatican II generation were the most
likely to say that they were attracted by their institute's common or institutional ministries (3 percent as compared to less than 1 percent among
the other age cohorts in both LCWR and CMSWR). Among the traits of
the individual sisters that respondents found attractive, the post-Vatican
II and Vatican II respondents of both conferences and both survey years
were the only generations to mention that the sisters were "hardworking"
(3 to 4 percent). No millennials in either conference found the sisters'
hardworking lifestyle attractive.

Some interesting common themes occur among the respondents to
the 2009 survey when they listed the aspects of ministry that challenged
them. Overwhelmingly, across generations and conferences, the respondents cited the difficulties of time management and balancing ministry
with community:

What do you find most challenging about religious life?

Balancing ministry, common life, family (millennial, LCWR).
Balancing time, being available for my sisters (millennial, CMSWR).

Not knowing how to manage the time—struggling with the word "no." I engage with too much activities outside the community to the point that if I am not doing it, nobody will. Wrong perception. The world will still spin without me (post-Vatican II, LCWR).

Our contemplative/active life often brings with it a tension which, given our apostolate of education and the seemingly ceaseless "doing," leaves less energy for "being"—which is what was the attraction to religious life in the first place (post-Vatican II, CMSWR).

The focus on work to the exclusion of quality community time (post-Vatican II, LCWR).

That there never seems to be enough hours in the day to complete all that needs to be done (post-Vatican II, CMSWR).

Balancing time—ministry, God, family, community, relationships, self (Vatican II, LCWR).

The struggle to balance a demanding job and a balanced prayer and community life (Vatican II, CMSWR).

Balancing spirituality and ministry was the most commonly mentioned of all the various balance issues. As chapter 6 noted, between 7 and 20 percent of the various generations, in both LCWR and CMSWR, mentioned this challenge. Lesser percentages (3–8 percent) mentioned the difficulty of balancing ministry and community.

A few respondents in both conferences complained about the inability to choose their ministry, or about superiors being overly concerned with ministry commitments to the detriment of the needs of the sisters:

What do you find most challenging about religious life?

Right now, having just come out of the novitiate, I am working full time at a ministry that I don't prefer and one that is different from almost every other sister's at the monastery who mostly minister in the same place. Because of this, I am not included in much of what concerns the sisters regarding ministry, and it is making the adjustment harder than it needs to be (post-Vatican II, LCWR).

Administrators/superiors more concerned with ministry than with the sisters who minister (post-Vatican II, CMSWR).

I do not organize or plan my own education and ministry (post-Vatican II, LCWR).

The emphasis on works and not on the person (Vatican II, CMSWR).

The youngest and oldest generations were less likely to voice these concerns, the young perhaps because they were still new in ministry, and the oldest perhaps because they were retiring or re-phasing in ministry.

Several respondents in LCWR institutes mentioned the stress and burnout involved in trying to cover ministerial tasks and internal institute commitments with ever-fewer numbers of sisters:

What do you find most challenging about religious life?

Sometimes it seems that as religious (at least in my congregation) we are trying to do more and more with fewer people. I fear burnout (post-Vatican II, LCWR).

Lower number of sisters—same ministries and work—workload is hard (post-Vatican II, LCWR).

The aging of our membership is difficult because we are not able to continue to minister as we have in the past. This requires restructuring (post-Vatican II, LCWR).

Because we are getting so few vocations, more "internal" responsibilities are falling on me, taking time and energy from my mission. We are forced to close missions the Church still needs, and pass up missions the Church needs, due to aging membership (Vatican II, LCWR).

Other LCWR respondents worried that the demands of their present ministries were compromising their ability to live community fully or to plan for the future:

What do you find most challenging about religious life?

Because so many of us are in inserted works, we often do not have the ability to be in charge of our own works so that we could better serve the poor! (post-Vatican II, LCWR).

Changing ministries—fear that we will lose the communal aspect of ministry as sisters seek their own jobs (post-Vatican II, LCWR).

Finding the balance between maintenance and mission—being stuck in the old and moving forward toward the new—caring for members and still having relevant ministry (Vatican II, LCWR).

Caring for retirement needs of aging members which is very important. I don't mean to minimize this effort, but there is a desire
for creating new ministries and sometimes the realities of numbers and needs hold us back (Vatican II, LCWR).

As a small community—many are much older and so we have fewer
resources with which to do unpaid ministry (Vatican II, LCWR).

To summarize, therefore, younger entrants to religious life are more
attracted by opportunities to live and minister in common: The type of
ministry was less important to millennials than the opportunity to minister *together*. On the other hand, certain challenges were common to all
ages and both leadership conferences in 2009: the challenge of living
communally and the difficulty of balancing work, prayer, and common
life. The attraction of community seems to be increasing among all age
cohorts over time: Respondents of all generations were much more likely
to cite this in 2009 than were the respondents who had entered their
institutes before 1980.

Conclusions

An essential element of religious life, at least for the past several centuries,
has been living together and working in a common ministry to serve the
People of God. The simple fact of community living has been a witness in
an increasingly individualistic society. And a common ministry—teaching
in parish schools or private academies, nursing in large hospitals or in
homes—was an essential part of the identity of many apostolic institutes.

But societal needs change over time, and the common ministries of
an institute may become less needed or appear less relevant. The prophetic dilemma mentioned in chapter 3 presents itself: When and how
should women religious change to meet these new needs? At the same
time, sisters feel the tension between the essential elements of religious
life: prayer, community living, and the demands of ministry. At various times over the centuries, one or the other of these had taken prece-
dence: The rules of cloister or the need to "get one's prayers in" may limit
the time for ministry; the busy-ness of ministry may usurp time for prayer
or drain energy from community presence. In reaction, subsequent generations have often emphasized (their elders would say *over*emphasized)
whatever elements had been subordinated in previous years. It is necessary for the members of each generation—and of religious institutes

disproportionately dominated by one generational mindset—to make a conscious effort to see religious life through the eyes of the other. Without this willingness to search for mutual understanding and to hear each other's truth, the prophetic witness of religious life, so necessary to the larger Church, will be weakened. Chapter 8 offers some recommendations for how this dialogue could most profitably be carried out.

Chapter 8

Conclusion

INVITING THE FUTURE

Maria took a deep breath and clicked the "Submit" icon, sending her application to the San Vicente Legal Clinic winging its way through cyberspace. The clinic was offering a semester internship in legal assistance for immigrants that would fulfill her practicum requirement at the law school. Maria felt relief; she had finally made one decision after researching several options.

Now it was time for the other choice. She toggled back and forth between the two other websites on her computer screen. There was a monastery of sisters ten miles from the clinic that invited seekers to a six-month live-in experience. The site showed several young sisters and novices, in a traditional habit, working in the garden, praying together in the chapel, and laughing at recreation. If any worked outside the monastery, they were not pictured—although the site's copy did mention that several of the sisters were teachers. No mention was made of any other apostolate.

Then there was the order of sisters who sponsored the San Vicente Legal Clinic. They were an international institute, with a motherhouse in Europe and several provinces in the United States. But there was only one community, with four sisters, in the region of the state where the clinic was located. The website supplied a picture of a vibrant local community; all four sisters appeared to be over seventy. "Are there any younger sisters elsewhere in this institute?" Maria wondered. "Are they even open to receiving new members?"

Back and forth, back and forth. Finally, she breathed a silent prayer to Mary and clicked the "Contact Us" button....

AS IS THE case with all human beings, the religious beliefs, values, and preferences of U.S. Catholics do not develop in a vacuum. Whether they see vowed religious life as a desirable life choice or as an obsolete and dying anachronism; whether they automatically assume that sisters and nuns are holier than laypeople or that they are naïve and psychologically stunted; whether they are indignant because sisters are unjustly oppressed by a sexist male hierarchy or because they have been seduced by radical feminism to flout the magisterium—all depend at least in part on the social locations that make such beliefs and values plausible. The aphorism of W. I. Thomas cited in chapter 1 reminds us that such beliefs can have real consequences for religious institutes and their members, as well as for the Church as a whole: "If [people] define situations as real, they are real in their consequences" (Thomas and Thomas 1928, 571–572).

How Catholics in general—and persons thinking of entering a religious institute in particular—define religious life is due partly to *period effects*: An economic boom or bust affects how they view material possessions; a scandal impacts their willingness to trust the institution in which the scandal took place; inventions like the television or the Internet influence how they react to people and events. Our study has discovered some period effects that influenced the women who entered religious life between 1965 and 1980, as compared to those who became sisters or nuns between 1993 and 2008. Chapter 6 noted that all age groups of the women who had entered religious institutes prior to 1980 were less likely to be attracted by the sisters' prayerfulness and spirituality than similar women who entered later. Specific religious practices such as Eucharistic Adoration, prayer in common, and Marian devotions were often considered "conservative" and "pre-Vatican II" in the 1965–80 period, and were therefore less appealing to those entering religious institutes at that time. Women of all generations who have entered since 1993, on the other hand, were more attracted by precisely these opportunities for prayer. Even women considering active, apostolic institutes were more likely to be seeking a balance between prayer/contemplation and ministry/service than those who had entered earlier. Chapter 7 noted another period effect in the value placed on common living: All age groups entering between

1965 and 1980 were less likely to value this aspect of religious life than those who entered their institutes after 1993.

But overlying such period effects are the effects of one's generational cohort. *Cohort effects* stem from the uniquely powerful impact that the familial, educational, religious, and societal experiences of one's childhood have on a person's worldview for the rest of her life. Each generation is a unique culture, as distinctly different as various ethnic, regional, or class cultures are from each other. Most Catholics of the pre-Vatican II generation grew up in an all-encompassing, unchanging Catholic culture, whose rituals and practices helped them cope with the uncertainties of the Great Depression and World War II. In contrast, most Vatican II Catholics were profoundly influenced in their youth by the fresh winds of change following the Council, as well as by secular social movements for Civil Rights, Women's Liberation, and an end to U.S. involvement in the Vietnam War. To this day, they remain interested in these issues and attached to the forms of religious expression that shaped their teen and young adult years. Many post-Vatican II Catholics, on the other hand, grew up without a stable religious anchor, in a larger society wracked by political corruption, economic stagnation, and environmental degradation. At least one study has found that they have been less likely to return to an active practice of Catholicism, even after they married and began to have children. In fact, many have abandoned religious practice at this stage in their lives—a historically unusual pattern for new parents who, in the past, had been more likely to resume their church connections once they had children to rear (Silk 2012).

Millennial Catholics have even less experience with and knowledge of their faith. Young Catholics of the millennial generation often relate more profoundly to the culture of their secular peers, many of whom profess no religion at all. While at least one study has found that millennial Catholics are less likely than average to have renounced their religion completely, they are also only half as likely as millennials in conservative Protestant denominations to be highly religious (Pearce and Denton 2011, 64). The percentage who attend Mass weekly has shrunk from 37 percent in 1972 to 15 percent in 2010, even though the percentage who attend at least monthly rose from 19 percent to 32 percent (Gray 2012). As millennials enter their late twenties, they have been less likely to marry in church ceremonies and less likely to baptize their children. While nearly eight in ten evangelicals and black Protestant millennials say that their religion is a very important part of their life, only 44 percent of Catholic millennials say the same (Jones, Cox, and Banchoff 2012).

Generational cultures, while powerful, are nevertheless not destiny. Persons who are of the same race, ethnicity, and social class often react to their common experiences in different ways; the same is true of individuals in the same age cohort. Each generation, in other words, contains an oppositional minority culture: traditionalists in a generation that embraces novelty, idealists among realists, religious "islands" in a secular sea. Although the majority of millennial Catholics may be only tenuously attached to their faith and its practice, studies have found that some 10 to 15 percent of their age peers have embraced the opposite: They attend Mass weekly, even daily, profess fervent loyalty to the pope and the magisterium, and prefer ornate devotional practices to the "Beige Catholicism" of their post-Vatican II childhoods (Barron 2011). It is this minority generational subculture, researchers have found, that is likely to populate Catholic seminaries today (Hoge and Wenger 2003, 132–133). Our research indicates that they form a disproportionate percentage of the millennial and post-Vatican II women entering religious life as well, in both LCWR and CMSWR institutes.

This has profound implications for the future of religious life in the United States and for institutes whose leaders belong to LCWR and CMSWR. On the one hand, LCWR institutes are failing to attract millennial entrants in any significant number, although a limited number of older Vatican II women continue to join them. Half of those who entered LCWR institutes between 1993 and 2008 were over the age of forty. This cannot continue; the Vatican II generation will age as the pre-Vatican II generation has, and it will be replaced by post-Vatican II and millennial Catholics—who will have much the same cohort mindset in 2030 that they have today. This means that the majority of forty- and fifty-year-old millennial women fifteen years hence will still be distant from the Church, if indeed they have not deserted it completely. Studies of the United States (Wittberg 2012), Italy (Magister 2012b), and Britain and Canada (Brown 2012) have shown that the majority of millennial Catholic women in these countries are actually *less* orthodox, *less* devout, and *less* observant in their religious practice than their male peers—the first generation for which this is true. They will be no more interested in religious life at age forty or fifty than they are today, unless religious communities can figure out how to attract them. Perhaps the coming post-millennial generation (those born after 1995) will be more attracted to religious life once they reach adulthood, but this is by no means certain.

CMSWR institutes face a different set of challenges. The traditionalist subculture of millennial Catholics appears to be primarily drawn to CMSWR institutes, several of which have been profiled in the popular media as bursting at the seams with young novices. But although 55 percent of CMSWR institutes report having three or more women in initial formation, only about one-fourth (27 percent) have more than ten new entrants; and an equal percentage report having no new sisters at all. These uneven proportions are not likely to change, as long as the institutes appeal only to the atypically traditionalist 10 or 15 percent of the millennial generation.

But attempting to attract entrants from the majority generational culture of millennial women would probably require greater ideological changes than most CMSWR institutes would be willing to make. While there are many reports of millennials' commitment to volunteer service with the poor and to Catholic Social Teaching, Studies show that the majority of millennial Catholic women, in addition to being only loosely attached to Catholicism overall, are:

- More consumerist and materialistic than previous generations. Eighty-one percent of millennial college freshmen in a recent survey said that being well off financially was an essential or very important personal goal—"an all-time high." Also at an all-time high was listing "to be able to make more money" as a reason to go to college—74.6 percent ranked this as very important, as compared to 50 percent of college freshmen in 1976. This percentage is actually higher at Catholic colleges (76.9 percent) than it is at other religious (68.3 percent) or nonsectarian (72.1 percent) colleges (Pryor et al. 2012, 4, 37). Admittedly, this may be because millennials graduate with higher indebtedness than previous generations.
- Tolerant of difference and diversity. Four-fifths of millennials had at least one friend of another race or ethnic group when growing up. The downside of this diversity is that millennials are reluctant to think critically, because that seems to be passing judgment on others. Most reject any dogmatic proclamation of a single truth, including the proclamations of Church leaders (Hegy 2011, 20; Institute of Politics 2012, 31). They are therefore less likely to support ending legalized abortion, banning the ordination of women, or restricting gay marriage, no matter what the Church may say about these issues. Only 21 percent of

millennials believe that religious values should play an important role in government laws or decisions (Institute of Politics 2012, 30).

- More likely to exhibit high self-esteem, whether or not it is warranted. The *average* millennial woman scored higher on a self-esteem scale than *three-fourths* of women did a generation ago; the difference for millennial men was even greater. Critics charge that parents' and teachers' efforts to encourage self-esteem in millennials when they were children have made them self-centered and even narcissistic as adults (Twenge 2006, 93).

Not only is it extremely unlikely that millennial Catholic women, if they hold these views, will be interested in entering a CMSWR institute, it is equally unlikely that the institute would be interested in accepting them—unless, of course, they change their generational mindset to one more acceptable to the institute's present members. This is something that millennial Catholic women are unlikely to do. Although it is true that each generation experiences age effects in their beliefs and values in addition to the period and cohort effects that influence them (i.e., there is a tendency for generations to soften their ideological stances as they age, with liberals becoming somewhat more conservative and conservatives becoming somewhat more liberal), it is nevertheless also true that the basic pattern of each generation's beliefs and preferences tends not to change (Mannheim 1952). In twenty years, the Vatican II cohort will still prefer the prayers and practices of their young adulthood. Even in their fifties, most millennials are still likely to be only loosely attached to their faith. With the exception of the fifteen or twenty CMSWR institutes that have been successful in recruiting from the traditionalist minority subculture of millennials, therefore, the future of religious life in the United States would appear to be in peril—unless concerted efforts are made to reach out to those who, surveys tell us, have considered religious life but did not choose to enter it.

The challenges faced by religious institutes of women in the United States have implications for the larger U.S. Church as well. Historically, religious orders have been the leaders in helping the Church adapt to societal and cultural changes (Finke and Wittberg 2000; Wittberg 1995, 31–42). Benedictine and other monastic traditions enabled the early Church to meet the challenges stemming from the end of the Roman persecutions, as well as from the subsequent barbarian invasions. The thirteenth-century mendicant orders helped the Church adapt to the rise of medieval commerce and trading towns. Sixteenth- and seventeenth-century apostolic groups such as the Jesuits, Vincentians, and Daughters of Charity addressed the challenges of the Reformation and the dislocations of a budding mercantile economy. In the nineteenth and twentieth centuries, religious institutes of women built systems of education, healthcare, and social service in response to the needs of those within and outside the Church. Today, the charitable works of women religious in the United States are described as "the most formidable influence in the tradition of Catholic philanthropy in our day" (FADICA 2010a). In all periods, it was the religious institutes that were at the forefront of the Church's response to societal ills.

If the Church is unable to articulate the Gospel message in a language that resonates with changing worldviews in the twenty-first century, it will become less and less relevant to the generations that inhabit it. In the past, this articulation was primarily the task of successive founding waves of religious institutes (Hostie 1983; Cada 1979). Religious institutes were also the primary bearers of the Church's missionary activities at the frontiers of the Christian world and beyond. But present-day religious institutes will not be able to lead the Church in evangelizing our current increasingly secular youth if they are composed only of a much older generation, or of a traditionalist minority already out of sync with most of their age peers. Worse still would be if religious institutes each began to emphasize that their version of religious life was more faithful to the "true" model than other religious institutes' versions were, thus reflecting the ideological polarization that has paralyzed the larger U.S. society (Bishop 2008). As chapter 5 noted, some of the open-ended responses to the 2009 survey seem to reflect this mindset.

An alternative, of course, is to give up altogether on attempts to reach out to and attract more millennial and post-Vatican II Catholics from the majority culture to religious institutes. At various times, writers on both ends of the ideological spectrum have advanced the idea of a faithful remnant (Arzillo 2012), a "fire in the ashes" (Chittister 1995) that would preserve religious life until a more propitious time. Perhaps the post-millennial (or a post-post millennial) generation will be more amenable to refounding or revitalizing religious institutes in 2050 or beyond. This, of course, is not assured. In the meantime, the Church risks losing much of its influence, not only over the larger society, but even over the schools, hospitals, and social service agencies once so firmly linked to the Catholic philanthropic tradition by the multitudes of sisters who served in them (Wittberg 2006, 147–165).

Another alternative is to focus on the ethnic groups—primarily Hispanic and Asian in the United States—that are still attached to a more traditional version of Catholicism. As we showed in chapter 4, only 15 percent of pre-Vatican II Catholics in the United States are Hispanic, but 54 percent of millennial Catholics are. Already, as chapter 1 noted, 16 percent of women in initial formation in the United States are Hispanic/Latina, and another 16 percent are Asian. Non-Hispanic whites comprised only 61 percent of new entrants in 2009. This percentage is likely to drop further in coming years. But, just as the children and grandchildren of previous immigrant groups became assimilated into U.S. culture in the past, the second and third generations of Hispanic and Asian Catholics in the United States are likely to do the same. And this assimilation would mean adopting the same beliefs, values, and priorities that have kept the current generation of white middle-class millennial Catholics from affiliating with their parents' and grandparents' religion. Unless the Church can figure out how to articulate its message to mainstream U.S. culture, it is not likely to keep a strong hold on Hispanic-American Catholics either. Will Catholicism's religious institutes take the lead in this effort as they have in the past? Or will they be too few, too small, and too culturally encapsulated to have an effect?

Implications

If the Church is to truly evangelize modern Western culture, as Pope Benedict XVI and Pope Francis (and, indeed, the Gospels themselves) have called it to do, then it must devise a way to reach that culture. This is the recurring challenge that the Church has faced time and again throughout its history. Each time the Church has met the challenge, not by merely repeating its age-old truths in the language, symbols, and practices of previous generations, but by engaging with the hopes, dreams, fears, and preoccupations of the coming one, and by devising a new language, new symbols, and new practices that articulate its timeless message in a form that resonates with them. And it has always been the religious institutes—male and female—that were the leaders in this rearticulation. Thus, the mendicant friars of the thirteenth century rearticulated Christian truths in new prayer forms (the rosary), new images (the Christmas crib), and new pastoral practices (the sermon, handbooks for priests hearing confessions). The sixteenth-century Jesuits popularized the retreat and the Spiritual Exercises; the Visitation and other seventeenth-century sisters initiated religious education for girls. Nineteenth-century Redemptorists and other male orders invented the parish mission, a Catholic equivalent to the revivals popular in Protestant churches (Taves 1986). Nineteenth-century American sisters created an entire separate school system to safeguard the faith of Catholic immigrants and decisively eliminated anti-Catholic hostility for a generation by their heroic nursing services on the battle-fields of the Civil War. Today's religious institutes cannot similarly evangelize mainstream modern culture if they do not catalyze and formulate a similarly creative rearticulation, one that will appeal to the deepest needs and hungers of millennial and post-millennial Catholics. If past history is any guide, unless religious institutes fulfill this role of rearticulation and evangelization, it will not be done, or it will be done less effectively. And the Church will be poorer as a result. But in order to do so, religious institutes will need to draw new generations of members from all the varied segments of millennial and post-millennial culture.

How might this be done? Religious institutes must first understand the beliefs, values, desires, and preoccupations that attract young people to, or repel them from, considering a religious vocation. These may be practical difficulties like the mounting college debts faced by so many college graduates, or deeper philosophical barriers like the millennials' instinctive disapproval of the Church's position on women's ordination. Understanding at a deep level means realizing that the beliefs of a younger generation may be "packaged" together in configurations that seem illogical to their elders (Converse 1964, 207–209). For example, as we pointed out in chapter 2, a love for Gregorian chant and Eucharistic Adoration may be "packaged" with a belief that priests should be married, a radical commitment to live and work with the poor, a desire to wear a full habit (in a mixed religious community of men and women), and an interest in the spiritual discipline of yoga. A generation with such a configuration of beliefs and interests is not likely to feel at home in a religious institute where these beliefs are assumed to be antithetical to each other.

Understanding the mindset of a generation's culture does not necessarily mean altering the foundational truths of one's own faith tradition. It instead involves devising ways to speak those truths in a language that the hearers will understand and accept. At times, as John Lofland discovered in his study of the early days of the Unification Church (Lofland 1977), this may entail initially attracting potential recruits through non-evangelization activities like social get-togethers or common projects, and presenting them with the faith's more difficult religious teachings only *after* they have developed friendships with and commitment to other Church members. This, admittedly, may seem manipulative but, as several sociologists have noted, we are more likely to act ourselves into believing something than we are to believe ourselves into acting in a given way (Perrow 1986, 134–135; see also Weick 1995, 24, 26).

Religious institutes therefore need to construct as many opportunities as possible for members of the different generations to meet with and get to know one another. These opportunities should involve activities that each generation would actually want to participate in (such as social events, service opportunities, or opportunities for reflection) or that meet a deeply felt personal need (such as Ignatian discernment training to help college students navigate the many decisions they must make as they enter adulthood). One-on-one opportunities should also be devised: the mentoring of a nursing, education, or social work student by a sister nurse, teacher, or social worker who can serve as a role model; oral history projects in which students collect and record the life stories of retired sisters; spiritual direction offered at reduced fees affordable to college students; and so on. Millennial "computer natives" might also be asked to work with religious sisters in mining the full potential of social networking: creating blogs, twitter feeds, podcasts, or even a virtual presence on sites like Second Life. All of these opportunities for interaction between older religious and young adult Catholics should be consistent, frequent, and ongoing in order to develop mutual understanding and appreciation between the generations.

Active invitational efforts are also absolutely necessary. Recent CARA surveys have found that 8 percent of never-married millennial women have considered a religious vocation at least a little seriously, but fewer than one-tenth were encouraged to do so by a sister (Gray and Gautier 2012, 2, 91). Concerted efforts are needed to discover the most effective ways of tendering this invitation and increasing the sisters' comfort levels while doing so. The former task will require conducting research: focus groups, surveys, and an extensive review of how other denominations and religious groups—including especially the 27 percent of CMSWR institutes with ten or more new entrants—extend such invitations and with what success. The latter task will require intentional training of the sisters in invitational practices: role-playing sessions, apprenticeships and mentoring by sisters and communities in successful invitational programs, and the like. The sisters must also be convinced—or re-convinced—that religious life has something valuable and essential to offer the millennial (and post-millennial) generations, in order to elicit their enthusiastic commitment to such invitational efforts. Our research found that some respondents in the 2009 survey felt that many of their sisters do not believe that future generations will be interested in joining them.

Paradoxically, if the present members of a religious institute are enthusiastically committed to a particular focus—be it protecting the unborn, advocating for the needs of women and children, reviving the Tridentine Mass, or developing and living an eco-spirituality—sufficiently strongly to motivate them to invite new members to join them, this may be a double-edged sword. Such a focus may also limit the institute's growth if it is or becomes less widely shared. Thus, one study of both the pro-life and pro-choice movements in twentieth-century United States found that their "moral worldviews" offered "a collective identity [and] a strong sense of purpose" that was extremely useful in mobilizing their followers. But since these moral worldviews were not widely shared outside of the movements, they were also "the central obstacle preventing the movement from winning allies" (Burns 2005, 278–279). Such perceived "extremism" may actually cause observers to adopt the opposite viewpoint, which is precisely the mechanism by which worldviews change from one generation to the next. Thus, institutes whose members engage in a rigorous schedule of traditional devotions may later come to be seen as irrelevant and "out of touch" with the pressing social needs of the world. A new set of socially activist institutes may later come to be seen as "not spiritual enough" or "workaholics" by a subsequent generation that desires more traditional devotions or a balance between prayer and work.

As a result of this oscillating dynamic, while the most successful religious institutes are those whose members feel strongly united around a single key focus, they may also be the ones that have the most difficulty adapting to the changed mindset of a subsequent generation. On the other hand, a more diffuse identity and purpose—one that allows for several different interpretations of the religious institute's charism—may blur internal divisions and inhibit the sisters from articulating a coherent reason why anyone should bother joining them at all (Burns 2005, 272). Encouraging the members of an institute to articulate a charism that provides a sufficiently distinctive group identity but is also sufficiently encompassing to appeal to a wide range of potential entrants (all the while maintaining unity among said members) will require the conscious efforts of both vocation personnel and institute leaders.

Another serious problem is the alienation of young Catholic women from the Church due to their deep conviction that they are second-class citizens within it. Although in the past, more women than men entered religious life, the ratio is now even or reversed (Wittberg 2012). A recent CARA study found that, while 13 percent of millennial Catholic men had considered entering the priesthood or religious life at some point, only 8 percent of millennial Catholic women had ever done so (Gray and Gautier 2012, 2):

> [T]he pattern over time indicates the possibility that there is a slow erosion of the likelihood of ever having considered a religious voca-tion among Catholic women in the last decade....If this decline is real, it is likely related to generational changes, with the older female Catholics, who may have been more likely to consider this in their youth, gradually being replaced by a younger generation of women who are not equally likely to consider this (Gray and Gautier 2012, 98).

The present millennial generations of Catholics in the United States—non-Hispanic whites, Latinos, and other races and ethnic groups—pose unique challenges for the Church, challenges that the Church *must* meet if it is to survive as a significant influence in twenty-first century society. In previous historical periods, new religious institutes were *youth movements*, founded precisely to enable the Church to meet the emerging strains and hungers of their day. Their success was measured in their ability to attract followers, not merely from an anomalous 10 or 15 percent of their gen-eration, but in waves of fervent adherents from a wide spectrum of soci-ety. The fourth-century Egyptian Church alone contained some 10,000 male hermits and 20,000 consecrated virgins. Twelfth-century Germany saw the opening of 100 new Benedictine monasteries for women; France gained forty and England eighty in the same century. The male Franciscan order grew from a handful to over 3,000 friars between 1209 and 1221; the Dominicans grew to 13,000 in the first fifty years after their found-ing. The Beguines comprised 15 percent of the entire adult female pop-ulation of Cologne in 1320. The Jesuits grew from less than a dozen to 15,500 between 1541 and 1629; the Daughters of Charity gained their first 800 women in fewer than twenty-five years. The explosive increase in the number of sisters in the nineteenth and early twentieth-century United States has already been mentioned in chapter 1; similar growth took place in Ireland (from 120 to 8,000 sisters), Quebec (from 673 to 9,600 sisters), France (which added 200,000 sisters, 116,000 of whom stayed in France), and elsewhere during the same period (Wittberg 1994, 31–39). It was these orders—filled with *young* people—that catalyzed the revival of the Church in their respective periods. Revitalized religious institutes and/or other ecclesial movements are necessary for a similar revival today. The attraction of each coming generation to religious life is essential for the very survival of the Church.

Millennial Catholics, of course, are not the last generation the Church must attract. A post-millennial generation is already passing through our high schools. While we do not yet know what worldview they will develop when they reach young adulthood, we do know that they will not be the same as the millennials. In a very short time, all religious institutes—LCWR, as well as CMSWR—will need to get to know this new generation. And this too will be a challenge. A CMSWR community twenty years from now, dominated by a middle-aged millennial leadership, will have the same difficulty in understanding the next generation as LCWR communities dominated by pre-Vatican II and Vatican II leadership had in understanding millennial and post-Vatican II youth.

An overlay of ethnic difference makes the challenges all the more complex, as white-dominated institutes must prepare to include women from many ethnic groups, with spiritual practices different from their own. New gifts for religious institutes—and for all of religious life—are contained in the lives of these new sisters. All of the challenges are worth the effort because religious life is essential to the mission of the Church in responding to the needs of the world.

Research Studies Used in This Book

The research incorporated in these pages comes from two major national studies of women religious, conducted ten years apart. The first study, which we refer to as the 1999 study, was comprised of three separate surveys—one of the leaders of institutes of women religious, and two of select groups of sisters who had entered those institutes after 1965. For the purposes of this book, we concentrated primarily on the responses in the 1999 study from the sisters who entered their institutes during the first fifteen years captured by the survey (1965 to 1980) and stayed in religious life, to draw a clearer comparison with the respondents in the second study.

The second study, which we refer to as the 2009 study, was comprised of two separate surveys—one of the leaders of both female and male religious institutes in the United States, and one of the men and women who had entered those institutes in the fifteen years immediately prior to the survey (between 1993 and 2008). We focused exclusively on the women's institutes in this second study: 725 institutes of women religious and 2,147 women who entered them after 1993.

Both studies attempted to gain information from the entire identified population of sisters, not a portion (or sample) of them. Thus, measurements of statistical significance are not meaningful here. The numbers and proportions reported in this book are characteristics of the represented populations (e.g., all institutes of women religious in 1999 and 2009, all women who entered religious life between 1965 and 1980 and stayed, and all women who entered religious life between 1993 and 2008 and stayed). We describe the methodologies of the two studies below and then compare some of the characteristics of the responding institutes of women religious at these two points in time.

1999 Study Methodology

The principal investigator for the 1999 study was Sister Mary Johnson, with funding from a grant from the Lilly Endowment. The study comprised three related surveys: one survey of the leaders of 818 religious institutes of women in the United States, one survey of 4,381 women who had entered those institutes after 1965 and remained in religious life, and a final survey of 2,082 women who had entered those institutes after 1965 but subsequently left religious life.

Institute Survey

The questionnaire for religious institutes was a single informant survey of 56 items, which asked about the characteristics of the religious institute (e.g., province, region, congregation, monastery), as well as the characteristics of members of the institute. The questionnaire also asked each institute for the names of all women who had entered the institute since January 1, 1966, those who were still members, as well as those who had left the institute. Two additional questionnaires were developed for distribution to these women. The "Stayers" questionnaire consisted of 178 items, and the "Leavers" questionnaire included 115 items.

To locate and identify the institutes of women religious in the United States, the researchers consulted the 1996 edition of *The Official Catholic Directory* (OCD). That volume listed 818 valid institutes of women religious in the United States. The institute survey was fielded in November 1997 and the surveys of "Stayers" and "Leavers" were fielded as the names came in from the institute surveys. Data collection concluded for this study in June 1998, and data analysis began at that point.

A total of 468 completed institute surveys were received. Out of the 818 original surveys that were mailed, nine were returned by the postal service as undeliverable, one institute left the United States and was no longer eligible for the survey, and twenty-six institutes had merged with another institute at the time of the survey, resulting in 782 eligible institutes. Another thirty institutes refused to participate in the study. Thus, the total response rate for the institute survey was 60 percent (468/782).

Responding institutes reported 69,953 total sisters, which corresponds to approximately 80 percent of the 87,443 sisters reported by the OCD in 1999.

"Stayers" Survey

A total of 285 institutes (61 percent of all responding institutes) sent back the names and addresses of sisters who entered the institute after 1965 and remained (the "Stayers"). A total of 101 institutes (22 percent of all responding institutes) sent back the names and addresses of sisters who had entered the institute after 1965 and had since left (the "Leavers"). Three institutes reported that they had no sisters enter since 1966, and eleven reported that they had no sisters who entered since 1966 who remained. Finally, thirty-four institutes reported that they had no sisters who entered since 1966 who had left.

In January 1999, some 4,381 surveys were mailed to sisters who entered their institutes after 1965 and remained. This was the total number of names and addresses provided by the institutes. Out of this total, 406 had been misidentified by their institutes and had actually entered in 1965 or earlier. Another sixty-eight were returned by the postal service as undeliverable, nine were too ill or infirm to complete the survey, twenty-eight refused, seven were deceased, twenty-eight were in the process of leaving their institutes, and nine were out of the country. Subtracting the unusable responses from the total resulted in a total population of 3,863 "Stayers."

After multiple follow-ups by postcard and letter, a total of 2,740 completed surveys were returned by this group, resulting in a response rate for the "Stayers" survey of 71 percent (2,740/3,863). The data collection for the "Stayers" survey was completed in May 1999.

2009 Study Methodology

The principal investigators for the 2009 study were Sister Mary Bendyna and Dr. Mary Gautier of CARA. This study was commissioned by the National Religious Vocation Conference (NRVC) and funded by grants obtained by NRVC for the project. The questionnaire for religious institutes was a single informant survey of 145 items, which asked about the characteristics of the religious institute (e.g., province, region, congregation, monastery), as well as the characteristics of members of the institute. The questionnaire also asked each institute for the names of all those currently in initial formation (candidates/postulants, novices, and those in temporary vows/commitment), as well as those who professed final/perpetual vows/commitment in the institute since 1993. An additional questionnaire of 190 items was developed for distribution to these "new members."

Institute Survey

Researchers used mailing lists provided by the Conference of Major Superiors of Men (CMSM), the Council of Major Superiors of Women Religious (CMSWR), and the Leadership Conference of Women Religious (LCWR) to obtain contact information for 718 institutes of men and women religious (251 units of men religious and 467 units of women religious). CARA also sent the institute questionnaire to superiors of monasteries of contemplative nuns (who do not belong to either LCWR or CMSWR), as well as to superiors of new or emerging communities of consecrated life using mailing lists that CARA compiled for previous research. The institute survey was fielded in April 2008 to a total of 976 entities, with extensive follow-up through the summer and fall. At the end of data collection for the institute survey in September 2008, CARA received completed responses from 591 religious institutes, for an overall response rate of 60 percent.

For comparability to the 1999 study, only institutes of women religious are included in this study. The 2009 study contacted 725 institutes of women religious and monasteries of contemplative nuns and received a response from 429 units. Out of the 725 original institutes contacted, seven were returned as undeliverable, and two were institutes based outside the United States and thus ineligible. An additional five were duplicates (institutes with membership in both CMSWR and LCWR), and one had merged at the time of the survey, resulting in 710 eligible institutes of women. Thus, the total response rate for the institute survey was 60 percent (429/710).

The responding institutes of women religious account for 47,114 women religious, or 80 percent of all women religious in the United States, as reported by the OCD for 2009. Many of the institutes or other entities that did not respond appear to be either small, mostly contemplative, communities that may not have had anyone in initial formation for some time, or those that are still in the process of becoming institutes of consecrated life.

"New Members" Survey

The second phase of the 2009 study consisted of a survey of "new members," that is, current candidates/postulants, novices, and those in temporary vows or commitment, as well as those who had professed final vows or commitment since 1993. The questionnaires were mailed in fall 2008 and winter 2009 to 3,965 new members (including 2,244 women "new members") who had been identified by their religious institutes. However, some surveys were returned as undeliverable, some responses were from transfers from another religious institute rather than new members as defined by the study, and some respondents were formed and based outside the United States and thus beyond the parameters of the study. When these were removed from the sample, CARA received a total of 985 usable responses from women religious "new members" for a response rate of 45 percent among women religious.

Surveys

Post-Vatican II Entrants' Study

Institute Survey, 1997

N=468

1. What kind of institute is yours? NR=0%
    11% 1. Monastic
    12   2. Contemplative
    68   3. Apostolic
    2   4. Other (Please specify)
    7   5. Evangelical
        1a. If apostolic, is it NR=20%
        15% 1. Diocesan
        84   2. Pontifical
        .4   3. Other (Please specify).
2. On the national level, are you a member of NR=4%
    76% 1. LCWR   2   4. Both
    7   2. CMSWR   5   5. Not applicable
    10   3. Neither
3. Where was your institute originally founded? N=456
4. What year was your institute founded?
    N=446 Avg=1740   Median=1842   Range=480–1995
    4a. If applicable, what year was your institute founded in the U.S.?
    N=363 Avg=1884   Median=1880   Range=1700–1995
    4b. If applicable, what year was your unit founded?
    N=274 Avg=1913   Median=1919   Range=1790–1997

5. How many sisters are members of your unit today?   Avg=150   Median=84
    5a. How many are active (full or part-time work)?   Avg=96   Median=55
    5b. How many are retired?   Avg=49   Median=22

6. How many women in your unit
    1. have made perpetual vows   N=451   Avg=140   Median=75
    2. have made a temporary commitment   N=461   Avg=2   Median=1
    3. are novices   N=462   Avg=1   Median=0
    4. are affiliates or postulants (pre-novitiate) N=462   Avg=1   Median=0
    5. are candidates (planning to enter)   N=462   Avg=1   Median=0
    6. are interested in exploring the
       possibility of entrance   N=462   Avg=2   Median=0

7. What is the age of your sisters? How many were born

Avg	Median			Avg	Median	
17	8	1. before 1912	11	5	5. 1946–1954	
33	16	2. 1912–1921	4	2	6. 1955–1964	
21	9	3. 1922–1927	1	0	7. 1965–1976	
58	29	4. 1928–1945	0	0	8. after 1976	

8. What is the age breakdown of those who entered <u>since January 1, 1966</u>? How many sisters were born

AVG	Median			AVG	Median	
0	0	1. before 1912	11	4	5. 1946–1954	
1	0	2. 1912–1921	4	2	6. 1955–1964	
1	0	3. 1922–1927	2	0	7. 1965–1976	
4	1	4. 1928–1945	0	0	8. after1976	

9. What is the racial breakdown of your congregation? How many sisters who were born in the U.S. are

AVG	Median		AVG PCT	Median PCT
125	54	1. Caucasian (White)	82%	98%
1	0	2. Black or African-American	1%	0%
2	0	3. Hispanic or Latina	4%	0%
0	0	4. Native American	.5%	0%
0	0	5. Asian-American or Pacific Islander	1%	0%
1	0	6. Other (please specify)	.3%	0%
14	5	9a. How many were born outside the U.S.?	12%	4%
		9b. Where were they born?		

10. What is the racial breakdown of sisters born in the U.S. who entered <u>since January 1, 1966</u>? How many sisters are

AVG	Median		AVGPCT	Median PCT
21	8	1. Caucasian (White)	68%	87%
0	0	2. Black or African-American	1%	0%
1	0	3. Hispanic or Latina	6%	0%
0	0	4. Native American	1%	0%
0	0	5. Asian-American or Pacific Islander	2%	0%
0	0	6. Other (please specify)	0%	0%
3	1	10a. How many were born outside the U.S.? 12%		0%
		10b. Where were they born?		

11. In which states of the United States and countries of the world are your sisters located? How many sisters are in each?

Location of Sisters in the United States (VII)

State	Sum	AVG	Median	Min	Maximum
AL	303	.65	.00	0	62
AK	56	.12	.00	0	8
AZ	447	.96	.00	0	37
AR	299	.64	.00	0	120
CA	3189	6.83	.00	0	411
CO	557	1.19	.00	0	114
CT	1476	3.16	.00	0	240
DE	160	.34	.00	0	59
FL	848	1.82	.00	0	129
GA	205	.44	.00	0	71
HI	35	.08	.00	0	7
ID	99	.21	.00	0	68
IL	4441	9.51	.00	0	318
IN	1585	3.39	.00	0	424
IA	1180	2.53	.00	0	368
KS	1227	2.63	.00	0	252
KY	1068	2.29	.00	0	190
LA	1001	2.14	.00	0	158
ME	432	.93	.00	0	131
MD	1372	2.94	.00	0	312
MA	2606	5.59	.00	0	363
MI	2267	4.85	.00	0	574
MN	2548	5.47	.00	0	421
MS	288	.62	.00	0	80
MO	2703	5.80	.00	0	451

State	Sum	AVG	Median	Min	Maximum
MT	128	.27	.00	0	41
NE	359	.77	.00	0	111
NV	58	.12	.00	0	16
NH	763	1.63	.00	0	209
NJ	2148	4.61	.00	0	310
NM	319	.68	.00	0	31
NY	6890	14.79	.00	0	926
NC	294	.63	.00	0	91
ND	268	.57	.00	0	96
OH	3677	7.87	.00	0	521
OK	143	.31	.00	0	28
OR	499	1.07	.00	0	225
PA	6212	13.30	.00	0	907
RI	356	.76	.00	0	95
SC	436	.93	.00	0	313
SD	410	.88	.00	0	142
TE	232	.50	.00	0	104
TX	2089	4.47	.00	0	266
UT	36	.08	.00	0	11
VT	174	.37	.00	0	82
VA	212	.45	.00	0	44
WA	653	1.40	.00	0	117
WV	249	.53	.00	0	106
WI	3076	6.60	.00	0	661
WY	30	.06	.00	0	11
DC	294	.63	.00	0	32
PR	190	.41	.00	0	41

Sum	AVG	Median	
15,176	39	2	11a. How many sisters serve in other countries?

11b. Please list the countries and number in each.

12. Do the majority of sisters in your unit have (check one) NR=1%

    49.9%   1. Master's degree or beyond
    32.7%   2. Bachelor's degree
    17%   3. High school diploma
    .4%   4. Less than high school

13. Do you have an associate program? NR=4%

    65%   1. Yes
    35%   2. No (Skip to 14)

Sum	Avg	Median
18,609	66	46	13a. If yes, how many associates do you have?

13b. How many associates are

| 15,697 | 57 | 40 | 1. female |
| 2,149 | 8 | 5 | 2. male |

13c. How many of the <u>female</u> associates are

| 12,350 | 49 | 34 | 1. white |
| 1,054 | 4 | 1 | 2. women of color |

13d. How many of the <u>female</u> associates are

2,138	11	7	1. under age 50
7,673	41	25	2. 50 and above
150	.6	0	13e. How many of the associates have entered your unit to become sisters since the program began?

14. Do you have a lay missioner program? NR=6%

   13% 1. yes

   87% 2. no (Skip to 15)

| 87 | 2 | 0 | 14a. If yes, how many lay missioners have entered your unit to become sisters since the program began? |

15. Were you founded to do one particular ministry? NR=6%

   48% 1. yes

   52% 2. no

   15a. If yes, what was that ministry?

   15b. If yes, are most of the active sisters (check one) NR=60%

   51% 1. still involved in that ministry

   49% 2. involved in a variety of ministries

16. Do you have a corporate work for which you are known? NR=9%

   64% 1. Yes

   36% 2. No

   16a. If yes, what is it?

17. Do you have sponsored institutions? NR=7%

   60% 1. Yes

   40% 2. No (Skip to 18)

| 1,370 | 5 | 3 | 17a. If yes, how many? NR=46% |
| 198 | 1 | 0 | 17b. If yes, how many vocations to your unit have come from these institutions in the last ten years? NR=49% |

18. What is the norm of dress for your unit? (check one) NR=2%

   16% 1. full habit   47% 3. wearing of institute symbol

   24% 2. modified habit   13% 4. no symbol or habit

Sum	Avg	Median
17,802	43	16	19. How many local communities do you have in your unit? NR=11%
933	15	14	19a. If only one, how many sisters live there? NR=87%

19b. If more than one, how many communities are comprised of NR=22%

8,820	24	4	1. one person	1,161	3	2	6. 6–10
3,638	10	5	2. two persons	335	1	0	7. 11–15
1,649	5	3	3. three persons	137	0	0	8. 16–20
1,271	3	2	4. four persons	372	1	1	9. over 20
669	2	1	5. five persons				

20. How many members have entered your unit <u>since January 1, 1966</u>? Please record the number who entered each year and the number of those who remain.

4,180 15% 5% 21. Please estimate the percentage of those who left who were asked to leave. NR=41%

427 1 1 22. Since 1966, how many left and later re-entered your unit? NR=16%

944 2 1 23. Since 1966, how many transferred in from other institutes? NR=14%

617 2 1 24. Since 1966, how many transferred out to other institutes? NR=14%

25. What is the structure of your vocation recruitment effort? Check all that apply.

21% 1. We have no formal structure. NR=1%

31% 2. Full-time vocation director(s). NR=1% How many?

    AVG=1 Median=1 NR=71%

39% 3. Part-time vocation director(s). NR=1% How many?

    AVG=2 Median=1 NR=65%

33% 4. Vocation team (please describe) NR=1%

16% 5. Other (please describe) NR=1%

26. Are any lay people involved in your vocation efforts? NR=3%

33% 1. yes

67% 2. no

26a. If yes, in what capacity? NR=74%

27. Does your unit have a stated numerical goal for new entrants for the 1997–98 year? NR=5%

7% 1. Yes

93% 2. No

27a. If yes, what is the goal? NR=93%

SUM AVG Median

4,309,517 14,461 7,300

28. What is the total budget for the vocation effort? NR=36%

AVG% Med% 28a. Of this, what percentage is directed to recruitment of

89%	100%	1. sisters	NR=58%
5%	0%	2. associates	NR=58%
1%	0%	3. lay missioners	NR=58%

11% 1% 29. What percentage of the total budget of your unit is directed to the vocation effort?   NR=57%

30. Which forms of the media do you use to encourage vocations to enter your unit?

    2% 1. billboards   NR=1%

    7% 2. TV   NR=1%

    5% 3. radio   NR=1%

    47% 4. parish bulletins   NR=1%

    63% 5. magazines (please specify)   NR=1%

    64% 6. other (please specify)   NR=1%

    6% 7. none   NR=1%

31. Do you have a homepage on the Internet? NR=22%

    45% 1. yes

    55% 2. no

32. Indicate how much stress you give to each element of your corporate identity as you deal with your various publics.

    AVG Median 1=Greatly stressed 2=Somewhat stressed 3=Not at all stressed

    1.4 1.0 1. community life   NR=9%

    1.3 1.0 2. mission   NR=12%

    1.5 1.0 3. communal prayer   NR=9%

    46 19 33. Over the last two years, how many inquiries has your unit received regarding entrance to the vowed life?   NR=16%

    44 45 34. What is the maximum age for entrance?   NR=42%

    20 20 35. What is the minimum age for entrance?   NR=15%

    16% 36. Does your unit have an image (unstated) of what the ideal candidate is supposed to look like and be like? What is that image?   NR=85%

37. Does your unit pray regularly for vocations to your institute? NR=3%

    90% 1. yes

    4% 2. no

    6% 3. unsure

    37a. If yes, how often?   NR=42%

    37b. If yes, what form does the prayer take?

38. Does your unit hold periodic structured gatherings for young adults? NR=6%

    48% 1. yes

    52% 2. no

    38a. If yes, please describe.

39. Do you have structured gatherings for women interested in entering?   NR=5%

    58% 1. yes

    42% 2. no

    39a. If yes, please describe.

40. What has been your most successful recruitment strategy over the last three years? Please describe.

41. In the last two years, how many women have you personally invited to think about entering? NR=26%

    AVG   Median

    7   3

42. How often is the topic of vocations on the agenda of your leadership meetings?   NR=14%

    14%   1. every meeting
    14%   2. at least 3/4 of all meetings per year
    18%   3. at least 1/2 of all meetings per year
    32%   4. at least 1/4 of all meetings per year
    20%   5. hardly ever
    2%   6. never

43. Estimate what percentage of your sisters are involved in recruitment of sisters?   NR=30%

    AVG%   Median%
    26%   10%

44. If applicable, estimate what percentage of your associates are involved in recruitment of sisters? NR=65%

    AVG%   Median%
    11%   0%

45. If applicable, estimate what percentage of your lay missioners are involved in recruitment of sisters? NR=88%

    AVG%   Median%
    5%   0%

46. What are prerequisites for entrance? (Check all that apply.)   NR=1%

    YES
    17%   1. College degree
    73%   2. No financial indebtedness
    96%   3. Physical exam
    96%   4. Interview(s)
    26%   5. HIV/AIDS testing
    78%   6. Psychological screening
    94%   7. Letters of recommendation
    86%   8. Sacramental history
    75%   9. Written autobiography
    43%   10. U.S. citizenship or permanent residency
    30%   11. Other (specify)
    13%   12. Other (specify)

47. What factors would deter you from accepting a woman for entrance?

48. What is the structure of your formation effort? (Check all that apply.)

    10% 1. We have no formal structure. NR=1%

    37% 2. Postulant director(s). NR=1% AVG Median

    35% 3. Full-time novice director(s). NR=1% .4 0 How many? NR=5%

    17% 4. Part-time novice director(s). NR=1% .2 0 How many? NR=3%

    28% 5. Full-time formation director(s). NR=1% .3 0 How many? NR=5%

    32% 6. Part-time formation director(s). NR=1% .4 0 How many? NR=6%

    31% 7. Other (please specify) NR=1%

49. Does your unit participate in an intercongregational formation experience? NR=7%

    70% 1. Yes

    30% 2. No

    49a. If yes, at what stage of the process? NR=40%

    AVG   Median

    $23,158 $14,000   50. What is the budget for your formation office (total for pre-final vows programs and personnel, etc.)? NR=57%

    14%   2%   50a. What percentage of the total budget is directed to formation? NR=66%

    7   8   51. On average, in the last fifteen years, how many years did it take a woman to pass from entrance to final vows? NR=14%

52. Do you have some kind of post-final vow structure or program to aid retention? NR=12%

    37% 1. Yes (Please describe)

    63% 2. No

53. Do you have some kind of post-Silver Jubilee structure or program to aid retention? NR=12%

    20% 1. Yes (Please describe)

    80% 2. No

    AVG Median

    43% 40% 54. Please estimate the percentage of your local communities in which you would be happy to place a new member. NR=35%

55. The following are attitudes about vocations. Please use the numbers 1 through 5 to indicate your level of agreement or disagreement with each statement. Use 3 if you do not know.

    1=Strongly agree 2 =Agree 3=Do not know 4=Disagree 5=Strongly disagree

SA	A	DK	D	SD	NR	
2	3	1	37	57	4	1. It is God alone who invites individuals to the religious life; it is not the job of a sister to invite anyone.
5	14	35	25	21	4	2. The future of my institute is Catholic religious, clergy, married and single people living and working together.

2	5	20	38	35	7	3. A new form of religious life will emerge in the U.S. in the not too distant future; then I will invite people to enter.
2	<1	2	29	67	4	4. It would be unjust to invite anyone to enter an institute today given the great financial problems we face.
1	5	11	52	31	4	5. Religious vocations for the near future will be from the Third World; all recruitment efforts should be directed there.
42	40	10	6	2	7	6. Recruitment of a new generation of sisters in the U.S. is an essential aspect of mission.
19	41	31	9	<1	6	7. The future of my institute in the U.S. is multi-ethnic and multi-racial young Catholic women as vowed sisters.
<1	4	36	36	24	6	8. The future of my institute is ecumenical and interfaith members.
<1	5	8	47	39	6	9. The majority of women interested in entering religious life today have been wounded by society and thus do not have the gifts or strength needed to be sisters and nuns.
<1	1	1	18	80	4	10. My institute has nothing to offer young people today.
1	<1	1	24	74	5	11. We must wait for the transformation of the Church before we can invite anyone to enter in this country.
35	36	3	17	9	9	12. We exist for mission, not to perpetuate ourselves.
<1	5	7	50	38	4	13. As religious we must decrease so that the laity might increase and take their rightful role in the Church.
1	3	4	47	45	6	14. Previous generations were badgered by sisters to think about entering; I would rather not invite and thus not be perceived as badgering people into entering.
<1	2	4	38	56	5	15. The recruitment of a new generation of religious runs counter to the Vatican II vision of a lay-centered Church.
<1	2	2	45	51	4	16. The age gap between the majority of our members and young people today is too great; therefore, we cannot invite the young to enter.
1	3	1	36	59	5	17. Our founding spirit and charism did not include invitation to entrance, it is not in our tradition as an institute.

<1	<1	<1	20	79	4	18. Since lay people are now involved in many aspects of ministry, religious life is not needed in this country.
21	47	20	10	2	8	19. We must invite the poor and marginalized to become sisters in our institute.
77	18	1	1	3	4	20. The ministry of vocation recruitment belongs to each sister in the institute not just those in formal positions.
<1	<1	1	17	82	4	21. Ours is no longer a way of life, there is nothing to invite people to.
<1	<1	3	42	55	5	22. Young people today are too conservative to be effective sisters.

56. What is the greatest challenge facing your unit with reference to vocations? What is the greatest challenge facing you regarding formation? (Use last page, too, if needed.)

Post-Vatican II Entrants' Study

Individual Survey-B (Stayers), 1999

N=2,740

Background Information

1. Full name and initials of present institute (and province, region, etc., if applicable)
2. What kind of institute is yours?   N=0%
   - 76%   1.) Apostolic
   - 4   2.) Contemplative
   - 8   3.) Monastic
   - 11   4.) Evangelical
   - 1   5.) Other (specify)
3. Is your institute   NR=3%
   - 88%   1.) Pontifical
   - 10   2.) Diocesan
   - 2   3.) Not applicable (both)
   - <1   4.) Other (specify): 17 Society of Apostolic Life
4. If applicable, does your congregation belong to
   - 85%   1.) LCWR
   - 4   2.) CMSWR
   - 5   3.) Both
   - 5   4.) Neither
   - 1   5.) Don't know
   - <1   6.) Not applicable
5. Of how many institutes have you been a member? N=2,648   Avg.=1   Median=1
   - 2%   None
   - 89   One
   - 9   Two
   - <1   Three
   - <1   Four

   5a. If more than one, what year did you <u>enter</u> your first institute?
   N=263   Avg.=1968   Median=1966

   5b. What year did you <u>depart</u> your first institute?
   N=253   Avg.=1978   Median=1979
6. Did you transfer from one institute to another?   NR=2%
   - 93%   1.) No
   - 7   2.) Yes

   6a. If yes, did you transfer from one type of religious life to another, e.g., apostolic to contemplative?   NR=94%
   - 78%   1.) No
   - 22   2.) Yes

7. What year did you enter your present religious institute?
   N–2,725 Avg.=1977 Median=1976
   49% 1966–1975
   32   1976–1986
   19   1987–1997
   <1   after 1997

8. Did you ever leave your institute and re-enter it later? NR=1%
   93% 1.) No
   7   2.) Yes
   8a. If yes, how many years later did you re-enter?
   N=184 Avg.=6 Median=3

9. What year did you make final vows, if applicable?
   N=2,387 Avg.=1982 Median=1982

10. What year were you born?
    N=2,736 Avg.=1951 Median=1950

11. How old are you? N=2,732 Avg.=47 Median=48
    17% Under 40
    56   41–50
    22   51–60
    5   61–85

12. Did you attend a Catholic elementary school in the U.S.? NR=0%
    28% 1.) No
    72   2.) Yes
    12a. If yes, for how many years?
    N=1,748 Avg.=7 Median=8

13. Did you attend a Catholic high school in the U.S.? NR=0%
    35% 1.) No
    65   2.) Yes
    13a. If yes, for how many years?
    N=1,605 Avg.=4 Median=4

14. Did you attend a Catholic college or university in the U.S. for your undergraduate degree?
    35% 1.) No NR=1%
    65   2.) Yes
    14a. If yes, for how many years?
    N=1,652 Avg.=4 Median=4

15. When you were in junior high and high school, for how many years did you attend religious education at your parish, such as C.C.D. classes?
    N=2,192 Avg.=1 Median=0

16. When you were in high school, were you ever involved in Catholic youth ministry or parish youth programs? NR=3%
    29% 1.) Often.
    28   2.) Occasionally
    43   3.) Never

17. Were you a convert to Catholicism? NR=0%
    92% 1.) No
    8 2.) Yes

18. During your elementary school years, did you live with both of your parents?
    NR=0%
    8% 1.) No
    92 2.) Yes

19. During your elementary school years, was your mother Catholic?
    NR=0%
    8% 1.) No
    91 2.) Yes
    1 3.) Not Applicable

20. During your elementary school years, was your father Catholic?
    NR=0%
    13% 1.) No
    85 2.) Yes
    2 3.) Not Applicable

21. How many times a month did your mother attend Mass?
    N=2,608 Avg.=6 Median=4

22. How many times a month did your father attend Mass?
    N=2,543 Avg.=4 Median=4

23. Were you born in the U.S.? NR=0%
    11% 1.) No
    89 2.) Yes

    23a. If not, in which country were you born?
        41 Mexico, 41 Philippines, Canada, Ireland, Vietnam

24. What was the first generation of your family to come to this country on your
    father's side?
    9% 1.) My father was first NR=1%
    28 2.) My grandparent(s) was first
    27 3.) My great-grandparent(s) was first
    18 4.) Beyond great-grandparents
    10 5.) Don't know
    7 6.) Not applicable

25. From which country(ies) did they come on your father's side?
    572 Ireland, 564 Germany, 209 Italy, 167 Poland, 163 England, 104 Canada

26. What was the first generation of your family to come to this country on your
    mother's side?
    8% 1.) My mother was first
    28 2.) My grandparent(s) was first
    29 3.) My great-grandparent(s) was first
    19 4.) Beyond great-grandparents
    10 5.) Don't know
    6 6.) Not applicable

27. From which country(ies) did they come on your mother's side? 694 Ireland, 521 Germany, 201 Italy, 148 Poland, 130 England

28. What is your race?

    89% 1.) White

    5   2.) Latina or Hispanic

    1   3.) African-American

    <1   4.) Native American

    3   5.) Asian or Pacific Islander

    0   6.) Caribbean Islander

    1   7.) Bi-racial (specify) 9 White/NA, 7 White/Hispanic, 6 White/Asian, 2 Hispanic/Asian

    <1   8.) Other (specify) 7 African, 4 multi-racial, 1 Garifuna

29. With which ethnic group do you most identify?   NR=25%

    489 White, 456 Irish, 195 German, 174 Italian, 45 None

30. Which language did you speak at home when you were growing up?

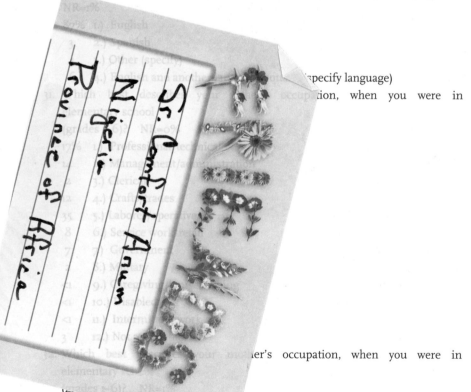

specify language)

31. Which best describes your _____ occupation, when you were in elementary school (grades 1-5)? NR=0%

    6% 1.) Professional/technical

    2   2.) Management/administration

    7   3.) Clerical

    1   4.) Crafts/trades

　5　　5.) Laborer/operative
　5　　6.) Service work/retail
　<1　7.) Government
　0　　8.) Military
　61　9.) Caregiving/housekeeping
　0　　10.) Disabled
　2　　11.) Intermittent work
　11　12.) Not applicable

33. Which category best describes your social class when you were in elementary school? NR=1%

　3%　1.) Poor
　39　2.) Working
　39　3.) Lower Middle
　18　4.) Upper Middle
　1　　5.) Upper

34. During elementary school, in which region of the U.S. did you grow up? NR=2%

　27%　1.) Northeast
　11　　2.) East
　5　　3.) South
　34　　4.) Midwest
　4　　5.) Southwest
　6　　6.) Rocky Mountain or Far West
　3　　7.) Northwest
　3　　8.) Combination of more than one
　7　　9.) Outside of the U.S. (specify): 36 Philippines, 29 Mexico, 20 Ireland, 11 Canada

35. During elementary school, where did you live?　　　　　　　NR=1%

　5%　1.) An inner-city
　33　2.) A city
　20　3.) A suburb
　21　4.) A town
　14　5.) A rural area
　7　　6.) Combination of more than one

36. What was the political affiliation of your father when you were in elementary school?　　　　　　　NR=3%

　51%　1.) Democrat
　22　　2.) Republican
　3　　3.) Independent
　1　　4.) Other (specify)
　15　　5.) Don't know
　8　　6.) Not applicable

37. What was the political affiliation of your mother when you were in elementary school? NR=2%

    55% 1.) Democrat

    17   2.) Republican

    5   3.) Independent

    1   4.) Other (specify)

    15   5.) Don't know

    7   6.) Not applicable

38. What is your current political affiliation?   NR=3%

    67% 1.) Democrat

    8   2.) Republican

    14   3.) Independent

    3   4.) Other (specify)

    8   5.) Not applicable

Vocation Story

39. How old were you when you first thought about being a Sister?

    N=2,671   Avg.=14 Median=12

40. How old were you when you decided to enter?

    N=2,712   Avg.=22 Median=20

41. How old were you when you actually entered?

    N=2,724   Avg.=24 Median=22

42. Did you experience a call from God to enter?   NR=2%

    5%   1.) No

    82   2.) Yes

    13   3.) Unsure

43. How many institutes did you consider seriously before entering yours? NR–0%

    45% 1.) Just my own

    33   2.) Two

    16   3.) Three

    6   4.) Four to six

    <1   5.) Seven to ten

    <1   6.) More than ten

44. How long did you discern the question of entering? NR=1%

    2%   1.) Less than a day

    4   2.) Less than a month

    20   3.) Less than a year

    49   4.) 1–3 years

    15   5.) 4–6 years

    5   6.) 7–10 years

    5   7.) Over 10 years

45. Was your encounter with the institute you entered through   NR=1%

  67% 1.) A Sister in the institute

  5   2.) An advertisement (specify)

  <1 3.) The Internet (specify)

  5   4.) A priest

  5   5.) A relative

  5   6.) A friend

  1   7.) A co-worker

  12 8.) Other (specify)

46. Were you educated by a Sister(s) from your institute while in (check all that apply):

  32% 1.) Elementary school

  25% 2.) Junior high school

  39% 3.) High school

  30% 4.) College

  4% 5.) Graduate school

  37% 6.) None of the above

47. Were you educated by Sisters from another institute at any point in your education? NR=1%

  29% 1.) No

  71 2.) Yes

48. Did you discern a particular charism in your institute before entrance? NR=1%

  31% 1.) No

  59 2.) Yes

  10 3.) Unsure

49. Aside from God, who most encouraged you to enter? NR=1%

  13% 1.) Family

  9   2.) Friends

  1   3.) Co-workers

  43 4.) Woman religious

  6   5.) Priest

  <1 6.) Lay teacher

  23 7.) Nobody

  2   8.) Former Sister

  2   9.) Other (specify)

50. Who most tried to discourage you from entering?   NR=3%

  36% 1.) Family

  14 2.) Friends

  3   3.) Co-workers

  2   4.) Woman religious

  1   5.) Priest

<1   6.) Lay teacher

40   7.) Nobody

<1   8.) Former Sister

4   9.) Other (specify)

51. Was the religious life formally presented, in class or in campus ministry, as an option for you to consider seriously while in (check all that apply):

    48% 1.) Elementary school

    37% 2.) Junior high

    49% 3.) High school

    12% 4.) College

52. How many relatives (by blood) do you have in your institute? 0=85% NR=6% N=2,564 Avg.=.3 Median=0

    52a. If any, is the closest relative a(n): NR=89%

    21% 1.) Sister

    28   2.) Aunt

    6   3.) Grandaunt

    40   4.) Cousin

    5   5.) Other (specify): 6 Second Cousins, 3 Distant Cousins, 2 Third Cousins, 2 Nieces

53. Did a Sister(s) invite you to enter?   NR=2%

    47% 1.) No

    53   2.) Yes

54. How many women did you invite to enter last year? 0=56% NR=4% N=2,626 Avg.=1.7 Median=0

55. Do you believe that God wants a new generation of sisters in the U.S.? NR=2%

    3% 1.) No

    76   2.) Yes

    21   3.) Unsure

56. What is your status at this time? NR=1%

    1% 1.) Pre-novitiate

    3   2.) Novitiate

    8   3.) First vows

    85   4.) Final vows

    3   5.) Member of society of apostolic life. We do not make final vows.

57. When did you enter? NR=2%

    5% 1.) During high school

    21   2.) Immediately after high school

    12   3.) After high school and some work experience

    9   4.) After some college

    14   5.) After some college and some work experience

    5   6.) Immediately after college

20   7.) After college and some work experience

2   8.) After some grad/professional school

1   9.) After grad/professional school

11   10.) After grad/professional school and some work experience

58. Before entrance, were you: NR=0%

94% 1.) Single

2   2.) Engaged

3   3.) Divorced

1   4.) Widowed

59. Do you have children?   NR=1%

96% 1.) No

4   2.) Yes

60. Were you a lay missioner of your institute before entrance?   NR=0%

82% 1.) No

2   2.) Yes

16   3.) We do not have such a program

61. Were you an associate of your institute before entrance?   NR=2%

85% 1.) No

8   2.) Yes

7   3.) We do not have such a program

62. Before entrance, did you work as a volunteer or paid worker
    (check all that apply):

20% 1.) In direct service to the poor in the U.S.

3   2.) In direct service to the poor in a Third World nation

8   3.) In efforts to bring about systemic change and social justice

40   4.) In parish or diocesan pastoral, administrative, liturgical or educative
        ministries

63. What was your occupation immediately before entrance?   NR=3%

35%	1.) Professional/technical	1	7.)	Government
6	2.) Management/administration	<1	8.)	Military
13	3.) Clerical	2	9.)	Caregiving/housekeeping
1	4.) Crafts/trades	<1	10.)	Disabled
3	5.) Laborer/operative	2	11.)	Intermittent work
8	6.) Service work/retail	29	12.)	Not applicable

64. Were you in a non-traditional occupation before entrance?   NR=4%

92% 1.) No

8   2.) Yes

64a. If yes, what was it?

65. Before entrance, did you ever serve as a <u>volunteer</u> staff member of a Catholic institution (check all that apply):

    36% 1.) Parish

    9% 2.) Hospital

    12% 3.) School/college

    11% 4.) Helping agency

    46% 5.) None

66. Before entrance, did you ever serve as a <u>paid</u> staff member of a Catholic institution (check all that apply):

    8% 1.) Parish

    6% 2.) Hospital

    13% 3.) School/college

    4% 4.) Helping agency

    68% 5.) None

67. How long did you work (not attending school) before entrance?
    NR=3%

    27% 1.) Did not work

    13   2.) Less than a year

    27   3.) 1–3 years

    11   4.) 4–6 years

    6   5.) 7–9 years

    8   6.) 10–15 years

    3   7.) 16–20 years

    5   8.) Over 20 years

68. Did you have educational loans to pay back before entrance?   NR=2%

    86% 1.) No

    14   2.) Yes

    68a. If yes, how much did the loans total? NR–89%

        N=302   Avg.=$5,456   Median=$4,000

    68b. If yes, did your institute assume some/all of the loans?   NR=88%

        70% 1.) No

        30   2.) Yes

    68c. If yes, what percentage of your loans did your institute assume? NR=96%

69. Were you required to get a physical exam before entrance?   NR=1%

    7%   1.) No

    93   2.) Yes

    69a. If yes, who paid for it?   NR=32%

        91% 1.) Myself

        8   2.) Institute

        1   3.) Both

70. Were you required to get psychological testing before entrance?   NR=1%

   32% 1.) No

   68   2.) Yes

   70a. If yes, who paid for it?   NR=47%

      40% 1.) Myself

      55   2.) Institute

      5   3.) Both

71. What is the highest level of education you have attained to date?   NR=1%

   <1% 1.) Less than high school diploma

   3   2.) High school diploma or equivalent

   5   3.) Some college

   10   4.) College degree

   8   5.) Some grad/professional school

   51   6.) Master's degree

   1   7.) RN

   4   8.) M.S.W.

   5   9.) Ph.D.

   1   10.) J.D.

   1   11.) M.D.

   3   12.) Enrolled in a graduate program

   8   13.) Other (specify)

72. What was the highest level of education you received before entrance?   NR=1%

   3%   1.) Less than high school diploma

   32   2.) High school diploma or equivalent

   21   3.) Some college

   25   4.) College degree

   5   5.) Some grad/professional school

   8   6.) Master's degree

   2   7.) RN

   1   8.) M.S.W.

   1   9.) Ph.D.

   <1   10.) J.D.

   <1   11.) M.D.

   2   12.) Enrolled in a graduate program

   <1   13.) Other (specify)

73. If you possess a Master's degree(s), in which field(s) is it?   NR=33%

74. If you possess a doctoral degree, in which field is it?   NR=92%

75. What is your primary ministry at this time?   NR=2%

76. What is your usual mode of dress in your ministry?   NR=0%

   11% 1.) Full habit

   13   2.) Modified habit

   38   3.) Institute symbol

   38   4.) No symbol or habit

77. In your ministry, do you use the title "Sister" to refer to yourself? NR=1%

    47% 1.) All of the time

    46   2.) Some of the time

    7   3.) Never

78. Have you ever been in leadership in your institute? NR=1%

    76% 1.) No

    13   2.) Yes, currently

    11   3.) Yes, in the past

79. Have you ever been in formation work (full- or part-time)? NR=1%

    81% 1.) No

    7   2.) Yes, currently

    12   3.) Yes, in the past

80. Have you ever been in vocation work (full- or part-time)? NR=0%

    75% 1.) No

    10   2.) Yes, currently

    15   3.) Yes, in the past

81. Since entrance, have you served in a Third World nation? NR=1%

    91% 1.) No

    9   2.) Yes

        81a. If yes, for how many years? 91%

            N=244   Avg.=4   Median=2

82. Many in the media presume that Sisters want to be priests. What is your view—do you personally feel called to the priesthood? NR=1%

    4% 1.) Yes

    14   2.) Yes, but in a different form

    75   3.) No

    7   4.) Unsure

83. Do you consider yourself a feminist? NR=3%

    38% 1.) No

    48   2.) Yes

    14   3.) Unsure

84. Check all of the following that you read weekly/monthly?

29%	1.) America	33%	6.) Review for Religious
5%	2.) Commonweal	73%	7.) Diocesan Newspaper
58%	3.) NCR	82%	8.) Publications of your institute
1%	4.) The Wanderer	7%	9.) Sisterlist on the Internet
14%	5.) Sisters Today		

Community and Ministerial Life

There is much discussion today about community life. For the purposes of this survey, community is defined as the people with whom you share common space and a kitchen. This definition does not include self-contained units wherein sisters meet periodically for meals and prayer. Sisters in those units would be considered to be living alone.

85. With how many Sisters of your institute do you now live?   NR=1%
     N=2,705 Avg.=9   Median=3
     19%   None
     16   One
     11   Two
     11   Three
     25   Four-Ten
     18   Eleven or more
86. With how many Sisters of your institute do you now work?   o = 4 2 %
     NR=4%
     N=2,639   Avg.=7   Median=1
87. If you had your preference right now, with how many Sisters would you prefer
     to live?
     (choose one)   NR=2%
     11%   1.) With none
     14   2.) With one other Sister
     12   3.) With two other Sisters
     45   4.) In a group of 4–7 Sisters
      6   5.) In a group of 8–10 Sisters
      2   6.) In a group of 11–15 Sisters
      4   7.) In a group of 16–20 Sisters
      6   8.) In a group of more than 20 Sisters
88. If you had your preference right now, with whom would you prefer to live?
     NR=2%
     9%   1.) No one   64   7.) Sister(s) of my own institute
     1   2.) An ecumenical group   <1   8.) Children
     <1   3.) An interfaith group   <1   9.) Teens/young adults
     <1   4.) Married couple(s)   <1   10.) Family member(s)
     1   5.) Single layperson(s)   5   11.) Inter-congregationally
     4   6.) Men and women religious   15   12.) Combination of Sisters and
                                                       one of the above (choose
                                                       number and insert on line)

89. Is the area in which you <u>live</u>:   NR=2%
     37%   1.) Urban
     14   2.) Inner-city
     33   3.) Suburban
     16   4.) Rural

90. Is the area in which you <u>work</u>:   NR=4%

   36% 1.) Urban

   19   2.) Inner-city

   29   3.) Suburban

   16   4.) Rural

91. In what kind of neighborhood do you <u>live</u> at the present time? NR=2%

   9%   1.) Poor

   34   2.) Working class

   28   3.) Lower middle class

   27   4.) Upper middle class

   3   5.) Upper class

92. In what kind of neighborhood do you <u>work</u> at the present time?
NR=7%

   18% 1.) Poor

   30   2.) Working class

   23   3.) Lower middle class

   27   4.) Upper middle class

   3   5.) Upper class

93. Do you <u>live</u> in a multicultural neighborhood?   NR=1%

   43% 1.) No

   57   2.) Yes

94. Do you <u>work</u> in a multicultural neighborhood?   NR=4%

   42% 1.) No

   58   2.) Yes

95. Is the neighborhood in which you <u>live</u> predominantly: NR=2%

   72% 1.) White

   9   2.) African-American

   1   3.) Asian

   7   4.) Latino

   11   5.) Other (specify): mixed or multi-cultural is modal response

96. Is the neighborhood in which you <u>work</u> predominantly: NR=6%

   65% 1.) White

   11   2.) African-American

   2   3.) Asian

   8   4.) Latino

   14   5.) Other (specify): mixed or multi-cultural is modal response

97. Do you <u>live</u> in a neighborhood where you, yourself, are a minority?
NR=2%

   77% 1.) No

   23   2.) Yes

98. Do you <u>work</u> in a neighborhood where you, yourself, are a minority?
    NR=5%

    74%   1.) No

    26   2.) Yes

99. Do you live in a(n):   NR=1%

    37%   1.) Convent

    4   2.) Apartment in a complex wherein other Sisters of my institute
               reside in other apartments

    12   3.) Apartment in a complex wherein no Sisters of my institute reside in
               other apartments

    26   4.) House

    9   5.) Monastery

    2   6.) Former Rectory

    o   7.) Catholic Worker house

    <1   8.) Housing project

    3   9.) Institution of some kind (specify)

    7   10.) Other (specify)

100. Do you work primarily in a(n):   NR=6%

    75%   1.) Catholic institution

    2   2.) Ecumenical institution

    1   3.) Interfaith institution

    3   4.) Government institution

    16   5.) Non-profit institution

    3   6.) For-profit institution

101. Do you work in an institution sponsored by your congregation?
    NR=3%

    53%   1.) No

    39   2.) Yes

    8   3.) Not applicable

102. Would you be willing to work in an institution sponsored by your
    congregation? NR=4%

    6%   1.) No

    83   2.) Yes

    11   3.) Not applicable

103. Do you live with (check all that apply):

    1%   1.) A married couple(s)

    4%   2.) Single person(s)

    1%   3.) Lay missioner(s)

    1%   4.) Teens/young adults

    1%   5.) Children

    1%   6.) An ecumenical group

   10%   7.) Sister(s) of another institute

   <1%   8.) Men and women religious

   1%   9.) Family member(s) of one of the Sisters

   78%   10.) Sister(s) of my own institute

   14%   11.) I live alone

   1%   12.) An interfaith group

104. Other than a name listed near the doorbell, is there any visible sign, symbol or structure that makes clear to the public that Sisters live in your home? NR=2%

   55%   1.) No

   44   2.) Yes

   1   3.) Unsure

105. How many of the ten houses closest to yours know that there are Sisters in your house?

   N=2,509   Avg.=7   Median=10

106. Do you live in close physical proximity to where you work (e.g., on campus, in the same compound, etc.)   NR=3%

   52%   1.) No

   48   2.) Yes

107. How close do you live to the nearest Sisters of your institute (those not living with you)? NR=4%

   67%   1.) Within 10 miles

   17   2.) 11–50 miles

   16   3.) More than 50 miles

108. Do you live in what is considered the house of another institute or group? NR=1%

   93%   1.) No

   7   2.) Yes

109. Do youth and young adults visit your home?   NR=1%

   21%   1.) Regularly

   60   2.) Once in a while

   19   3.) Never

110. Is hospitality to young people who are discerning their vocation held as a value of your community?   NR=1%

   6%   1.) No

   84   2.) Yes

   10   3.) Unsure

111. Do you have a guest room in your community?   NR=1%

   11%   1.) No

   75   2.) Yes

   14   3.) There is extra space for a guest but not a room

112. How many rooms in your home are considered community rooms?
     NR=9%
     N=2,500   Avg.=3   Median=2
     112a. Of those, how many do not have a television set in them?   NR=23%
     N=2,102   Avg.=2   Median=1
113. Is there a common prayer space in your community?
     NR=6%
     60% 1.) Yes, with the Blessed Sacrament
     19   2.) Yes, without the Blessed Sacrament
     21   3.) No
114. If you live alone, what do you consider to be your primary community?
     NR=79%
     14% 1.) Family
     13   2.) Co-workers
     17   3.) Friends
     48   4.) Your institute
     8   5.) Other

IF YOU LIVE ALONE, PLEASE SKIP THE FOLLOWING QUESTIONS 115
TO 139.

14% Live Alone (NR reported below does not include these 14 percent who
live alone)

115. Which holidays are regularly celebrated together by your community on the day
     itself?
     (Check all that apply.)
     53% 1.) Thanksgiving
     55% 2.) Christmas
     58% 3.) Easter
116. How often is a meal eaten together by your community?   NR=5%
     35% 1.) More than once a day
     24   2.) Once a day
     11   3.) Monday-Friday
     19   4.) Monday-Thursday
     7   5.) Twice a week
     2   6.) Once a week
     2   7.) Few times a month
     <1   8.) Few times a year
     <1   9.) Never
117. How often do you pray (not the blessing of meals) with the members of your
     community?
     37% 1.) More than once a day NR=5%
     14   2.) Once a day
     17   3.) Monday-Friday

13   4.) Monday-Thursday

6   5.) Twice a week

4   6.) Once a week

4   7.) Few times a month

3   8.) Few times a year

2   9.) Never

118. Please choose the style of common prayer that you use most frequently as a community:

26%   1.) Prayer of Christians (red book) NR=8%

14   2.) 1988 New Companion to the Breviary (gray book)

13   3.) 1997 People's Companion to the Breviary (2-volume psalter)

20   4.) Common prayer book of your congregation

10   5.) Scripture sharing

14   6.) Creative, non-conventional

3   7.) We do not have common prayer

119. Is music used regularly in common prayer?   NR=5%

26%   1.) Tapes and CDs

16   2.) Singing of psalm(s) or song(s)

<1   3.) Playing of instruments

42   4.) We use music and we sing

13   5.) We do not use music or sing

3   6.) We do not have common prayer

120. Do you as a community pray for vocations to the vowed religious life? NR=4%

32%   1.) Daily

19   2.) Weekly

8   3.) Monthly

33   4.) Once in a while

8   5.) Never

121. How often is Eucharistic liturgy celebrated in your community? NR=5%

36%   1.) Daily

6   2.) More than once a week

6   3.) Weekly

1   4.) More than once a month

3   5.) Monthly

16   6.) Few times a year

32   7.) Never

122. How often is a Communion service held in your community? NR=7%

    5%   1.) Daily

    3   2.) More than once a week

    5   3.) Weekly

    2   4.) More than once a month

    1   5.) Monthly

    24   6.) Few times a year

    60   7.) Never

123. How often do you have formal community meetings?   NR=5%

    17%   1.) Weekly

    12   2.) Semi-monthly

    33   3.) Monthly

    28   4.) Few times a year

    10   5.) Never

124. How often does the community spend a day of prayer together?
NR=6%

    28%   1.) Monthly

    39   2.) Few times a year

    33   3.) Never

125. How often does your community spend a day of relaxation together?
NR=6%

    26%   1.) Monthly

    56   2.) Few times a year

    18   3.) Never

126. In the course of this year, how often did your community spend a weekend away
together in order to relax?   NR=5%

    12%   1.) Few times a year

    15   2.) A couple of times a year

    17   3.) Once

    56   4.) Never

127. In the course of this year, did.your community go on vacation together?
NR=5%

    16%   1.) Yes, all were able to go

    12   2.) Yes, some were able to go

    72   3.) No

128. What is the form of governance for your community?   NR=6%

    52%   1.) Collegial

    13   2.) Coordinator

    34   3.) Local Superior

129. Are there written goals for the community?　　　　NR=5%

    31%　　1.) No

    66　　2.) Yes

    3　　3.) Unsure

    129a. If yes, are they reviewed annually?　NR=33%

    9%　　1.) No

    87　　2.) Yes

    4　　3.) Unsure

130. How many Sisters have not yet made final vows in your community? (Indicate NA if not applicable).　NR=34%

    N=1,432　　Avg.=2　Median=1

131. Do you live with your best friend?　　　　NR=6%

    77%　　1.) No

    23　　2.) Yes

132. The following questions ask about Sisters in your community. To the best of your knowledge, how many of the Sisters in your community, including yourself, are:

N	Avg	Med		N	Avg	Med.	
488	5	2	1.) Above 90 years	1380	3	2	6.) 40–49 years
724	10	3	2.) 80–89 years	830	3	1	7.) 30–39 years
1022	10	2	3.) 70–79 years	467	2	1	8.) 20–29 years
1287	8	2	4.) 60–69 years	298	<1	0	9.) Under 20 years
1554	6	2	5.) 50–59 years				

133. To the best of your knowledge, in terms of length of time in the house, how many Sisters in your community, including yourself, have lived there for:

N	Avg	Med		N	Avg	Med.	
200	6	1	1.) Over 60 years	517	4	2	5.) 20–29 years
208	6	2	2.) 50–59 years	924	4	2	6.) 10–19 years
235	6	2	3.) 40–49 years	1153	4	2	7.) 5–9 years
324	5	2	4.) 30–39 years	1553	4	3	8.) Less than 5 years

134. How long ago did the Sisters in your community, including yourself, enter religious life?

    On each line, indicate the number of Sisters who entered:

N	Avg	Med		N	Avg.	Med.	
314	4	1	1.) Over 70 years ago	1365	4	2	5.) 30–39 years ago
574	6	2	2.) 60–69 years ago	1182	2	1	6.) 20–29 years ago
909	6	2	3.) 50–59 years ago	920	2	1	7.) 10–19 years; ago
1157	5	2	4.) 40–49 years ago	703	3	1	8.) 9 years ago or less

135. Are you the youngest Sister in the community?   NR=4%

    53%   1.) No

    47   2.) Yes

136. In terms of years in religious life, are you the newest Sister in the community? NR=4%

    58%   1.) No

    42   2.) Yes

137. How many years ago did the last person enter into your community? NR=10%

    N=2,093   Avg.=7   Median=2

138. With reference to ministries in the community, the sisters are NR=5%

    80%   1.) In a variety of ministries

    16   2.) In the same ministry

    4   3.) Not applicable

139. Would your community be a good one for a sister in formation (who has not made final vows)?   NR=4%

    14%   1.) No

    72   2.) Yes

    14   3.) Unsure

140. Is there a pet in the community? NR=1%

    11%   1.) Dog

    9   2.) Cat

    75   3.) Neither

    5   4.) Both

141. How many communities have you lived in since entrance?   NR=2%

    N=2,692   Avg.=6   Median=6

142. How many full-time ministries have you had since entrance?   NR=5%

    N=2,609   Avg.=3   Median=3

143. If applicable, please estimate the percentage of communities in your institute in which you would be happy to see a newer member placed.   NR=27%

    N=2,010   Avg.=39%   Median=30%

144. How many years have you lived in this community? NR=3%

    N=2,655   Avg.=8   Median=5

Spiritual and Religious Structures

145. Were you a participant in a post-Final Vow retention program of your institute? NR=3%

    29%   1.) No

    9   2.) Yes

    7   3.) I have not made Final Vows

    55   4.) We do not have such a program

146. Were you a participant in a post-Silver Jubilee retention program of your institute? NR=11%

    96% 1.) No

    4 2.) Yes

147. Have you been a participant in an institute gathering of Sisters who have entered since Vatican II or a gathering of Sisters 55 years of age and younger? NR=2%

    48% 1.) No

    52 2.) Yes

148. Have you been a participant in an inter-congregational gathering of Sisters who have entered since Vatican II or a gathering of Sisters 55 years of age and younger? NR=2%

    67% 1.) No

    33 2.) Yes

149. Do you participate in a feminist spirituality group on a regular basis? NR=1%

    90% 1.) No

    10 2.) Yes

150. How often do you attend Mass? NR=<1%

    35% 1.) Daily

    20 2.) 4–6 times a week

    16 3.) 2–3 times a week

    24 4.) Weekly

    2 5.) Monthly

    3 6.) Rarely

    <1 7.) Never

151. Did you attend *daily* Mass before entrance? NR=<1%

    62% 1.) No

    38 2.) Yes

152. Where do you usually attend Sunday Mass? NR=1%

    36% 1.) Parish in whose geographical boundaries I live

    17 2.) The parish where I work

    21 3.) Another parish

    18 4.) In my residence

    8 5.) None of the above

153. In the last six months, have you been active in any group or committee in the parish you attend? NR=7%

    62% 1.) No

    38 2.) Yes

154. In the last year, have you done the following? (Check all that apply).

    52%   1.) Made a 6–8 day directed retreat

    39%   2.) Made a private retreat

    24%   3.) Made a preached retreat

    61%   4.) Gone to a spiritual director

    68%   5.) Made a day(s) of recollection

    7%   6.) Participated in a 12-step meeting

    6%   7.) Participated in a charismatic prayer meeting

    40%   8.) Gone to a social justice meeting

    41%   9.) Gone to Eucharistic Adoration

155. How long do you spend in <u>personal</u> (not communal) prayer every day? NR=1%

    49%   1.) Less than an hour

    40   2.) 1 hour

    9   3.) 2 hours

    2   4.) 3 hours

    <1   5.) 4 hours

    <1   6.) More than 4 hrs.

156. Think of your five closest friends. How many of the five are members of your institute?

    N=2,676   Avg.=3   Median=3

157. Please rate the following regarding how well each supports your vocation: 1=Not at all supportive 2= Moderately unsupportive 3=Not applicable 4=Moderately supportive 5=Very supportive

1	2	3	4	5	
1	3	9	21	66	1.) The community in which you live
<1	1	2	14	83	2.) Your friends in the institute
<1	3	3	35	59	3.) Friends outside the institute
2	5	2	34	56	4.) Family
1	3	1	24	71	5.) The leadership of your institute
<1	3	2	35	60	6.) The membership of your institute
<1	2	22	31	45	7.) Sisters in other institutes
2	3	13	34	48	8.) Co-workers

158. Who of the following do you consider to be a member of your institute? (Check all that apply.)

    97%   1.) A sister who has made final vows   59%   4.) A postulant

    95%   2.) A sister who has made temporary vows   33%   5.) A candidate

    87%   3.) A novice   15%

            6.) A woman who was formerly a vowed Sister in your institute (not now an associate)

159. Does your institute have the following? (Check all that apply.)

    84% 1.) associates/oblates

    73% 2.) benefactors

    17% 3.) lay missioners

160. Which of the following do you consider to be members of your institute? (Check all that apply.)

    50% 1.) associates/oblates

    11% 2.) benefactors

    7% 3.) lay missioners

    17% 4.) former Sisters in your institute

161. Do you believe that a person has to be Catholic in order to be a member of your institute?

    16% 1.) No   NR=3%

    74 2.) Yes

    10 3.) Not sure

162. Please rate your level of satisfaction with how actively the following are invited by your institute to be Sisters. 1 = Not at all satisfied 2 = Moderately dissatisfied 3 = Don't know/Not applicable 4 = Moderately satisfied 5 = Completely satisfied

1	2	3	4	5	
20	20	17	26	17	1.) Women of color
17	19	23	24	16	2.) Poor women
17	17	29	22	15	3.) Immigrant women
7	13	13	40	27	4.) Working class women
4	8	10	42	36	5.) Professional women

163. Using the scale in the above response, please rate your level of satisfaction with how well your institute is:

1	2	3	4	5	
10	22	8	43	16	1.) Inviting a new generation of Sisters
7	18	8	48	19	2.) Forming new Sisters
7	16	7	50	21	3.) Retaining Sisters

164. Rate how much encouragement to enter is given to each of the following groups by your institute: 1 = Strongly discouraged 2=Somewhat discouraged 3= We do not have such a program 4 = Somewhat encouraged 5 = Strongly encouraged

1	2	3	4	5	
2	2	2	29	66	1.) Women who want to be vowed sisters
2	3	15	31	49	2.) Women who want to be associates
2	2	69	13	13	3.) Women who want to be lay missioners

165. There is discussion about a "new form of religious life." Is that term used in your institute at assemblies, in discussions, etc.?   NR=2%

    27% 1.) Frequently

    47 2.) Once in awhile

    26 3.) Never

166. Do you think that you know what the term "new form of religious life" means? NR=2%

　　29%　1.) No　31　　　　2.) Yes　40　　　3.) Unsure

　　166a. If yes, please specify what it means? NR=68%

167. Do you know what Sisters in your institute mean when they use the term "new form of religious life"? NR=3%

　　23%　1.) No

　　16　　2.) Yes

　　44　　3.) Unsure

　　17　　4.) That term is not used

　　167a. If yes, please specify what they mean?　　　　NR=83%

168. Rate the following possible responses to the statement—The heart of religious life is:

　　Please use 1 = Strongly agree 2 = Agree 3 = Don't know 4 = Disagree 5 = Strongly Disagree

1	2	3	4	5	
57	33	4	5	2	1.) The vows
49	35	4	9	2	2.) Communal living
36	46	3	13	2	3.) Ministry
63	31	1	3	1	4.) Personal prayer
51	40	3	5	1	5.) Communal prayer

169. Rate the emphasis of each of the following in your formation, 1 = Greatly stressed 2 = Somewhat stressed 3 = Not at all stressed

1	2	3	
57	34	9	1.) Mission
54	40	6	2.) Ministry
77	21	2	3.) Communal living
84	14	2	4.) Personal prayer
80	18	2	5.) Communal prayer

Please rate each of the following three questions: 1 = Definitely a violation 2 = A minor violation 3= Don't know 4 = Mayor may not be a violation depending on circumstances 5 = Not at all a violation

170. Using the above scale, rate each of the following in regard to the violation of the vow of poverty.

1	2	3	4	5	
42	16	2	38	2	1.) Not living simply
45	18	2	34	2	2.) Not sharing what one has
26	13	3	52	7	3.) Not turning in money gifts or turning over ownership of goods or property
59	5	3	30	4	4.) Producing income for oneself
76	8	3	10	3	5.) Not having a concern for the poor

171. Using the above scale, rate each of the following in regard to the violation of the vow of chastity (celibacy)?

I	2	3	4	5	
85	3	1	10	1	1.) Engagement in genital sexual activity
52	13	2	31	3	2.) Involvement in an exclusive relationship
12	6	4	47	31	3.) Not living communally
25	15	9	46	5	4.) Allowing the sharing of one's love to be limited in some way
60	12	7	17	5	5.) Not having a concern for the unloved

172. Using the above scale, rate each of the following in regard to the violation of the vow of obedience?

I	2	3	4	5	
40	14	5	29	12	1.) Not praying regularly
24	6	2	63	6	2.) Not obeying a superior
33	15	11	37	5	3.) Not assuming collegial authority
33	13	6	45	4	4.) Not listening to the call of one's Sisters
49	12	13	18	8	5.) Not having a concern for those who are not free

173. Which one element of your formation program continues to be foundational to your religious life?

174. Which one element do you wish you received more of during your formation?

175. Rate the emphasis on each in your formation. 1 = Greatly stressed 2 = Somewhat stressed 3 = Not at all stressed

I	2	3	
13	39	48	1.) Creation theology/spirituality
8	36	58	2.) Feminist theology/spirituality
12	40	48	3.) Liberation theology/spirituality
60	35	5	4.) Traditional theologies/spiritualities
84	13	4	5.) Other (specify)

176. Which theologies/spiritualities are influential in your life today? 1 = Very influential 2 = Somewhat influential 3 = Not at all influential

I	2	3	
41	44	14	1.) Creation theology/spirituality
32	50	19	2.) Feminist theology/spirituality
33	48	19	3.) Liberation theology/spirituality
37	53	11	4.) Traditional theologies/spiritualities
83	14	3	5.) Other (specify)

177. Why did you enter the form of religious life you did, e.g, apostolic, contemplative, etc.?

178. Why did you enter your particular institute?

179. Why do you stay?

Center for Applied Research in the Apostolate and the National Religious Vocation Conference

Survey of Religious Institutes and Societies of Apostolic Life

INSTITUTES OF WOMEN RELIGIOUS ONLY, 2009
N=429

Type of Institute or Society

1. Gender of members: N/A 1. Men 100% 2. Women.
2. Canonical Status:
   - 4% 1. Public association of the faithful
   - 94 2. Religious institute
   - 2 3. Society of apostolic life   NR=4%
3. Status of the institute or society: NR=4%
   - 13% 1. Diocesan right
   - 87 2. Pontifical right

Character or lifestyle of the institute or society (check all that apply):
   - 70% 4. Apostolic   3   7. Eremitic
   - 28 5. Contemplative   12   8. Evangelical
   - 4 6.Conventual   18   9. Monastic

Demographic Data

Please indicate the <u>number</u> *in each category in your* <u>unit</u>:
Avg=.55   10. Pre-candidates/aspirants (before entrance)
Median=0
Avg=.42   11. Candidates/postulants (before novitiate)
Median=0
Avg=.75   12. Novices
Median=0
Avg=1.66   13. Temporary vows/commitment
Median=0
Avg=110   14. Final/perpetual vows/commitment
Median=55

Items 15–19 applied to men's institutes only

*Please indicate the <u>number</u> of **candidates/postulants, novices, and temporary professed** in your <u>unit</u> who were born in each decade:*

	Candidates/ Postulants	Novices	Temporary Professed
Before 1940	20. Avg=.00	27. Avg=.00	34. Avg=.03
1940–1949	21. Avg=.02	28. Avg=.03	35. Avg=.08
1950–1959	22. Avg=.06	29. Avg=.09	36. Avg=.22
1960–1969	23. Avg=.06	30. Avg=.09	37. Avg=.31
1970–1979	24. Avg=.11	31. Avg=.19	38. Avg=.49
1980–1989	25. Avg=.21	32. Avg=.24	39. Avg=.45
1990 or later	26. Avg=.02	33. Avg=.00	40. Avg=.03

*Please indicate the number of **finally professed members** in your <u>unit</u> who were born in each decade:*

Avg=12.5	41. Before 1920	Avg=6.5	45. 1950–1959
Avg=28.3	42. 1920–1929	Avg=2.4	46. 1960–1969
Avg=34.8	43. 1930–1939	Avg=.84	47. 1970–1979
Avg=24.4	44. 1940–1949	Avg=.13	48. 1980 or later
Avg=70	49. <u>Average</u> age of **finally professed members**		
Med=74	50. <u>Median</u> age of **finally professed members**		

*Please indicate the <u>number</u> of **candidates/postulants, novices, and temporary professed** in your <u>unit</u> in each racial or ethnic category:*

Avg=.16	51. African American/Black/African
Avg=.47	52. Asian/Pacific Islander
Avg=1.8	53. Caucasian/White/Anglo
Avg=.49	54. Hispanic/Latino(a)
Avg=.02	55. Native American/American Indian
Avg=.03	56. Other:_____

*Please indicate the <u>number</u> of **finally professed members** in your <u>unit</u> in each racial or ethnic category:*

Avg=.64	57. African American/Black/African
Avg=2	58. Asian/Pacific Islander
Avg=99	59. Caucasian/White/Anglo
Avg=3	60. Hispanic/Latino(a)
Avg=.16	61. Native American/American Indian
Avg=.06	62. Other:_____

Vocation Ministry

63. Does your unit have a **vocation director**?

   85   1. Yes   15 2. No NR=1

64. *If yes*, which best describes the **vocation director**?

   98   1. A member of your unit

   .5   2. A member of another unit of your institute, society, or federation

   0   3. A member of another institute or society

   .3   4. An associate

   .5   5. A lay person who is not a member or associate

65. Is the **vocation director** engaged in vocation ministry:

   44   1. Full-time   56   2. Part-time   NR=17

66. Does your unit have a **vocation team**, i.e., more than
    one person directly responsible for vocation ministry?

   56   1. Yes   44   2. No   NR=7

   Avg=4   67. Number of members of the **vocation team**

If your unit has a vocation team, please indicate if it includes the following (check all that apply):

   53   68. Member(s)

   8   69. Associate(s)

   4   70. Other lay person(s) who is/are not member(s) or associate(s)

71. If your unit has a **vocation director and/or team**,
    what is the scope of his/her/their responsibilities?

   95   1. Your unit only

   4   2. More than one unit of your institute, society, or federation (e.g., two or
         more provinces)

   1   3. More than one institute or society NR=15

Please indicate if your unit sponsors or co-sponsors the following discernment programs (check all that apply):

   25   72. Discernment groups

   51   73. Discernment retreats

   71   74. "Come and See" experiences

   12   75. Discernment house

   56   76. Live-in experiences

   32   77. Ministry/mission experiences

Please indicate if your unit has used any of the following for vocation promotion in the last five years (check all that apply):

   73   78. Advertising   6 81. TV

   85   79. Website/Internet   8 82. Radio

   91   80. Print materials   18 83. Other:_____

Please indicate if your <u>unit</u> sponsors or co-sponsors vocation promotion or discernment programs specifically targeted toward these age groups (check all that apply):

41 84. Elementary school

58 85. High school

63 86. College

69 87. Young adults (20s and 30s)

29 88. Mature adults (over age 40)

Please indicate if your <u>unit</u> requires the following for admission (check all that apply):

94   89. Medical assessment   66 91. Behavioral assessment

80   90. Psychological testing   69 92. Background check

Formation/Incorporation Ministry

Please indicate the <u>number</u> of individuals in each category in your <u>unit</u>. If your unit has been reconfigured since 1990, please include the numbers for the units that are now part of your unit:

Avg=11   93. Total number who entered since Jan.1, 1990

Avg= 6   94. Of the total in #93, number who remain

*Of those who entered and then **departed** since 1990, please indicate the <u>number</u> who departed at each stage:*

Avg=2   95. During candidacy/postulancy

Avg=2   96. During novitiate

Avg=1   97. During temporary vows/commitment

Avg=.3 98. After final/perpetual vows/commitment

Please indicate the typical <u>number</u> of years that are required for each period of initial formation or incorporation in your <u>unit</u> (if less than a year, please specify the number of months):

Avg=1   99. Pre-candidacy/aspirancy (before entrance)

Avg=1   100. Candidacy/postulancy (before novitiate)

Avg=2   101. Novitiate

Avg=4   102. Temporary vows/commitment

Does the unit have the following requirements for admission to <u>candidacy/postulancy</u>?

Yes No

90   11   103. <u>Minimum **age**</u> (*please specify*): Avg=20

76   24   104. <u>Maximum **age**</u> (*please specify*): Avg=44

82   20   105. Minimum **education**

59   51   106. Minimum **work experience**

107. *If yes to #105 and/or #106*, please describe:

Do **candidates/postulants** in your <u>unit</u> spend all or part of their formation with religious others from:

Yes   No
38   62   108. Other units of your institute, society, federation
29   71   109. Other institutes or societies

Do **novices** in your <u>unit</u> spend all or part of their formation with others from:

Yes   No
52   48   110. Other units of your institute, society, federation
44   56   111. Other institutes or societies

Do those in **temporary vows/commitment** in your <u>unit</u> spend all or part of their formation with others from:

Yes   No
51   49   112. Other units of your institute, society, federation
27   73   113. Other institutes or societies

Reconfiguration

Yes   No
16   84   114. Has your unit reconfigured since 1990?
19   81   115. Is your unit in the process of reconfiguring?

116. *If yes to #114 and/or #115*, please describe:

Ministry

Active/apostolic institutes or societies only (#117–127):
Please indicate the <u>number</u> of members of your <u>unit</u> who are:
Avg=59 117. Active in a full-time ministry
Median=35
Avg=24 118. Active in a part-time ministry
Median=13
Avg=50 119. Retired from active ministry
Median=26

Of members who are active *(not retired from active ministry)*, <u>number</u> engaged in the following types of ministry:
Avg=25 120. Education
Median=11
Avg=11 121. Health care
Median=5
Avg=13 122. Pastoral ministry (e.g., parish, campus)
Median=7
Avg=4 123. Spiritual direction/retreat work
Median=2

Avg=7 124. Social work/social service
Median=3
Avg=2 125. Social justice/advocacy
Median=1
Avg=16 126. Internal ministry
Median=10
Avg=15 127. <u>Number</u> of members serving in a ministry
Median=6 sponsored or co-sponsored by your unit

Community Life and Prayer

Please indicate the number of active members (not retired from active ministry) of your unit who:

Avg=17   Median=3 128.   Live alone
Avg=20   Median=9 129.   Live in communities of 2 or 3
Avg=15   Median=6 130.   Live in communities of 4 to 7
Avg=23   Median=9 131.   Live in communities of 8+

Please indicate which of the following characterize the regular prayer life of a majority of members of your unit (check all that apply):

89   132. Daily Eucharist
82   133. Liturgy of the Hours
48   134. Non-liturgical common prayer
26   135. Common meditation
63   136. Faith sharing

Contemplative institutes only (#137–139):
Please indicate the <u>number</u> of members of your unit who are:
Avg=13   137. Able to participate fully in prayer life
Avg= 3   138. Able to participate somewhat in prayer life
Avg= 1   139. Unable to participate in prayer life

Religious Habit

Yes No   **NR=3**
63   37   140. Do members of your unit wear a habit?

141. *If yes*, please describe:

142. *If yes to #140*, is wearing the habit: **NR=4**
       55 1. Required in all or most circumstances
        9 2. Required only at certain times (e.g., ministry, prayer)
       34 3. Optional
        2 4. Other: _____

143. **If wearing the habit is optional**, how many
       members wear it all or most of the time?
         6 1. None   **NR=1**
       73 2. A few (less than 25%)
       12 3. Some (25–49%)
         7 4. Many (50–74%)
         3 5. Most (75% or more)

144. Please describe any special vocation promotion or recruitment efforts
     your religious institute or society of apostolic life has undertaken in
     recent years. Attach additional sheets if necessary.

145. Please describe any special formation/incorporation programs your reli-
     gious institute or society of apostolic life has undertaken in recent years.
     Attach additional sheets if necessary.

As part of this study for NRVC, CARA will survey those who have entered religious institutes and societies of apostolic life in the last two decades. Please list
the names and contact information (address, city, state, and ZIP) for all those
currently in initial formation (candidates/postulants, novices, and those in temporary vows/commitment) as well as those who **professed final/perpetual vows/
commitment in your unit since 1993**. Please attach additional sheets if necessary.

Please provide the information below for the person completing this survey so
we may contact you for clarifications about your responses:

    Name and Title:
    Institute/Society and Province:
    Phone, FAX, and E-mail:

Thank you for taking the time to complete this survey.
CARA/Center for Applied Research in the Apostolate at Georgetown University
2300 Wisconsin Ave., NW, Suite 400, Washington, DC 20007
Phone: 202-687-8080 Fax: 202-687-8083

Center for Applied Research in the Apostolate and the National Religious Vocation Conference

Survey of New Members

Women Religious Only, 2009 N=985

Percentage response for each item, calculated out of 100%, unless otherwise noted. NR (Non-response) separately calculated out of 100%.

Please use the responses below for questions 1–15.
1=Not at All   3=Somewhat
2=Only a Little   4=Very Much

How much did the following attract you to <u>religious life</u>*?*

1	2	3	4	NR	
2	3	13	83	2	1. A sense of call to religious life
0	3	20	76	3	2. A desire for prayer and spiritual growth
3	9	28	60	4	3. A desire to be part of a community
2	7	27	64	3	4. A desire to be of service
10	18	28	45	5	5. A desire to be more committed to the Church

How much did the following attract you to <u>your religious institute</u>*?*

1	2	3	4	NR	
15	19	27	39	6	6. The life and works of your founder/ess 4 10 28 58 4
					7. The mission of the institute
1	6	22	71	4	8. The spirituality of the institute
1	6	26	67	3	9. The prayer life of the institute
2	7	28	63	4	10. The community life of the institute
6	14	36	44	7	11. The ministries of the institute
12	16	19	53	5	12. The institute's fidelity to the Church
4	6	20	69	5	13. The example of members of the institute
24	13	25	38	9	14. A personal invitation by a member
6	7	26	62	6	15. Welcome and encouragement by members

How did you first become acquainted with your religious institute? Check all that apply.

- 30 16. In an institution where members served, e.g., school
- 19 17. Through working with a member of the institute
- 5 18. Through a relative in the institute
- 17 19. Through a friend in the institute
- 31 20. Through the recommendation of a friend or advisor

6   21. Through a vocation fair
2   22. Through a vocation match or placement service
10   23. Through an event sponsored by the institute
5   24. Through a media story about the institute or member
17   25. Through print or online promotional materials
25   26. Other:_____

Did you participate in any of the following before you entered your religious institute? Check all that apply.

18   27. Diocesan vocation programs
60   28. Spiritual direction
54   29. Discernment retreat
55   30. "Come and See" experience
35   31. Live in experience with the institute
21   32. Ministry or mission experience with the institute
13   33. Regular meeting with a discernment group
36   34. Regular meeting with a vocation director
32   35. Regular meeting with a member(s) of the institute
41   36. Regular visits to communities

Please use the responses below for questions 37–52.
1=Not at All   3=Somewhat
2=Only a Little   4=Very Much

How helpful were the following when you were discerning your call to religious life?

1	2	3	4	NR	
78	13	6	4	22	37. General Catholic or diocesan websites
75	12	8	5	23	38. Vocation discernment websites
60	11	14	15	21	39. Websites of religious institutes
48	18	24	10	17	40. Newspaper or magazine articles
41	18	24	17	15	41. Print or online promotional materials, e.g., brochures, posters, ads
69	15	10	6	21	42. CDs, DVDs, or videos
70	12	10	8	24	43. Diocesan vocation programs
18	7	19	56	15	44. Spiritual direction
27	5	14	54	19	45. Discernment retreat
27	5	14	54	19	46. "Come and See" experience
40	4	8	48	28	47. Live in experiences
43	10	15	33	30	48. Ministry or mission experience
63	11	14	13	35	49. Meeting with a discernment group
23	8	21	48	21	50. Meeting with a vocation director
10	4	19	67	17	51. Meeting with a member(s) of the institute
11	4	15	70	12	52. Visits to communities

Please use the responses below for questions 53–120.
1=Not at All   3=Somewhat
2=Only a Little   4=Very Much

How much did these influence your decision to enter your religious institute?

1	2	3	4	NR	
45	18	25	13	9	53. The size of the institute
40	14	23	24	7	54. Its geographic location(s)
54	12	15	19	26	55. Its internationality, if applicable
2	5	26	68	4	56. Prayer life or prayer styles in the institute
2	4	24	70	4	57. Community life in the institute
6	6	26	63	7	58. The lifestyle of members
73	13	10	4	11	59. The racial/ethnic background of members
43	20	24	12	9	60. The ages of members
13	11	34	41	8	61. The types of ministry of its members
25	6	13	57	5	62. Its practice regarding a religious habit

How much encouragement did you receive from the following when you first considered entering your religious institute?

1	2	3	4	NR	
3	6	24	68	6	63. Members of your institute
10	6	22	61	15	64. Vocation director/team
12	5	20	63	26	65. Spiritual director, if applicable
18	13	30	38	16	66. Other men and women religious
31	15	20	33	15	67. Diocesan priests
29	16	26	29	11	68. Your parents, if applicable
31	21	25	23	12	69. Your siblings, if applicable
32	26	26	16	14	70. Other family members
23	16	29	32	12	71. People in your parish
28	19	31	22	13	72. People in your school or workplace
23	7	21	49	28	73. Friends within the institute
15	16	33	37	11	74. Friends outside the institute

How much encouragement do you currently receive from the following in your life and ministry as a member of your religious institute?

1	2	3	4	NR	
<1	5	15	80	2	75. Members of your institute
2	6	17	76	3	76. The leadership of your institute
11	8	16	65	18	77. Novice/formation director/team
7	3	15	75	31	78. Spiritual director, if applicable
6	9	30	55	12	79. Other men and women religious

23	14	21	42	14	80. Diocesan priests
12	9	18	61	19	81. Your parents, if applicable
12	12	27	49	12	82. Your siblings, if applicable
14	15	30	42	13	83. Other family members
16	11	22	51	20	84. People in your parish
11	9	26	54	17	85. People in your school or workplace
3	6	25	66	13	86. People with whom you minister
4	6	24	67	12	87. People to whom you minister
1	4	16	80	10	88. Friends within the institute
4	9	30	57	9	89. Friends outside the institute

How important to you are these types of prayer?

I	2	3	4	NR	
5	7	13	75	1	90. Daily Eucharist
7	7	15	70	1	91. Liturgy of the Hours
5	13	33	49	7	92. Non-liturgical common prayer
13	14	20	53	5	93. Common meditation
15	12	14	59	2	94. Eucharistic Adoration
16	14	21	50	2	95. Other devotional prayer, e.g., rosary
4	11	28	57	4	96. Faith sharing

How important to you are these aspects of community life?

I	2	3	4	NR	
2	3	10	85	2	97. Living with other members
0	1	8	91	2	98. Praying with other members
4	9	22	65	2	99. Working with other members
1	3	13	83	2	100. Sharing meals together
3	4	19	75	2	101. Socializing/sharing leisure time together

How much do you prefer living in these settings?

I	2	3	4		
66	15	11	8	8	102. Alone
26	27	28	18	10	103. In a small community of two or three
11	12	33	44	9	104. In a medium-sized community of 4 to 7
12	11	26	52	6	105. In a large community of 8 or more
2	4	26	68	4	106. With members of different ages
3	9	37	51	8	107. With members of different cultures
12	13	28	47	13	108. With members in different ministries
11	11	23	56	9	109. With only members of your institute
13	14	36	37	34	110. With members of other units of your institute, e.g., other provinces
35	27	28	10	19	111. With members of other institutes
51	20	18	11	22	112. With associates

How much do you prefer ministry in these settings?

1	2	3	4	NR	
3	9	22	67	10	113. With other members of your institute
8	14	36	43	35	114. With members of other units of your institute, e.g., other provinces
9	21	45	25	19	115. With members of other institutes
5	9	27	59	14	116. In a ministry sponsored by your institute
18	17	34	32	18	117. In a parish or diocesan ministry
14	20	41	25	20	118. With an organization that is Catholic but is not sponsored by your institute
31	31	29	9	20	119. With an organization that is religious but is not Catholic
50	25	19	7	20	120. With an organization that is not religious

> *Please use the responses below for questions 121–139.*
> **1=Poor   3=Good**
> **2=Fair   4=Excellent**

How would you rate the following in <u>your religious institute</u>?

1	2	3	4	NR	
4	15	35	46	2	121. Efforts to promote vocations
3	11	29	56	2	122. Welcome and support of newer members
4	13	32	51	2	123. Formation/incorporation programs
4	12	33	51	3	124. Opportunities for ongoing formation
3	10	28	60	5	125. Educational opportunities
4	15	35	46	9	126. Preparation for ministry
1	4	25	70	1	127. Opportunities for spiritual growth
2	6	30	63	2	128. Opportunities for personal growth
3	7	27	64	2	129. Sense of identity as religious
2	8	24	66	4	130. Sense of identity as institute members
1	7	26	67	2	131. Fidelity to the Church and its teachings
0	3	22	75	1	132. Faithfulness to prayer and spiritual growth
1	5	28	66	5	133. Focus on mission
0	3	23	75	5	134. Commitment to ministry
1	8	29	63	2	135. Response to the needs of our time
3	11	36	50	7	136. Efforts to promote social justice
3	13	37	47	2	137. Quality of community life
2	10	32	56	4	138. Communal prayer experiences
4	11	44	41	2	139. Relationships with one another

Yes No

69 31 1 140. Do members of your institute wear a habit?

141. *If yes to #140, is wearing the habit*   NR=3

   74 1. Required in all or most circumstances

    4 2. Required only at certain times, e.g., ministry, prayer

  18 3. Optional

   3 4. Other:_____

142. *If yes to #140, and wearing the habit is* _optional_,
how many members wear it all or most of the time?

   o 1. None   NR=1

  73 2. A few (less than 25%)

  18 3. Some (25–49%)

   4 4. Many (50–74%)

   5 5. Most (75% or more)

143. *If yes to #140, and wearing the habit is* _optional_,
how frequently do you wear it?   NR=4

  77 1. Never

   2 2. Once in a while

   6 3. Only at certain times, e.g., ministry, prayer

  15 4. In all or most circumstances

Yes No   NR=7

23 77 144. If your institute does not have a habit, would you wear one if
that was an option?   NR=6

90 10 145. Were you employed before you entered?

146. *If yes to #145, were you employed* NR=6
   81 1. Full-time   19 2. Part-time

73 27 147. Were you engaged in ministry before you entered?   NR=6

148. *If yes to #147, were you engaged in ministry*

  36 1. Full-time   NR=4

  10 2. Part-time

  54 3. Volunteer

Were you involved in any of the following before *you entered? Check all that apply.*

  37   149. Youth ministry or group

  29   150. Young adult ministry or group

  27   151. Campus ministry or group

  52   152. Liturgical ministry, e.g., lector, extraordinary minister

  36   153. Music ministry, cantor, choir

  42   154. Faith formation, catechetical ministry, RCIA

  54   155. Other volunteer work in a parish or other setting

  47   156. Retreats

  13   157. World Youth Day

  36   158. Faith-sharing group

8   159. Religious institute volunteer program, e.g., Mercy
or Jesuit Volunteer Corps

160. What is your current status in your religious institute?

   2   1. Candidate/postulant   NR=<1

   9   2. Novice

   27   3. Temporary vows/commitment

   62   4. Final/perpetual vows/commitment

161. Are you: 0 1. Male 100 2. Female NR=<1

162. If male, are you (or do you expect to be) a

   N/A 1. Brother   N/A 2. Priest   NR=N/A

163. What best describes your racial or ethnic background?

   3   1. African American/Black/African NR=1

   8   2. Asian/Pacific Islander

   79   3. Caucasian/White/Anglo

   8   4. Hispanic/Latino(a)

   <1 5. Native American/American Indian

   1   6. Other:_____

Yes No   NR=1

82 18   164. Were you born in the U.S.?

         165.   *If no to #164*, country of birth:

         _____

Please provide the following information:

   Avg=1965   166. Year you were born

   Avg=1997   167. Year you entered your religious institute

   Avg=2004   168. Year you professed/expect to profess final vows/perpetual
                  commitment

   N/A   169. Year you were ordained/expect to be ordained to the
                  priesthood

   Avg=20   170. <u>Age</u> you first considered religious life

   Yes   No

   14   86 171. Did you enter another religious institute before this one?

   Avg=11   172. *If yes*, number of years in that institute.

   89 11   173. Were you raised Catholic?

   Avg=26   174. If you became Catholic as an adult, <u>age</u> you entered the
                  Catholic Church

   10 90   175. Were you ever married?

   7   93   176. Do you have any children?

   4   96   177. Were you ever home-schooled?

   Avg= 8   178. *If yes*, number of years home-schooled

Did you attend any of the following <u>before</u> you entered? Check all that apply.

51 179. Parish-based religious education/CCD/RCIA

56 180. Catholic elementary or middle school

42 181. Catholic high school

38 182. Catholic college or university

12 183. Ministry formation program

6 184. Other:_____

185. What was the <u>highest</u> level of education you NR=1
     completed <u>before</u> you entered your religious institute?

13 1. High school or less   18 4. Master's degree

20 2. Some college   4 5. Doctoral degree

43 3. Bachelor's degree   2 6. Other:_____

186. If you continued your education after you entered,
     what is the <u>highest</u> level of education you completed?

1 1. High school or less   51 4. Master's degree

12 2. Some college   5 5. Doctoral degree

19 3. Bachelor's degree   12 6. Other:_____

187. Would you be willing to participate in a focus group?

65 1. Yes   35 2. No

---

188. What most attracted you to your religious institute?

---

190. What do you find most challenging about religious life?

---

189. What do you find most rewarding or satisfying about religious life?

Thank you for taking the time to complete this survey.
CARA/Center for Applied Research in the Apostolate at Georgetown
University

2300 Wisconsin Ave., NW, Suite 400, Washington, DC 20007

Phone: 202-687-8080 Fax: 202-687-8083

Notes

1. Groups of vowed religious women have been variously referred to as "orders" (which properly applies only to orders of cloistered nuns), "communities" (which may also apply to local convents within a larger entity), and "congregations" (which may be confused with a local parish). To avoid this confusion, we usually use the term "institute" to refer to all autonomously governed orders/congregations/societies of religious women who profess canonical vows.

2. Giving Voice describes itself on "A Giving Voice Update" as "a network of passion for God, all God's people and religious life now and as it emerges in the future."

3. See also www.aNunsLife.org, which was founded in 2006 and describes itself as "a place where you can talk with Catholic sisters and nuns and lots of other people on topics such as spirituality, prayer, community, ministry, and more."

4. The study reported that 350,000 never-married men indicated they had considered becoming a priest or brother.

5. Formation is the period of time between entrance into the institute and the profession of perpetual vows, a period of nine years on average.

6. The age structure of the world population varies by continent. For example, the age structure of many European countries varies from that of the United States. Europe's total population is estimated to decrease from 740 million in 2012 to 732 million in 2050, whereas the U.S. population is still growing, albeit more slowly than before (World Population Data Sheet 2012).

7. The median age of religious order priests and brothers is sixty-five (Bendyna and Gautier 2009, 28).

8. Among the seventy-four contemplative communities that responded to the CARA survey that are members of neither LCWR nor CMSWR, none reported more than six women in formation, and 42 percent reported that they have no one currently in formation.

CHAPTER 2

1. Respondents were asked: How essential is each of these items to *your* vision of what the Catholic faith is? A list of nineteen elements was read to each respondent in a phone interview. Other response categories were: important but not essential to the faith; not important to the faith; unaware it is part of the faith. Religious orders and the papacy followed five other elements as being essential to the faith. The elements and the percentage of young adults who saw them as essential are: belief that God is present in the sacraments—65 percent; charitable efforts toward helping the poor—58 percent; belief that Christ is present in the Eucharist—58 percent; devotion to Mary the mother of God—53 percent; and belief that God is present in a special way in the poor—52 percent.
2. A few institutes also have fourth vows. For example, the Sisters of Mercy profess a fourth vow of service.
3. One function of the young adult associate group is to provide peer support for the younger sisters in the institute (Garcia 2011).
4. From the *Annuarium Statisticum Ecclesiae* (the Statistical Yearbook of the Church). In 2010, there were 66,375 sisters in Africa; 72,985 in North America; 43,374 in Central America; 78,839 in South America; 165,308 in Asia (4,744 of whom are in the Middle East); 286,042 in Europe; and 9,012 in Oceania. In contrast to the total of 721, 935 religious sisters in the world in 2010, there were 135,227 religious priests and 54, 665 religious brothers.

CHAPTER 3

1. One recent example of a visitation to an entire country is Ireland. To address the Church sex- abuse crisis and the response of the Irish government, the Vatican announced an apostolic visitation of Ireland on March 20, 2010, which included seminaries, religious institutes, and dioceses. The *Summary of the Findings of the Apostolic Visitation in Ireland* was released on March 20, 2012.
2. Quinn, personal communication, April 2012.
3. As of this writing, the Vatican has made no comment regarding the results of the apostolic visitation.
4. In response to the doctrinal assessment, the following was contained in a statement released by the Board of LCWR on June 1, 2012: "Board members concluded that the assessment was based on unsubstantiated accusations and the result of a flawed process that lacked transparency. Moreover, the sanctions proposed were disproportionate to the concerns raised and could compromise their ability to fulfill their mission. The report has furthermore caused scandal and pain throughout the church community, and created greater polarization" ("LCWR Board Meets to Review CDF Report," June 1, 2012, www.lcwr.org).
   On April 15, 2013, Archbishop Gerhard Muller, the prefect of the Congregation for the Doctrine of the Faith (CDF), announced that Pope Francis had "reaffirmed

the findings of the assessment and the program of reform for this conference of major superiors" (Carol Glatz, *Catholic News Service*, "Pope Francis reaffirms Vatican's call for reform of U.S. nuns' group," April 15, 2013, www.catholicnews.com).

In response to Muller's announcement, one editorial contained the following report: "More than a few experienced Vatican watchers have advised caution in jumping to conclusions.... They suggest the Vatican has other ways to bring things to a salutary end" ("Pope Francis Should Meet with the Sisters," April 22, 2013, www.ncronline.org).

5. The other controversies, according to Gibson, were "Rome's censoring of Mercy Sister's Margaret Farley's theological writings, the USCCB's investigation of the Girl Scouts for alleged ties to Planned Parenthood, and the bishops' fight against the Obama administration's contraception mandate."

6. The terms "consecrated life" and "religious life" are sometimes used interchangeably in Church documents, adding to the lack of clarity discussed in chapter 2.

7. O'Malley, in his Murnion lecture, stated that "[i]n other words, the documents of Vatican II are not a grab-bag of discrete units. When examined not one by one, but as a single though complex corpus, the pervasiveness of certain issues clearly emerges and vindicates the intuition that the Council had a message to deliver to the Church and to the world that was bigger than any document considered in isolation.... Among such issues was rapprochement, or reconciliation.... [According to Pope John XXIII, the Council] should, more generally, 'make use of the medicine of mercy rather than of severity' in dealing with everyone. It should eschew as far as possible, the language of condemnation" (Initiative Report: Catholic Common Ground Initiative, October 2012, 1–2).

8. These include the following documents: *Religious and Human Promotion* was released in 1978. *Mutuae Relationes* was also released in 1978 and is subtitled *Directives for the Mutual Relations between Bishops and Religious in the Church*. *The Contemplative Dimension of Religious Life* was written in 1980. The Sacred Congregation for Religious and Secular Institutes issued *Essential Elements in the Church's Teaching on Religious Life as Applied to Institutes Dedicated to Works of the Apostolate* in 1983, the same year as the revised Code of Canon Law was promulgated. In 1984, Pope John Paul II issued the apostolic exhortation *Redemptionis Donum*. In 1990, *Directives on Formation* was issued. *Fraternal Life in Community* was promulgated in 1994. *Consecrated Life: A Sign of the Church's Vitality* was the "final message" of the 1994 World Synod of Bishops on Consecrated Life. *Verbi Sponsa* was issued in 1999 and focuses on contemplative nuns, not active sisters. Two instructions were disseminated by the Sacred Congregation for Religious and Secular Institutes: in 2002, *Starting Afresh from Christ: A Renewed Commitment to Consecrated Life in the Third Millennium*, and in 2008, *The Service of Authority and Obedience*.

9. The term "religious life" is used in the title of the congress; the term "consecrated life" is used in the title of the conference's final document. This points to the lack of clarity we noted earlier in this chapter and in chapter 2.

CHAPTER 4

1. These categories are taken from Wittberg (2012, 122–123).

CHAPTER 6

1. Note that not all religious institutes were required by their founders to say the Divine Office. In fact, some were explicitly told not to do so. A lower percentage valuing this item does not necessarily reflect a departure from the spirit of an institute's founder.

CHAPTER 7

1. The term "convent," in fact, originally applied to the residences of these peripatetic male friars, *not* to the residences of sisters.
2. Citing the threats of dyadic and familial withdrawal to group life, Kanter continued: "It is also one tenet of community life that as little as possible should belong exclusively to any one person; instead everything should be shared, affection as well as material possessions" (Kanter 1972, 86).
3. Sometimes, zoning regulations are an issue as well. Some municipalities prohibit more than two unrelated adults from living under the same roof.
4. The one exception was a small percentage (4 percent) of CMSWR post-Vatican II respondents who expressed this preference.
5. The strong bond possible in a dyadic construction is explained by Simmel: "This dependence of the dyad upon its two individual members causes the thought of its existence to be accompanied by the thought of its termination much more closely and impressively than in any other group, where every member knows that even after his [sic] retirement or death, the group can continue to exist.…This fact is bound to influence the inner attitude of the individual toward the dyad, even though not always consciously nor in the same way" (Simmel 1950, 123–124).
6. These may be exclusive coalitions between two of the three members that exclude the third, or "rejoicing thirds" where one member pits the other two against each other in order to reap benefits from both (Simmel 1950, 154–162).
7. Simmel describes the isolation of an individual vis-à-vis a group: "The feeling of isolation is rarely as decisive and intense when one actually finds oneself physically alone, as when one is a stranger, without relations, among many physically close persons, at a 'party,' on a train, or in the traffic of a large city (Simmel 1950, 119).

8. The twelfth recommendation of this Congress reads: "Young people, in particular, thirst for community as an expression of mission and as a place for sharing faith and relationships.... Every institute has to keep developing means of
ongoing formation so that community life is more human and meaningful. The
community has to be open and hospitable" (http://www.fransalians.com/wcrl/
final_document.htm).

References

Arzillo, Francesco. 2012. "How to Read the New 'Signs of the Times.'" www.chiesa. espressonline.it. Accessed December 31, 2012.

Barron, Robert. 2011. *Catholicism: A Journey to the Heart of Faith.* New York: Random House.

Beal, John P., James A. Coriden, and Thomas J. Green (eds.). 2000. *New Commentary on the Code of Canon Law.* Commissioned by the Canon Law Society of America. Mahwah, NJ: Paulist Press.

Beaudoin, Tom. 1998. *Virtual Faith: The Irreverent Spiritual Quest of Generation X.* San Francisco: Jossey-Bass Publishers.

Belluck, Pam. 2001. "Nuns Offer Clues to Alzheimer's and Aging." *New York Times,* May 7. http://www.nytimes.com/2001/05/07/us/nuns-offer-clues-to-alzheimer-s-and-aging.html. Accessed December 29, 2012.

Bendyna, Mary E. 2000. *Partners in Mission: A Profile of Associates and Religious in the United States.* Englewood Cliffs, NJ: North American Conference of Associates and Religious.

Bendyna, Mary E. (ed.). 2006. *Emerging Communities of Consecrated Life in the United States* (2nd ed.). Washington, DC: Center for Applied Research in the Apostolate.

Bendyna, Mary E., and Mary L. Gautier. 2009. *Recent Vocations to Religious Life: A Report for the National Religious Vocation Conference.* Washington, DC: Center for Applied Research in the Apostolate.

Berkley Center for Religion, Peace and World Affairs (Georgetown University) and the Public Religion Research Institute. 2012. "Millennial Values Survey," April 19.

Bishop, Bill. 2008. *The Big Sort: Why the Clustering of Like-Minded America Is Tearing Us Apart.* Boston, MA: Houghton Mifflin.

Briggs, Kenneth. 2006. *Double-Crossed: Uncovering the Catholic Church's Betrayal of American Nuns.* Garden City, NY: Doubleday.

Brooks, David. 2013. "The Empirical Kids." *New York Times,* March 29, A 23.

Brown, Callum G. 2012. *Religion and the Demographic Revolution.* Studies in Modern British History. Suffolk, UK: Boydell Press.

Bruce, Tricia C. 2011. *Faithful Revolution: How Voice of the Faithful Is Changing the Church*. New York: Oxford University Press.

Burns, Gene. 2005. *The Moral Veto*. New York: Cambridge University Press.

Cada, Lawrence, et al. 1979. *Shaping the Coming Age of Religious Life*. New York: Seabury Press.

Canon Law Society of America (Washington, DC). 1983. *Code of Canon Law: Latin-English Edition*.

Carroll, Colleen. 2002. *The New Faithful: Why Young Adults are Embracing Christian Orthodoxy*. Chicago: Loyola University Press.

Caspary, Anita M., IHM. 2003. *Witness to Integrity: The Crisis of the Immaculate Heart Community of California*. Collegeville, MN: Liturgical Press.

Center for Applied Research in the Apostolate (Washington, DC). 1999. *Emerging Religious Communities in the United States*.

Chittister, Joan. 1995. *The Fire in These Ashes: A Spirituality of Contemporary Religious Life*. Kansas City, MO: Sheed and Ward.

Confoy, Maryanne. 2008. *Religious Life and Priesthood: Perfectae Caritatis, Optatam Totius, Presbyterorum Ordinis*. Mahwah, NJ: Paulist Press.

Converse, Phillip. 1964. "On the Nature of Belief Systems in Mass Publics," in David E. Apter (ed.), *Ideology and Discontent*, 206–245. New York: Free Press.

Council of Major Superiors of Women Religious. 2009. *The Foundations of Religious Life: Revisiting the Vision*. Notre Dame, IN: Ave Maria Press.

D'Antonio, William V., James D. Davidson, Dean R. Hoge, and Mary L. Gautier. 2007. *American Catholics Today: New Realities of Their Faith and Their Church*. Lanham, MD: Rowman & Littlefield Publishers.

D'Antonio, William V., and Anthony Pogorelc, SS. 2007. *Voices of the Faithful: Loyal Catholics Striving for Change*. New York: Herder & Herder, Crossroad Publishing.

D'Antonio, William V., Michele Dillon, and Mary L. Gautier. 2013. *American Catholics in Transition*. Lanham, MD: Rowman & Littlefield Publishers.

Denham, Ann, and Gert Wilkinson. 2009. *Cloister of the Heart: Association of Contemplative Sisters*. Bloomington, IN: Xlibris.

Ebaugh, Helen Rose Fuchs. 1993. *Women in the Vanishing Cloister: Organizational Decline in Catholic Religious Orders in the United States*. New Brunswick, NJ: Rutgers University Press.

Ewens, Mary. 1989. "The Vocation Decline of Women Religious: Some Historical Perspectives," in Laurie Felknor (ed.), *The Crisis in Religious Vocations*, 165–180. New York: Paulist Press.

Farrell, Pat, O.S.F. 2012. "Navigating the Shifts." Presidential Address to the Assembly of the Leadership Conference of Women Religious, St. Louis, MO., August 10.

Finke, Roger, and Rodney Stark. 1992. *The Churching of America 1776–1990: Winners and Losers in Our Religious Economy.* New Brunswick, NJ: Rutgers University Press.

Finke, Roger, and Patricia Wittberg. 2000. "Organizational Revival from Within: Explaining Revivalism and Reform in the Roman Catholic Church." *Journal of the Scientific Study of Religion* 39, No. 2: 154–170.

Foundations and Donors Interested in Catholic Activities, Inc. 2010a. *"The Leadership and Philanthropy of Women Religious: A Tradition Embraces the Future."* Washington, DC: FADICA, Inc.

Foundations and Donors Interested in Catholic Activities, Inc. 2010b. *"The Leadership and Philanthropy of Women Religious: Global Partnerships for Human Progress."* Washington, DC: FADICA, Inc.

Froehle, Bryan T., and Mary L. Gautier. 2000. *Catholicism USA: A Portrait of the Catholic Church in the United States.* Maryknoll, NY: Orbis Books.

Garcia, Sister Elsa, CDP, and Sister Gloria Ann Fiedler, CDP. 2011. "Five Winning Ways to Extend Contact with Young Adults," *Horizon*, Vol. 36, No. 3: 30–32.

Gautier, Mary L., and Melissa A. Cidade. 2012. *Educational Debt and Vocations to Religious Life: A Report for the National Religious Vocation Conference.* Washington, DC: Center for Applied Research in the Apostolate.

Gautier, Mary L., Paul M. Perl, and Stephen J. Fichter. 2012. *Same Call, Different Men: The Evolution of the Priesthood since Vatican II.* Collegeville, MN: Liturgical Press.

Gautier, Mary L., and Carolyne Saunders. 2013. *New Sisters and Brothers in Perpetual Vows: A Report to the Secretariat of Clergy, Consecrated Life and Vocations, United States Conference of Catholic Bishops.* Washington, DC: Center for Applied Research in the Apostolate.

Gibson, David. 2012. "Catholic Bishops Debate Hiring a Spokesperson." http://ncronline.org/print/news/vatican/catholic-bishops-debate-hiring-spokesperson. Accessed April 2, 2013.

Gottemoeller, Doris, RSM. 1997. "The Priesthood: Implications in Consecrated Life for Women," in Paul K. Hennessy (ed.), *A Concert of Charisms: Ordained Ministry in Religious Life*, 127–138. New York: Paulist Press.

——. 2005. "Living in Community: Continuing the Conversation." *Review for Religious* 64(3): 269–280.

Gray, Mark M. 2012. "Young Adult Catholics Haven't Lost God's Number." Washington DC: Center for Applied Research in the Apostolate.

Gray, Mark M., and Mary L. Gautier. 2012. *Consideration of Priesthood and Religious Life among Never-Married U.S. Catholics.* Washington DC: Center for Applied Research in the Apostolate.

Hegy, Pierre. 2011. *Wake Up, Lazarus: On Catholic Renewal.* Bloomington, IN: iUniverse.

Hoge, Dean R., William D. Dinges, Mary Johnson, SNDdeN, and Juan L. Gonzales, Jr. 2001. *Young Adult Catholics: Religion in the Culture of Choice.* Notre Dame, IN: University of Notre Dame Press.

Hoge, Dean R., and Jacqueline E. Wenger. 2003. *Evolving Visions of the Priesthood: Changes from Vatican II to the Turn of the New Century.* Collegeville, MN: Liturgical Press.

Holy See. 2012. *"Summary of the Findings of the Apostolic Visitation in Ireland."* Rome: March 20.

Hostie, Raymond, SJ. 1983. *The Life and Death of Religious Orders: A Psycho-sociological Approach.* Washington, DC: Center for Applied Research in the Apostolate.

Institute of Politics. 2012. *"Survey of Young Americans' Attitudes toward Politics and Public Service,"* 21st ed. Cambridge, MA: John F. Kennedy School of Government, Harvard University.

John Paul II. 1996. *Vita Consecrata* (Post-Synodal Apostolic Exhortation). Rome: March 25.

Johnson, Mary. 1998. "The Reweaving of Catholic Spiritual and Institutional Life." *The Annals of the American Academy of Political and Social Science,* 558, July: 135–143.

——. 2001. "Religious Life in the USA: Community as a Key Bridge to Young Adults." *Social Compass* 48 (2): 229–236.

——. 2006a. "Religious Education in Its Societal and Ecclesial Context," in Robert P. Imbelli (ed.), *Handing on the Faith: The Church's Mission and Challenge,* 13–29. New York: Herder & Herder, Crossroad Publishing.

——. 2006b. "Collective Identity and Distinctiveness: The Case of U.S. Conferences of Apostolic Women and Men Religious." in T. Frank Kennedy, SJ (ed.), *Inculturation and the Church in North America,* 179–197, New York: Herder & Herder, Crossroad Publishing.

Johnson, Mary, and Patricia Wittberg. 2012. "Reality Check: A Fact-Based Assessment of Vocations to Religious Life," *America* 207(10) October 15.

Jones, Robert P., Daniel Cox, and Thomas Banchoff. 2012. *A Generation in Transition: Religion, Values, and Politics among College-Age Millennials.* Washington, DC: Public Religion Research Institute.

Kanter, Rosabeth Moss. 1972. *Commitment and Community: Communes and Utopias in Sociological Perspective.* Cambridge, MA: Harvard University Press.

Klinenberg, Eric. 2012. *Going Solo: The Extraordinary Rise and Surprising Appeal of Living Alone.* New York: Penguin.

Kohles, Sarah, OSF. 2013. "Our Shared Mission," Giving Voice February 2013 E-Newsletter. www.giving-voice.org. Accessed March 11, 2013.

Lofland, John. 1977. *Doomsday Cult: A Study of Conversion, Proselytization, and Maintenance of Faith.* New York: Irvington.

Magister, Sandro. 2012. "Religious Illiteracy. The First to Send Back to School are the Adults." http://chiesa.espresso.repubblica.it/articolo/1350276?engy. Accessed June 25, 2012.

Mannheim, Karl. 1952. "The Problem of Generations," in *Essays on the Sociology of Knowledge*, 276–320. New York: Oxford University Press.

———. 1955. "Ideology and Utopia," in *Collected Works*, Vol. I. New York: Mariner Books.

Masini, Eleonora Barbieri. 1998. "Women Religious, Builders of an Alternative Future, Journeying Onward in New Solidarities," in *International Union of Superiors General*, n. 108.

McPherson, Miller, Lynn Smith-Lovin, and Matthew E. Brashears. 2006. "Social Isolation in America: Changes in Core Discussion Networks over Two Decades." *American Sociological Review* 71: 353–375.

Morris, Charles. 1997. *American Catholics: The Saints and Sinners Who Built America's Most Powerful Church*. New York: Times Books.

Neal, Marie Augusta, SNDdeN. 1984. *Catholic Sisters in Transition: From the 1960s to the 1990s*. Wilmington, DE: Michael Glazier.

———. 1990. *From Nuns to Sisters: An Expanding Vocation*. Mystic, CT: Twenty-Third Publications.

Nygren, David J., and Miriam D. Ukeritis. 1993. *The Future of Religious Orders in the United States*. Westport, CT: Praeger Publishers.

Oates, Mary J. 1995. *The Catholic Philanthropic Tradition in America*. Bloomington and Indianapolis, IN: Indiana University Press.

Official Catholic Directory. 1910–2010. Berkeley Heights, NJ: P. J. Kenedy & Sons.

O'Malley, John W. 2008. *What Happened at Vatican II*. Cambridge, MA: Belknap Press of Harvard University Press.

———. 2012. "Vatican II: Celebrating 50 Years—The Significance of Gaudium et Spes," the Catholic Common Ground Initiative Murnion Lecture, Catholic University of America, Washington, DC, June 1, in "Initiative Report, Catholic Common Ground Initiative, " October.

Orsy, Ladislas, SJ. 2009. *Receiving the Council: Theological and Canonical Insights and Debates*. Collegeville, MN: Liturgical Press.

Paul VI. 1964. *Lumen Gentium* (Dogmatic Constitution of the Church). Rome: November 21.

———. 1965. *Perfectae Caritatis* (Decree on the Adaptation and Renewal of Religious Life). Rome: October 28.

———. 1966. *Ecclesiae Sanctae* (Apostolic Letter, *Motu Proprio*, On the Implementation of the Decrees *Christus Dominus, Presbyterorum Ordinis*, and *Perfectae Caritatis*). Rome: August 6.

———. 1966. *Evangelica Testificatio* (Apostolic Exhortation on the Renewal of Religious Life According to the Teaching of the Second Vatican Council). Rome: June 29.

Pearce, Lisa D., and Melinda L. Denton. 2011. *A Faith of Their Own: Stability and Change in the Religiosity of America's Adolescents*. New York: Oxford University Press.

Perrow, Charles. 1986. *Complex Organizations: A Critical Essay*, 3rd ed. New York: Random House.

Pew Research Center (Washington, DC). 2007. *How Young People View Their Lives, Futures and Politics: A Portrait of "Generation Next."*

———. 2012. "Young, Underemployed, and Optimistic: Coming of Age, Slowly, in a Tough Economy," Pew Social and Demographic Trends. www.pewsocialtrends. org. Accessed March 2012.

Population Reference Bureau (Washington, DC). 2012. *World Population Data Sheet.*

Pryor, John H., Kevin Eagan, Laura Palucki Blake, Sylvia Hurtado, Jennifer Berdan, and Matthew H. Case. 2012. *The American Freshman: National Norms Fall.* Los Angeles: Cooperative Institutional Research Program at the Higher Education Research Institute, Graduate School of Education and Information Studies, University of California.

Putnam, Robert D. 1995. "Bowling Alone: America's Declining Social Capital." *Journal of Democracy* 6(1): 65–78.

———. 2000. *Bowling Alone: The Collapse and Revival of American Community.* New York: Simon and Schuster.

Putnam, Robert D., and David E. Campbell. 2010. *American Grace: How Religion Divides and Unites Us.* New York: Simon and Schuster.

Quiñonez, Lora Ann, and Mary Daniel Turner. 1992. *The Transformation of American Catholic Sisters.* Philadelphia: Temple University Press.

Reese, Thomas J., SJ. 1989. *Archbishop: Inside the Power Structure of the American Catholic Church.* San Francisco: Harper & Row.

———. 2004. "The Impact of the Sexual Abuse Crisis," in Francis Oakley and Bruce Russett (eds.), *Governance, Accountability and the Future of the Catholic Church.* New York: Continuum.

Roof, Wade Clark. 1993. *A Generation of Seekers: The Spiritual Journeys of the Baby Boom Generation.* San Francisco: HarperSanFrancisco.

———. 1999. *Spiritual Marketplace: Baby Boomers and the Remaking of American Religion.* Princeton, NJ: Princeton University Press.

———. 2009. "Generations and Religion," in Peter B. Clarke (ed.), *The Oxford Handbook of the Sociology of Religion.* New York: Oxford University Press.

Sack, Kevin. 2011. "Nuns, a 'Dying Breed,' Fade From Leadership Roles at Catholic Hospitals." *New York Times*, August 20.

Sacred Congregation for Religious and for Secular Institutes. 1983. *Essential Elements in the Church's Teaching on Religious Life as Applied to Institutes Dedicated to Works of the Apostolate.* Rome: May 31.

Sacred Congregation for Religious and for Secular Institutes, and Sacred Congregation for Bishops. 1978. *Directives for the Mutual Relations between Bishops and Religious in the Church.* Rome: May 14.

Schneiders, Sandra M., I.H.M. 2000. *Finding the Treasure: Locating Catholic Religious Life in a New Ecclesial and Cultural Context.* Mahwah, NJ: Paulist Press.

———. 2001. *Selling All: Commitment, Consecrated Celibacy, and Community in Catholic Religious Life.* Mahwah, NJ: Paulist Press.

———. 2013. *Buying the Field: Catholic Religious Life in Mission to the World.* Mahwah, NJ: Paulist Press.

Secretaria Status. 2010. *Annuarium Statisticum Ecclesiae (Statistical Yearbook of the Church).* Vatican City: *Libreria Editrice Vaticana.*

Shenker, Barry. 1986. *Intentional Communities: Ideology and Alienation in Communal Societies.* London: Routledge.

Silk, Mark. 2012. "GenX Catholic Debacle." www.religionnews.com/blogs/mark-silk/gen-s-cathoic-debacle. Accessed June 24, 2012.

Simmel, Georg. 1950. *The Sociology of Georg Simmel,* Kurt H. Wolff, trans. New York: Free Press.

Smith, Christian. 1998. *American Evangelicalism, Embattled and Thriving.* Chicago: University of Chicago Press.

Smith, Christian, and Patricia Snell. 2009. *Souls in Transition: The Religious and Spiritual Lives of Emerging Adults.* New York: Oxford University Press.

Steinfels, Peter. 2003. *A People Adrift: The Crisis of the Roman Catholic Church in America.* New York: Simon and Schuster.

Stewart, George C., Jr. 1994. *Marvels of Charity: History of American Sisters and Nuns.* Huntington, IN: Our Sunday Visitor Publishing Division.

Sullivan, Melanie-Prejean. 2009. *Whispers, Nudges, & A Couple of Kicks: A Guide for Those who Teach and Practice Discernment.* Louisville, KY: Bellarmine University Press.

Synod of Bishops. 1994. "Consecrated Life, A Sign of the Church's Vitality." www.CatholicCulture.org.

Taves, Anne. 1986. *The Household of Faith: Roman Catholic Devotion in the Mid-Nineteenth Century.* Notre Dame, IN: Notre Dame University Press.

Thomas, William I., and Dorothy S. Thomas. 1928. *The Child in America: Behavior Problems and Programs.* New York: Knopf.

Twenge, Jean. 2006. *Generation Me: Why Today's Young Americans Are More Confident, Assertive, Entitled—and More Miserable than Ever Before.* New York: Free Press.

United States Catholic Conference, Inc. (Washington, DC). 1994. *Catechism of the Catholic Church.*

United States Conference of Catholic Bishops. 1986. "U.S. Religious Life and the Decline of Vocations." *Origins* (Dec. 4), Vol. 16, No. 25: 467–470.

Veysey, Lawrence. 1973. *The Communal Experience.* Chicago: University of Chicago Press.

Weber, Max. 1963. *The Sociology of Religion.* English trans. (from the 4th ed.). Boston: Beacon Press.

Weick, Karl. 1995. *Sensemaking in Organizations.* Thousand Oaks, CA: Sage.

Weigel, George. 2012. "The Sisters: Two Views." http://www.eppc.org/publications/pubID.4758/pub_detail.a. Accessed June 8, 2012.

Wittberg, Patricia. 1994. *The Rise and Fall of Catholic Religious Orders: A Social Movement Perspective.* Albany, NY: State University of New York Press.

————. 2006. *From Piety to Professionalism—And Back? Transformations of Organized Religious Virtuosity*. Lanham, MD: Lexington Books.

————. 2012. "A Lost Generation?" *America* 206(5), February 20: 13–18.

World Congress on Religious Life. 2004. "What the Spirit Says Today to Consecrated Life." http://www.fransalians.com/wcrl/final_document.htm. Accessed October 25, 2011.

Zablocki, Benjamin. 1980. *The Joyful Community*. Chicago: University of Chicago Press.

Zagano, Phyllis. 2011. "Ministry by Women Religious and the U.S. Apostolic Visitation." *New Blackfriars* 92(1041): 591–606. http://onlinelibrary.wiley.com/doi/10.1111/j.1741–2005.2011.01422.x/full. Accessed April 10, 2012.

Index